The Music
of
Friends

75 Years
of the
Chamber Music Conference
and Composers' Forum of the East

The Music of Friends

75 Years of the
Chamber Music Conference
and Composers' Forum of the East

David W. Webber

Chamber
Music
Conference

The Music of Friends:
75 Years of the Chamber Music Conference and Composers' Forum of the East
by David W. Webber

Copyright © 2020 The Chamber Music Conference and Composers' Forum of the East, Inc.
First Edition

Chamber Music Conference
P.O. Box 130
Arlington, MA 02476

Visit us at cmceast.org

Book design and cover design by Laura Lis Scott, Book Love Space

Front cover photos by Claire Stefani; back cover photos by
Alice Berman (top right) and Claire Stefani

Library of Congress Control Number: 2020911141

ISBN: 978-1-7345306-0-5 (paperback)
ISBN: 978-1-7345306-1-2 (ePub)

Contents

For more information about the Chamber Music Conference,
including additional archival material and photographs relating to
the conference's history, please visit cmceast.org/history75.

The author's acknowledgments, notes on sources, background on the writing
of this history, and author's note appear at the end of this book.

Foreword

This book is the story of a remarkable musical community. For seventy-five years, musicians have gathered each summer at the Chamber Music Conference to study, rehearse, perform, compose, play, and hear chamber music. The components of the conference have varied in details and emphasis over time, but three aspects have remained fundamental: the coaching of serious amateur participants in chamber music by a faculty of professional concert artists; a series of concerts, free and open to the public, performed by the faculty; and residencies by distinguished composers, whose works are studied by both participants and faculty.

Attending the conference becomes a cherished rite of summer for many participants and faculty alike, and some return annually for decades. The high return rate produces a strong sense of continuity, while the influx of new participants and faculty each year brings fresh vitality to the conference. For regular attendees, the conference is as meaningful for the opportunities to form and enjoy friendships as it is for its musical offerings. Sharing a love of music and a passion for learning, and drawn closer by myriad lifelong friendships, the conference community is very tight-knit, even though it assembles for only a few weeks of the year, and this is a major reason the conference has endured as an institution. The story of the conference is truly a story of "the music of friends."

If you are a current or past attendee of the conference, this history will inspire an appreciation for our past and for the participants, faculty, composers, and staff whose vision and dedication made possible the conference of today, and I hope that for some of you, it also inspires a commitment to become more involved and to help ensure that the conference thrives far into the future. If you have not attended the conference, I hope this history leads you, or a musician you know, to join us someday, perhaps as a participant in our coaching program or as an audience member at our concerts.

The board of directors of the conference commissioned this book to celebrate our seventy-fifth anniversary, a milestone that would also have marked the beginning of a new chapter for us: our first year in residence at Colgate University, after over sixty years—with only one interruption—at Bennington College. However, as the book goes to press, the world is facing a public health crisis, the COVID-19 pandemic, which has claimed thousands of lives and disrupted almost every aspect of society, and our 2020 season has been canceled. We are saddened by the devastating impact of the pandemic, but hopeful for a brighter future. History has shown that the conference is resilient. When this crisis has passed, however long that takes, our community will come together again, and I expect that we will value the experience of making music with friends more than ever before.

On behalf of the entire conference community, I would like to thank David Webber and the members of the editorial board for the enormous effort that they have poured into this history. Particularly noteworthy is the wealth of information David has uncovered about the formative years of the conference; quite possibly, some of this information would have been lost forever had he not undertaken this project now. I am grateful for his indefatigable and careful research.

—Mike Kong
Chair, Board of Directors
The Chamber Music Conference

Prelude: A Personal Perspective

It's not the vistas that have drawn the faithful each summer to the campus of Bennington College, though the view from the "end of the world" over the green sloping hills can be sublime. It's not the perfect swimming lake, either: most never made the one-mile trek to float in its glassy perfection. As for the lumpy beds and institutional stir-frys, the less said the better.

But then the devotees of the Chamber Music Conference who have thronged to this corner of Vermont year after year, sometimes for decades, were never looking for a vacation. What has drawn adult musicians to the conference is the promise of transformation.

The rest of the year, life is tempered by factors like status, looks, and age. But for the duration of the conference a meritocracy rules where groups form based on nothing but skill. The transformation begins at registration, with the ritual donning of the neck wallet. In an instant, doctors, accountants, and engineers turn into clarinetists, violists, and pianists.

The community of participants is united in an almost monastic devotion to music. The day is given over to coaching sessions where participants pore over previously assigned works under the guidance of professionals. There are rehearsals, and scheduled periods of free-play during which old friends reunite to revisit a beloved work, and impromptu ensembles of near-strangers sight-read through unknown terrain—some at come-hell-or-high-water speed, others with frequent stops and loud counting. Some get up early to fit in practice before the first morning coaching session; or stay behind in a sweltering attic room late in the evening in order to clean up that one tricky passage, or make sense of a coach's new fingering.

In many ways the transformation is a return. For amateur players, that one week in the summer is a stolen reunion with their first love. It's a return to a level of devotion they brought to music as teenagers, or at conservatory, before practical considerations and life intervened and led them to other careers. For the handful of professional orchestral musicians and teachers who come, it's a rare chance to revisit the intimacy of small-ensemble playing.

And for the art form itself, the conference creates a return to the conditions for which much of this music was written: private gatherings of skilled amateurs bringing music to life for the sheer love of it. The paradox: that music-making so full of imperfections can feel so pure.

Among amateur chamber musicians, Benningtonians, as devotees of this conference will surely be known for years even after the impending move to Colgate University, are a special breed, who play best when barefoot and tune to A=441 Hz "because that way nobody is happy."

I remember my first reading at Bennington in the summer of 2013. I was visiting as a journalist, researching a story about contemporary composers who write with amateurs in mind. (The CMC has led the way in this field for years with a robust commissioning program and residencies.)

I had recently picked up the violin after a thirteen-year hiatus and it was with uneasy foreboding that I accepted the invitation to join in a reading of Dvořák's second piano quintet. The scherzo became a blurry wild ride during which I "fell off" numerous times and scrambled to join back in, only to lose my spot again. But in the gorgeous slow dumka movement there were wondrous moments, free from thought, when everything came together. At the end I vowed to get into shape to return as a participant.

Terror, elation, and a chastened assessment of my limitations would become recurrent components of my emotional journey each time I attended the conference. Often, I'd cycle through them in a single coaching session.

Transformation is accelerated at the conference because learning happens on so many levels. There are the fellow players who pull us along and inspire us to produce sounds we didn't know we had in us, at tempos we hadn't deemed possible. There are the coaches who find the right words to unlock a technical block or give shape to a phrase. And there is the music itself that nudges us to try on new roles and expressions: the bonhomie of Haydn; the acerbic wit of Shostakovich; the fainting-couch elegance of Brahms.

And learning isn't all musical, either. Summiting masterpieces of the chamber repertoire is a group effort that can require astute psychology and empathetic communication skills.

I can't think of many social endeavors that create such an intimate bond among adults of such different backgrounds and ages. At the conference, I am always inspired by the older participants. It's not just the sight of one of them cheerfully lugging a cello case up the hill in the heat, and then shredding a difficult passage with impeccable intonation. It's the stories of players who returned to their instrument later in life and worked their way back to ever more difficult repertoire. In a world that worships youth and prizes quick gratification, the cultivation of amateur chamber music—in companionship with people of different ages—offers a more generous perspective.

And then there's the bond that links generations of players across centuries. I can't know what it felt like to be a teenager in Berlin in 1825. But to join in a late-evening play-through of the Mendelssohn Octet on the last night of camp, the room electric with fierce concentration and glee, is to tap into the same energy that must have coursed through the Mendelssohns' salon at the first reading. Did they get through it without messing up?

I don't know, but I'm going to practice until I do. Even if it takes a few decades.

—Corinna da Fonseca-Wollheim
Contributing Music Critic for the *New York Times* and Founder, Beginner's Ear

The Music of Friends

of

Friends

75 Years
of the
Chamber Music Conference
and Composers' Forum of the East

Ottetto.

Allegro molto vivace

I. A Common Language of Music

By chance, in my 30s, I was introduced to chamber music, and it became a significant part of my life. I loved the idea of small groups of instrumentalists, one person playing each part, one instrument responding to another, a conversation among friends. And, it was a great personal and musical joy to discover a summer chamber music camp for adults, where I met many other amateurs who also spoke the common language of music.

—Judith Ensign,
conference administrative director and participant,
"Echoes of a Violin"
(unpublished manuscript, 2018)

FOR SEVENTY-FIVE YEARS, the love of music making has flourished at the Chamber Music Conference. A four-week summer program for—and by—amateur musicians, it combines outstanding, intensive chamber music coaching, seminars, and concerts (free and open to the public) by the conference's professional faculty. A composer residency and commissioning program ensures that new

Manuscript score of the opening of Felix Mendelssohn's Octet, dated October 15, 1825.

music is an integral component, with works by resident composers performed by both faculty and participant ensembles. Informal chamber music reading sessions are highly popular, often involve a mix of amateurs and professional faculty, and are an opportunity for long-time friends or new acquaintances to return to familiar masterpieces or explore unknown works. Today, the summer conference brings together more than 350 conferees—a mix of amateur and professional performing musicians, as well as composers—who immerse themselves in the joy of making chamber music.

Over these seventy-five years, the conference's sites have included five college campuses. The conference has taken place over a total of 220 weeks, has hosted close to 500 composers, and has been staffed by more than 430 professional musicians. It has cycled through six names, gone through a complete corporate reorganization, and been led by eight music directors. The original two-week program doubled to four weeks and was reformulated to integrate resident composers into the amateur music-making context. The founders and early leaders of the organization have been succeeded by new generations of chamber music enthusiasts.

But the story of the conference is more than the organizational structure and leadership changes, the various sites, and the ongoing governance and operational issues. These changes made the development and even the survival of the conference possible, but they were merely the means to a greater end: the creation of a vital community, organized around the love of playing chamber music.

Each summer, many of the same musicians return to the conference—many count their attendance in decades, not years—to join in making music with their friends. When in

1999 Senior Composer-in-Residence Chen Yi was commissioned by the conference to write a work for a participant ensemble, it was no surprise that she titled it *The Joy of the Reunion*—a reference to the warm greetings among friends coming together to make music once again.

Musicians at the conference look forward to meeting new musicians and forging new friendships—after all, everyone was once a newcomer. And notable among the newcomers are children and other family members of conferees, as chamber music has traditionally been an intergenerational, intrafamilial activity.

Those attending the conference never know when a spontaneous, shared musical experience will resonate deeply enough to be sought out and relived in subsequent years. Some years ago, participant oboist Bobby Kipp, who had already attended for more than a decade, set up a free-play session with a violist newcomer, Nimmi Kavasery. It was easy for Kipp to pull together the flute, bassoon, horn, violin, and cello to join her and Kavasery for a reading of the P.D.Q. Bach *Schleptet* ("Peter Schickele, editor"). The humorous *Schleptet* proved a welcome diversion from the serious work of the morning coaching session. The next summer, Kavasery approached Kipp with the enthusiastic question, "Are we going to do the *Schleptet* again?" Indeed, Kavasery and Kipp have returned to the *Schleptet* in subsequent years, making it something of an annual tradition. Such traditions among conferees are actually quite common, as players return to the same favorite work year after year.

A Working Vacation

Conference participants embrace a schedule that can be as grueling as it is rewarding. Most participants attend for one week, perhaps two, as few have the stamina for more. Participant hornist David Kemp summed it up well in a piece he wrote for the *New York Times* Travel Section in 1981. "I wonder why I am working so hard on my vacation when I could be cooling my feet in an icy mountain stream,"[1] he facetiously lamented, describing faculty bassoonist Jane Taylor's unrelenting efforts to have him master a particularly challenging phrase in the Nielsen Wind Quintet.

For most participants, the conference is a part of their lives not just for one or two weeks in the summer, but throughout the year. As soon as one summer's conference is complete, participants work on planning groups and repertory to be requested for the next summer. Eager participants can apply as early as December for the next summer's session, although the actual deadline is not until early spring.

Once accepted, applicants may submit requests for works they would like to be coached on. As participants attend over the years and get to know other players, they have the option to mutually agree to request to be coached as a group, perhaps specifying a particular work. By no means do all participants make such requests, nor is pre-forming a group necessary for a highly rewarding coaching experience. But this aspect of the conference—providing, at least to some degree, personalized coaching schedules—is one ingredient of the conference's recipe for success.

By June, participants receive their coaching assignments and obtain copies of the parts and scores for those works. Participants are expected not only to learn their own parts as thoroughly as possible, but also to become familiar with the other players' parts and the overall structure of the piece.

The Daily Schedule

The coaching sessions are the core activity. Each participant typically has a morning and an afternoon session during the six days, Monday through Saturday, of the conference's week, which adds up to twenty-one coaching hours. Four works are assigned, with each work receiving three sessions led by the same faculty coach. (The first week of the conference—the "intensive week"—has a slightly different schedule, with only three coaching assignments, but with the same total of twenty-one coaching hours, plus scheduled time for groups to rehearse without their coaches.) Some participants fill every available minute when not being coached with free-time playing, with the result that they are playing eight or more hours every day.

Musicians can also attend the conference as "auditors." Auditors may observe coaching sessions and participate in unlimited free-playing sessions, as well as attending concerts and lectures. This option appeals to both newcomers and returnees who do not have the time to prepare pieces for coaching sessions, who cannot spend an entire week at the conference, or who want to play chamber music without coaching.

A Synergistic Community

Along with the satisfaction and sense of accomplishment that comes from the musical learning, growth, and increased confidence that the conference supports, the magic of the conference is the almost ineffable, if fleeting, experience of what some

Jacob Glick coaches the Bartók sixth string quartet in 1984.

Photo by Alice Berman

might call "being in the zone," when, for example, a phrase is played so well and effortlessly that the player might "wonder where it came from."[2] Or, a sudden sense of uncanny, deep emotional connection gives the sensation of goosebumps or brings joyful tears to one's eyes.

The intensity of the chamber music immersion experience is perhaps what makes for this magic, allowing musicians to tap into creativity and expressiveness they did not know they possessed. Yet this personal experience occurs in a shared context and would not exist if not for the contribution of the other players within each ensemble.

One of the secrets of chamber music coaching is drawing out from each player their very best, most focused "in the zone" performance, which in turn contributes to the synergistic direction for the group. Former Music Director Shem Guibbory credits his predecessor, Jacob Glick, with building this part of the conference's culture. Glick believed deeply in the potential for every musician—amateur or not—to grow, thrive, and learn. At the same time, he championed the idea that playing chamber music is such a potentially profound human experience that it should not be left merely to professionals.

Guibbory recalls a coaching session decades ago on Max Bruch's Eight Pieces, opus 83, during a hot, energy-sapping afternoon. Playing through the piece, the cellist, who was certainly not the most advanced of amateur players, unexpectedly began playing like never before, rendering an utterly exquisite performance. Guibbory could sense, as the pianist and violinist glanced meaningfully out of the corners of their eyes, that this was a transformational moment for the entire group, "a moment of grace." When the reading was over, the cellist looked up and said simply, "I felt that was pretty good."

Reflecting on that cellist's experience, Guibbory noted that "we are all that person."

The Music of Friends

The social aspect of playing chamber music, so much in evidence at the conference, has as its antecedent the historical circumstances in which much of this music was created and first played. Consider this story: four amateur musicians (that is, *Kunstfreunden*—literally, "friends of the arts") have been invited by their host, Baron von Fürnberg, to his summer home in the countryside of Weinzierl, not far from Vienna, "to make a little music," as they did from time to time. The baron, wanting to hear something new, asked that one of the violinists, a composer yet in his teens, compose "something that could be performed by these four amateurs."[3]

When originally published more than two hundred years ago, this story was intended to document the birth of the string quartet—the composer-violinist in the group was none other than Franz Joseph Haydn, and among the pieces played was his first string quartet, opus 1, no. 1. Whether apocryphal or not, this story—sourced to Haydn himself—captures the conviviality of amateur music making, even in an aristocratic setting.

Today, we can view the Haydn quartets as the fountainhead of the conference's core chamber music repertory. Not only was this music conceived for playing in an intimate social setting, as opposed to a public concert venue; it often reflects a similar kind of musical sensibility. As Goethe famously wrote, a string quartet is like "a conversation among four intelligent people."[4]

Although the string quartet, and related string-based ensembles, took the lead historically, wind instruments were not by any means neglected. Think of Mozart's celebrated clarinet quintet or his flute quartets, which, by the way, were written for an amateur flutist. Wind instruments soon came into their own, both in mixed wind-string ensembles—think now of Beethoven's Septet or Schubert's Octet—and in wind-only quartets and quintets from innovators such as Reicha and Danzi.

"Joyous and Lively in the Extreme"

The annals of music history contain many accounts of the social context of amateur music making. As early as 1757, when Haydn was supposedly inventing the string quartet for his friends at Baron von Fürnberg's, the composer and violinist/violist Carl Ditters von Dittersdorf was at a chamber music party of his own. He reported how he was joined by his two brothers, plus a cellist friend, to read through six new quartets by Franz Xaver Richter. Between quartets, they had a "jolly" time drinking "rare good coffee," and smoking "the finest tobacco."[5]

In another account from about twenty-five years later, Dittersdorf appears again, as related by the Irish tenor Michael Kelly, who was a guest at that party. Dittersdorf, on second violin, was joined by Haydn, first violin; Mozart, viola; and the composer Johann Baptist Wanhal on cello. Kelly noted that as players they were "tolerable," although, in a facetiously huge understatement, he added that "there was a little science among them."[6] While Kelly neglects to tell us what we would most like to know about this quartet—*what music did they play?*—he instead reports on the social aspect of the occasion: "after the musical feast was over, we sat down to an excellent supper, and became joyous and lively in the extreme."

A year later, what is perhaps the most famous chamber music party in history took place when Haydn was a guest at Mozart's home in Vienna, an occasion reported on by Mozart's father, Leopold.[7] Joined by two amateurs, the Barons Anton and Bartholomäus Tinti, they read Mozart's latest quartets, the last three (K. 458, 464, and 465) of a set of six published together as opus 10 and dedicated to Haydn.

Mozart was apparently a regular guest at a weekly musical salon at the Vienna home of the botanist Baron von Jacquin. The evenings were reportedly dedicated to "conviviality," while "young people chatted away, joked, made music, played little games, and had a great time."[8] During one of these evenings in 1786, Mozart played viola, along with Anton Stadler on clarinet and the baron's daughter, the amateur pianist (and Mozart's student) Franziska von Jacquin, on a new work Mozart had written for himself and his friends, the "Kegelstatt" Trio, K. 498.

By the early nineteenth century, chamber music was increasingly written for public performance by professional musicians in concert venues, not for private readings by amateurs. A good marker for that might be Beethoven's opus 59 "Razumovsky" quartets, which, although dedicated to an amateur violinist, Count (later Prince) Andrey Kirillovich Razumovsky, were written with specific professionals in mind. Longer and more difficult than his previous quartets, these quartets were likely beyond the reach of most amateurs of the time, and were first performed by a professional quartet in a concert setting.

Despite the shift toward professionalization of chamber music, however, it persisted as a non-public social activity. Such was the appreciation of playing chamber music at home with friends that Louis Spohr, a professional violinist and prolific composer of chamber music, had to knock out a wall when renovating his country house to have a room big enough so he could host "a quartet circle" with other music-loving families in the neighborhood. Spohr hosted three quartets every week and "concluded the evenings with a frugal supper."[9]

Even the curmudgeonly Johannes Brahms showed some warmth for amateurs playing his new chamber works in their homes. Brahms's close friend and the dedicatee of his opus 51 string quartets, the amateur violinist Theodor Billroth—a prominent physician, known today as a pioneer of modern abdominal surgery—was committed to these chamber music sessions ("music at home has its attractions!"[10]). Brahms often joined in. On one such occasion Brahms even recommended to Billroth that he include a certain Doctor Jurenak from Pest, "an excellent amateur and charming person," to participate in a first reading of the String Quartet no. 3 in B-flat Major, opus 67. Later, when setting up a reading of his new Quintet no. 1 in F Major, opus 88, Brahms asked Billroth, as an apparent after-thought, to invite a friend, the amateur cellist Josef Gänsbacher: "I am just thinking of Dr. G., who would also like to play, but can stand it if he's just an auditor."[11]

From this perspective, the narrative of the Chamber Music Conference begins not seventy-five, but well over two hundred years ago. At today's conference the string quartets of Richter are not a part of the repertory, but neither—although only in more recent years—is the smoking of fine tobacco. Rare good coffee, however, is as important as it was to Dittersdorf's string quartet. Whether the campus cafeteria serves up something like the excellent fare enjoyed by Michael Kelly in the company of Haydn and Mozart, or something more akin to Spohr's frugal supper, can be debated. And that dedication to conviviality, so much a part of the chamber music scene enjoyed by Mozart and so many others? It is alive and well today for the musicians who share the common language of music at the conference.

Seventy-five years ago, its story began.

II. Founding and Early Years: Middlebury College

Another minor geographical question: where is Vermont?

—Pierre Boulez, letter to John Cage, June 1950

IN 1948, THEODORE STRONGIN, a flutist, composer, and music critic, arrived too late for dinner on the first Sunday evening of the conference. He dropped his suitcase in the hallway (after extracting his flute) and ran to join a chamber music reading session. That suitcase—and his appetite—"stayed in the hallway just inside the front entrance until two a.m. while he played with other (better fed) players."[12] For the rest of Strongin's two weeks at the conference, it was the same story: "supper, sleep and sometimes even breakfast were in jeopardy." Not much has changed since these early years.

But in the first year—1946—what came to be known as the "Bennington" Conference was hosted by Middlebury College, a long-established liberal arts college in Vermont's Champlain Valley, about ninety miles north of Bennington.

Le Château, a building on the campus of Middlebury College, was the conference's first home, 1946-1950.

Courtesy of Middlebury College Special Collections

The conference's founder was a visionary Middlebury College music professor, Alan Carter.

The Conference's Founder: Alan Carter

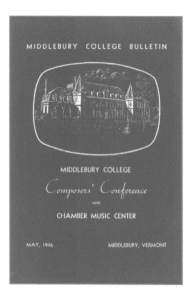

The first conference in 1946 was heralded by this Middlebury College Bulletin, *featuring a cover image of Le Château, the French department building used by the conference.*

Courtesy of Middlebury College Special Collections

Carter's musical career in Vermont, spanning more than four decades, is a story of ambitious innovation, with the founding of the conference just one of his achievements.

Carter was born in Greenwich, Connecticut, in 1904. His father was a prominent New York City physician, and the family lived on West 55th Street. As Carter recounted later, "practically every evening when I came home from 'playing' in the park I would hear on entering the house the strains of some Brahms trio, cello sonata, piano quartet, but always with a piano as my mother was an excellent amateur pianist and it was she who attracted some of the best musicians in New York to our house."

Carter began violin studies at age six. While in his teens, after an audition in which his mother accompanied him on a Schumann violin sonata, he was accepted as a student with the illustrious Hungarian violinist (and Joseph Joachim student) Leopold Auer, who had recently arrived from Europe.[13]

By 1923, Carter was attending the Mannes School of Music, and he then studied in Europe for four years. After his return, he assembled his Cremona String Quartet, in which he played viola, and Edwin Ideler (also an early conference staff member), first violin. The Cremona practiced as much as possible, gave a few poorly paying concerts, and in return for the loan of a set of Stradivarius instruments, as Carter recalled later, "would make music with wealthy amateurs certain evenings each week. . . . Amateur instrumentalists make up for lack of technical proficiency with contagious enthusiasm and a wealth of chamber

Alan Carter and the VSO

When Alan Carter founded the Vermont State Symphony Orchestra (VSO) in 1934, it was an almost entirely amateur ensemble, with musicians coming from across the state: a bass-playing lawyer from Woodstock; a tuba-playing paper-hanger from Rutland; a trombone-playing barber from Burlington. And, unlike any professional orchestra of the time, about one-third of the musicians were women. Carter continued to grow the VSO—no simple task, given the need to rehearse different orchestra sections in different locations, combining them only in the dress rehearsal. The VSO had no home hall or location, but performed throughout Vermont.

By 1939, Carter was ready to take the VSO on their first performance outside Vermont, to the New York World's Fair. He obtained one thousand dollars from the Vermont legislature for the trip, making the VSO the first state-supported orchestra in the nation.[14] The VSO World's Fair program was pure Carter, featuring three works by living American composers: Arcady Dubensky's *Anno 1600*;

During the 1960s, the VSO frequently broadcast their concerts. Here, in an undated photograph, Alan Carter conducts the orchestra in the studios of WCAX-TV, with Virginia deBlasiis, concertmaster, and George Finckel, principal cellist.

Courtesy of Vermont Symphony Orchestra

Robert McBride's ballet suite, *Showpiece;* and *Danza*, by John Alden Carpenter (most likely they were the first performances of these works in New York City). These were followed by a familiar, but highly challenging, crowd-pleaser—in what must have been a true barn-burner of a performance—Tchaikovsky's Fourth Symphony. As the *New York Times* commented, this program from the Vermont hinterlands "may, if anything, surprise urban professional musicians with its enterprise and discernment."[15] With the resulting national headlines (coverage ranged from *Newsweek* to *The Ladies' Home Journal*), the World's Fair concert was a publicity coup and an immense personal success for Carter. He would continue to conduct the VSO for the next forty years.

music knowledge seldom equaled by the most respected professional chamber music players of our time."[16]

Carter found his way to Barnard, Vermont, in the early 1930s, looking for a new beginning after economic hard times. In 1934, he married Barbara Kent, a daughter of the artist Rockwell Kent. In an informal concert space set up in a barn, Carter's chamber music concerts were soon drawing audiences from nearby Woodstock.[17] That same year, Carter founded the Vermont State Symphony Orchestra. In 1939, when he was already among the most prominent musicians in Vermont, Carter joined the music faculty of Middlebury College.

The Birth of the Conference

In 1946, Carter launched what he called the "Composers' Conference and Chamber Music Center." Summer concert series, including some with resident composers, were already popular in New England. In 1941, Carter and Otto Luening had co-founded the Vermont Festival of the Arts, sometimes called the Green Mountain Festival, at Middlebury College. The three-day festival included concerts by the Vermont State Symphony and what was reported to be the first English-language performance in the United States of Mozart's *The Impresario*, as well as a lecture by Virgil Thomson on "Contemporary Music." Not far away, in Saratoga Springs, New York, the Yaddo American Festival of Contemporary Music, which ended in 1952, had been guided by Aaron Copland in its early years. Yaddo included composers and performing artists, and involved innovative recording of new music for study purposes. Luening, who also attended Yaddo, saw a parallel between Yaddo and the new Middlebury conference in bringing "composers and expert chamber-music players" together.[18] But what made this conference different was the idea of bringing more experienced composers together with younger composers, trying out new works in rehearsal and concert, and adding the involvement of amateurs.

Carter's model for a summer music program was the Bread Loaf Writers' Conference, a two-week summer program of Middlebury College's Bread Loaf School of English, located in the Green Mountain National Forest in Ripton, Vermont, and within view of Bread Loaf Mountain. Four-time Pulitzer Prize-winning poet Robert Frost, who lived on a nearby farm, was a fixture at Bread Loaf. Carter reportedly asked Frost for advice about running a similar composers' conference. Frost, consistent with his persona as a thrifty Vermont farmer, gave advice that Carter no doubt did not want to hear: that a literary group such as the Bread Loaf Conference needed only one or two people to do the teaching, but that a music conference would require too many paid staff to be financially successful.[19] Obviously, Carter dismissed this advice, but Frost had put his finger on an issue that was to vex Carter and the conference for years.

Publicity for the conference start-up was through a League of Composers mailing list, well-placed news items—such as a notice that appeared in the *New York Times*[20]—and word of mouth. By this time, Carter had an extensive personal network among both professionals and amateurs.

As announced in the 1946 Middlebury College *Bulletin*, there were to be two programs, one for composers and the other for amateur players, although precisely how these programs might overlap, if at all, was unclear. The first—the Composers' Conference—was "to provide experienced criticism of scores and a program of discussion, instruction, and performance." The second—which was "an adjunct" to the Composers' Conference—was the Chamber Music Center, which would provide "contact between the composer and the student of music . . . making available ample chamber music material for both amateur and accomplished students of music." The staff would "offer personal and group instruction and coaching in the art of music making."

Beyond the descriptions of the program in the *Bulletin* and similar publications, information about many aspects of the amateurs' experience is lacking. Not surprisingly, Middlebury College did not preserve any internal or administrative documents pertaining to the conference. Thus, there are no concert programs—assuming any were printed—or participant lists, which might tell us how many amateurs were in attendance and who they were. What we do know is that the amateur music scene was a vibrant and very active one. According to one attendee's account, "the halls begin resounding at 9 A.M., and continue doing so until some indefinite, ghostly hour, well along toward morning."[21]

The conference was housed in the college's French Department building, Le Château, inspired by the Pavillon Henri IV of the Château de Fontainebleau, which provided dorm rooms as well as space for concerts. As Ernest Lubin, a composer who attended in 1950, dryly commented, however, "there was almost too much music, and one hopes that in a future year it may be possible to house the living quarters and the practice quarters separately."[22]

Early Conference Staff

For the inaugural summer in 1946, Carter, as "Director of the Conference," recruited an impressive staff, filling out a string quartet and piano ensemble, plus two staff composers, to join him for the two weeks. Perhaps most notable among the staff was Otto Luening, described in a lengthy *Baker's Biographical Dictionary of Musicians* article as a "multifaceted American composer, teacher, flutist, and conductor."[23] The other composer was Richard Donovan, professor of music at Yale. Donovan served in leadership roles at the Yaddo Festival and the American Composers Alliance, and his *Passacaglia on Vermont Folk Tunes* dates from his third year at the conference.

Edwin Ideler, one of the two violinists on staff, was concertmaster of the Louisville Symphony Orchestra. Previously, he had taught at Mannes and the Manhattan School, and performed chamber music extensively throughout New England (playing first violin in Carter's Cremona String Quartet), resulting in an award of the Elizabeth Sprague Coolidge Medal for eminent services to chamber music.[24]

The conference staff for the first year. Back row: Edwin Ideler, violin; George Finckel, cello; Alexander Broude, music publisher and amateur cellist; Raul Spivak, piano; Otto Luening, composer. Front row: Richard Donovan, composer; Alfred Frankenstein, music critic; Alan Carter, conference director and viola; and Virginia deBlasiis, violin.

Courtesy of Middlebury College Special Collections

Violinist Edwin Ideler coaches a group during the conference's first summer at Bennington.

The other violinist, Virginia "Ginny" deBlasiis,[25] grew up in a musical family in Glens Falls, New York, where she and her sister, Giovannina, a conservatory-trained pianist, ran their own chamber music series, which continues to this day. She studied violin at both the Curtis Institute and Juilliard, and was concertmaster of the VSO. She was a staff violinist for more than two decades and served as a trustee of the conference for many years. Another deBlasiis sister, the cellist Elizabeth "Bess" deBlasiis Karrick, who graduated from Yale and later studied at Juilliard, first attended the conference at Middlebury, and later served on the conference's board. Karrick was active in amateur circles, having played in the well-known music sessions in the Stockbridge home of violinist Helen Rice,[26] a founding member of the ACMP (today, the Associated Chamber Music Players, a worldwide network of amateur chamber musicians). Karrick and others made it clear early on that "amateur" was not incompatible with a high level of skill in playing.

The staff cellist, George Finckel, who performed regularly in a trio with the two deBlasiis sisters, was on the faculty of Bennington College and was the most prominent cellist in the southern Vermont area.

The staff pianist was the Argentinian Raul Spivak, who had made his Carnegie Hall recital debut in 1944, and often presented new solo piano works of South American composers in his New York City performances in the mid-1940s.[27]

The Conference's Godparent: Otto Luening

If Carter was the father of the conference, then Otto Luening was one of its godparents. Luening, a versatile and well-connected musician, was involved with the conference for more than three decades in various capacities—as staff composer, board

George Finckel

George Finckel, pictured here in his antique whalebone chair, was on the conference staff from the first year at Middlebury College. He was the patriarch of the Finckel family of cellists: George's two sons, Michael and Chris, both became professional cellists with significant careers in classical chamber music, as did his nephew, David Finckel.

George's son Michael joined the conference staff in the 1970s, and has had an extensive career as a cello soloist, composer, teacher, and conductor. Like his father, he served as principal cellist of the Vermont Symphony Orchestra. A founding member of the Trio of the Americas and the Cabrini Quartet, he performed under Pierre Boulez on the New York Philharmonic's Rug Concert series, was a member of Steve Reich and Musicians, and has been for many years the music director of the Sage City Symphony, a community orchestra in Bennington, Vermont.

George's son Chris has enjoyed a career as the cellist for the Manhattan String Quartet (and was on the conference faculty in 1988), and his nephew David Finckel was the cellist for the Emerson String Quartet for almost twenty-five years, later becoming the co-artistic director of the Chamber Music Society of Lincoln Center.

George Finckel was well-known not just as a cellist, but also for his sideline antiques shop, Finckel's Antiques, that he and his wife, Marianne "Willie" Wilson Finckel, a pianist and double bassist who was also on the Bennington College faculty, ran out of the barn on their property.[28] Staff violist Melvin Berger recalls that Finckel once arrived for a rehearsal bearing a very odd-looking, hand-held antique-seeming contraption with various handles and knives. His colleagues were absolutely baffled—perhaps as Finckel intended—about what this device could possibly be, until he explained: "this is what farmers use to castrate a bull."

Otto Luening

Although Otto Luening was born in Wisconsin, his family moved to Europe when he was twelve, and he later played flute and percussion in the Zurich Tonhalle Orchestra (under the baton of Richard Strauss, among others), acted and stage managed for James Joyce's English-language theater group, and was closely associated with the composer and virtuoso pianist Ferruccio Busoni. Luening composed chamber music for traditional ensembles, as well as film scores and orchestral and vocal works. He was a well-known opera conductor and is often remembered for his pioneering work in electronic music, much of which took place at the conference.

In his 1980 autobiography, Luening recalled that "besides the invaluable music contacts and the fund-raising experience that the conference gave me, I composed a number of works for particular performers."[29] Among these was George Finckel, who, Luening wrote, "had a strong influence on the string composing; I wrote many cello works for him and got to know all the possibilities of that fine instrument." Among those works was Luening's 1946 Suite for Cello and Piano.

Otto Luening, left, upon his retirement from the conference board of directors in 1984, receives a commemorative plaque for his almost forty years of service from board President Lionel Nowak, in Greenwall Auditorium, Bennington College.

member, and advisor. Highly regarded as a conductor as well as a composer, Luening had an impressive list of academic appointments: Eastman School of Music (1925–28), Bennington College (beginning 1934), Columbia University (beginning 1944), where he later was co-director of the Columbia-Princeton Electronic Music Center (today, the Computer Music Center), and then Juilliard (1971–73). Over the years, many of Luening's composition students or former students were at the conference,

Poet Robert Frost at the Bread Loaf School of English, 1945. Alan Carter consulted Frost about using the Bread Loaf Writers' Conference as a model for the summer music conference that Carter started the next year.

Courtesy of Middlebury College Special Collections

and Luening and his circle at Columbia University exercised considerable influence over conference activities.

The First Summer, 1946

That first summer of 1946, enthusiasm for the conference among those attending must have been almost unbounded, although ultimate implementation of some plans proved challenging. Alexander Broude, president of the music publishing firm Broude Brothers and on the side an accomplished cellist, announced that each year his firm would publish "a work submitted for the conference and selected by the composition faculty."[30] Carter's father-in-law, Rockwell Kent, offered to design the format for these annual publications. Kent was not new to this role of boosting one of his son-in-law's projects. In 1935, he had designed the program cover for the VSO's first concert, an image of an angelic figure in a gossamer skirt, floating in a starry sky while playing the violin and majestically peering down at the Green Mountains. The winning piece that first summer was Halsey Stevens's Sonatina for Flute and Piano, originally composed in 1943, and which was duly published by Broude Brothers, with a cover acknowledgment to the conference, though without being graced by a Rockwell Kent design. But after the first summer, the project seems to have lost steam. No other works appear to have been published in the series.

In the conference's early years, composers were encouraged to bring their completed or in-progress compositions for feedback from the composition staff, with the works then performed, if possible, given limits on instrumentation.

That first summer of 1946, as reported by Alfred Frankenstein in a brief but informative notice in the League of Composers periodical *Modern Music*, "the sport and game of making music was exemplified with great gusto and high spirits" in conference composer Frederick Harold Chapman's Theme and Variations for two violins.[31] Chapman, who later was an influential teacher and composer in Hampton, Virginia, had written this work for his wife and brother-in-law to play without him after he was drafted into military service in 1942.[32]

Another work premiered at the conference in 1946, a quartet movement by Héctor Alberto Tosar Errecart, a prominent Uruguayan pianist and composer, exhibited a "poignant and urgent expressionism." Tosar Errecart's presence at the conference was likely through staff pianist Raul Spivak.

Mathilde McKinney's Trio for violin, viola, and piano was "an interesting and spirited example of *Gebrauchsmusik*"—literally, "music for use," that is, music written for that specific occasion and perhaps with those (possibly amateur) performers in mind. McKinney was for many years professor of piano at Westminster Choir College.

Halsey Stevens's Quintet for flute, piano, and strings showed an "exquisite refinement of texture . . . subtleties of form and . . . vivid melodiousness." Stevens had just commenced what was to be an influential three-decade career teaching composition at the University of Southern California (among his students was Donald Crockett, who became the conference's senior composer-in-residence in 2002). The next summer, in 1947, Stevens joined the conference's composition staff.

Expanding the Conference Staff

During the next four years at Middlebury, the conference's staff was gradually expanded with many notable performers and composers. In 1948, the violinist Maurice Wilk, of the Bach Aria Group, joined the conference. New composers that year included Everett Helm, a composer, critic, and music historian based in Germany whose Piano Concerto was premiered by the Berlin Philharmonic three years later;[33] Normand Lockwood, who as a teenager studied with Ottorino Respighi in Rome and later in Paris with Nadia Boulanger, and was teaching at Columbia University at the time; and Edmund Haines, who received a Pulitzer award for his First Symphony in 1941, and was teaching at Sarah Lawrence College, where he spent most of his career.[34] The music publisher Alexander Broude returned.

By 1949, the conference's dozen staff members included, in addition to the returning members, Jean Berger, faculty pianist at Middlebury College; Dan Farnsworth, who joined George Finckel as a staff cellist; and composer Ingolf Dahl, chair of the music department at the University of Southern California. Dahl was joined by composer and pianist Esther Williamson (later Ballou), who as a 1937 graduate of Bennington College had studied with Luening. She went on to attend Mills College and the Juilliard School of Music, where she was on the faculty from 1943 to 1950.[35]

Also in 1949, the oboist Robert Bloom was in attendance, joining his Bach Aria Group colleague Maurice Wilk. Bloom was to remain affiliated with the conference for many years, including serving on the board during the 1950s. Among the foremost oboists of his generation, Bloom was a founding member of the Bach Aria Group. As a result of his association with Luening, who was his musical colleague at the conference, Bloom was inspired to write several chamber music works, primarily during the 1950s. Composers at the conference, in turn, with a player of Bloom's stature in their midst, wrote works with him in mind, such as Luening's *Legend* for oboe and strings (1950) and *Three Nocturnes* for oboe and piano

(1951); Lionel Nowak's Sonata (1949) and Quartet for oboe and strings (1952); Roger Goeb's two wind quintets (1952 and 1955); and Jean Berger's *Sonata da Camera* (1949), published by Broude Brothers. In 1950, composer Roger Goeb, who was to have a significant role in shaping the composer side of the conference, joined the composition staff.

Although directories of staff and participants have not survived from the Middlebury years, apparently "scholarships" (typically, a waiver of fees for room and board) were awarded for composers, and sometimes for instrumentalists as well. As evidenced by a notice in the *New York Times* in 1949, seven scholarships were awarded for that summer.[36]

Carter seems to have had a knack for choosing young musicians of great potential, including:

Helen Laird (voice and composition), who went on to have a distinguished singing career and served as the dean of Temple University School of Music;

Bernard Garfield (bassoon), a prolific composer who later founded the New York Woodwind Quintet and served for forty-three years as principal bassoonist of the Philadelphia Orchestra;

Barbara Ann Garvey (violin), who later became a leading authority on seventeenth-century violin technique;

Robert Nagel Jr. (composition), a distinguished trumpeter and composer who taught at Yale School of Music, New England Conservatory, and

Juilliard, among others, and founded the New York
Brass Quintet; and

Douglas Townsend (composition), a music historian
and composer who edited the *Musical Heritage
Review* and held teaching appointments at
Brooklyn College and the City University of New
York, among others.

Carter did not limit conference staff to composers and
professional performers. He included Alfred Frankenstein,
music and art critic of the *San Francisco Chronicle*, and former
professional clarinetist, who was to share his insights about
the role of the music critic. Music publisher Alexander Broude
presented on publication, performing rights, and related matters. Carter Harman, a composer (he had studied composition
with Otto Luening at Columbia) who was also a music critic
for the *New York Times* (and later for *Time* magazine) was
on the staff.[37] Richard Dana, amateur flutist and founder of
the Music Press, Inc., and publisher of notable contemporary
works, such as the Virgil Thomson and Gertrude Stein operas
Four Saints in Three Acts and *The Mother of Us All*, was a staff
member in 1949.[38]

Conference participants attended demonstrations of folk
music by Pete Seeger, joined by Marguerite Olney, the archivist who assembled the renowned Flanders Ballad Collection
at Middlebury, one of the greatest folk music archives in the
nation. Including professional journalists and publishers on
the conference staff was a savvy publicity strategy on Carter's
part. In addition to Frankenstein's report in *Modern Music*,
other press notices appeared as well.

A Remarkable Experiment

What we know today as the Chamber Music Conference was configured somewhat differently: "The Conference" was the composer side of the program, with, in the early years, a composition staff of three to six composers and as many as twenty younger or amateur composers. The other side, "The Center," was staffed by professional "interpretative" musicians, who coached the amateur players, but who also were assigned to read the new works written or revised on the spot by the composers. By the fifth year of the conference, as composer Ernest Lubin described them, activities seem to have coalesced into an informal schedule: "Each morning after breakfast, while the [amateur] instrumentalists divide into chamber music groups under the guidance of the instrumental faculty . . . the composers meet together to discuss one aspect or another of their problems." After lunch, there was a reading session of the composers' works, with feedback provided by the staff composers and performing musicians. The next day, the edited works could be brought back and read again. The afternoons were apparently free for the amateurs to rehearse their morning pieces or to read other works. In the evening, in the "grand salon of the château" there would be a chamber music and orchestral concert during which works by the composers present were played, together with other contemporary pieces, and "occasionally a concerto of Bach or Vivaldi."

The innovative Bread Loaf Conference, which had inspired Carter's founding of his conference, brought writers to Middlebury for intensive summer workshops. But according to Lubin, this new music conference represented an "even more remarkable experiment," as it embraced the "wisdom of Alan

Carter's philosophy of laissez-faire"—composers were free to participate as they wished, and they were under "no obligation of any kind."

The Early Recordings

In 1948, as announced in bold-faced text in the annual Middlebury College *Bulletin* promoting the conference, an important new feature was added: audio recordings would be made of the new works included in the final concert as well as amateur musicians' rehearsals and performances. These recordings were to be available for purchase for a "nominal fee." From that summer on, such recordings were routinely made on what was then state-of-the-art reel-to-reel audio equipment. For students and not-yet-established composers, having a recording of their work, in a reading or live performance by the top-notch professional musicians at the conference, was a valuable addition to their portfolios.

At least in some sense, the conference was now on the map. Years later, Luening related how notable musicians might drop by, giving as an example violinist Nathan Milstein, who showed up at Middlebury one morning. He reported: "at a moment's notice we gave Bach's G Major *Brandenburg* Concerto ... with Edmund Haines at the piano, a very spirited reading."[39]

Pierre Boulez, Composer-in-Residence?

The conference caught the attention of John Cage, and he recommended it to a young French composer he had become friends with during a previous visit to Paris—Pierre Boulez. At the time, twenty-four-year-old Boulez was just at the start of a career that would establish him as one of the dominating figures in twentieth-century music. Cage was better known at the time, but still two years away from conceptualizing the piece he considered his most important—4'33"—four minutes and thirty-three seconds of silence for unspecified instrument(s), written in 1952.

"You are invited to spend two weeks in Middlebury, Vermont in August (all expenses paid and 85 dollars on top – it's not a lot); it's a 'Composers' Conference,'" Cage wrote to Boulez in June 1950.[40] Cage immediately added, reducing the warmth of his implicit endorsement by quite a few degrees, "I can't say whether it is interesting because I've never been there." (Cage's view that the conference's offer of an $85 honorarium was "not a lot" was not entirely fair; for the conference at the time, it was far more than regular staff were customarily paid.)

Boulez responded with enthusiasm ("excellent news you gave me. Extraordinary!!") and a series of detailed questions, about the what, where, and when of his visit, including his confession ("it will make you blush") that he did not know where Vermont was.

Writing again, Cage, eager to get Boulez to the conference, reported that Alan Carter "will be delighted to have you present this summer."

"You can do what you like for it, discussions, anything, but they want you to play some of your music," he added. Helping Boulez on the geography question, slightly, he added in a postscript that "Vermont is a bit closer to the North Pole than N.Y.C."

They planned some remarkable presentations (Boulez insisted that he would only speak French, believing his English was inadequate) on Ravel, Schoenberg, Stravinsky, Webern, "rhythm and dodecaphony," and Boulez's Second Sonata for piano.

But Boulez, on tour in South America, was unable to get a visa from the U.S. consulate in Buenos Aires. "They made me fill in excessively detailed forms and took my fingerprints sixteen times," he lamented, after the visa did not arrive. Having given up on finding Vermont, wherever it may have been, he sailed for Paris, asking Cage to "please tell Middlebury that it really isn't my fault if I can't come, but the idiocy on the part of a Consulate."

Cage, however, did not give up. "I have told the whole story to Mr. Carter (Middlebury), telling him that we still have hopes that you will arrive here for the Conference." He even had Aaron Copland telegraph the U.S. embassy in Paris. But despite Cage's exhaustive efforts to make the trip happen, Boulez made other commitments once he was back in Paris.

Sadly, we will never know how Boulez might have reacted upon arriving at the 1950 conference and coming *face à face* with the French-inspired Le Château. Boulez expressed his hope to Cage that he might come the next year, but by then the conference had left Middlebury and Le Château for the Jennings music building—with its own upper-class dignity—at Bennington College.

III. The Early Bennington Years: A Cooperative Venture, 1951 to 1960

Bring composers and amateurs together, O.K.?

—George Grossman, staff violist, letter to conference
director Alan Carter, June 1954

AFTER THE CONFERENCE'S FIFTH SEASON drew to a close at Middlebury College in 1950 (alas, without Boulez or Cage in attendance), composer Ernest Lubin, who had attended the conference that summer, filed a report in the *New York Times*:

[A]s it exists now, the conference has a valuable contribution to make to our musical life, and one that is not duplicated anywhere else. This is the kind of thing that can be a stimulus to America's coming of age creatively.[41]

In a photo published in Vermont Life *in 1955, Alan Carter conducts the conference chamber orchestra in the Carriage Barn. Carter's annual welcome letter to attendees typically stated that dress at the conference was "always informal" except for the "semi-formal" public concerts.*

Photo by John F. Smith Jr., courtesy of
Middlebury College Special Collections

The move roughly ninety miles to the south to Bennington College brought the conference closer to the urban centers, particularly New York City and its environs, where many participating musicians resided. At the same time, the Vermont location in the foothills of the Green Mountains offered a bucolic summer retreat for musical urbanites. And if there was some concern that the conference had outgrown the Middlebury facilities, Bennington, whether this was known at the time or not, was to prove capable of hosting the conference through many years of growth.

From its opening in 1932, Bennington College had focused on the arts—the performing arts especially. Otto Luening had led the music program at Bennington from 1934 to 1944, when he left for Barnard College. Conference cellist George Finckel was also on the college faculty. Long before the conference's arrival on campus, the college had hosted its own summer programs, including the now-legendary Bennington School of the Dance, which started in 1934 under the direction of faculty member Martha Hill.[42] Five years later, through Luening's efforts, the college had expanded the eight-week program into the Bennington School of the Arts, adding a festival week with recitals of both contemporary chamber music and older repertory. Among the attendees at those concerts in 1940 was composer Frank Wigglesworth, who later began a long-term affiliation with the conference. The conference was thus settling in at a college with a reputation for summer arts programming.

Bennington, as a women's college (men first matriculated in 1969, although the theater program had admitted men prior to that), was unusual in its non-traditional educational philosophy, including off-campus "field study" as part of a "learn by doing" approach. The College's atmosphere of artsy, free-spirited

36

creativity was defined in a 1937 *Life* magazine pictorial essay by Alfred Eisenstaedt,[43] whose photos have been occasionally displayed in the campus Commons building over the years. In that essay, Bennington is presented as a progressive educational haven, bohemian yet glamorous, for daughters of some of America's wealthiest and most famous families. The article's lead image is of a winsome Peggy Hepburn ("it costs Peggy Hepburn $1,675 a year to look out this window," reads the caption), one of the two sisters of Hollywood's Katharine who were attending at the time.

Mimi Wallner, a music major in the class of 1940 who would attend the conference in 1949, was among the other students featured in the article. Eisenstaedt captures her deep in thought, with the caption explaining that "workshirt and blue jeans are popular at Bennington," adding that "during 'field' periods she studies piano in New York."

In 1950, the year before the conference arrived, the U.S. State Department featured Bennington College in a film intended to showcase its progressive educational philosophy, and included a scene in which students perform Schubert's Cello Quintet in the Carriage Barn. What better location for a composer conference and amateur chamber music summer program? Perhaps the only drawback, as wryly noted by staff cellist Alexander Kouguell, who joined the conference in 1958, was that "we never did have air conditioning."

The Setting

When conference staff and participants arrived in the summer of 1951, the brick Commons building towered over the campus, with the eleven original "colonial" college houses—all built in the 1930s—arrayed in parallel lines, and bearing the names of

Mimi Wallner, "Copyist and Autographer"

Mimi Wallner first attended the conference at Middlebury in 1949 as a composition and double bass scholarship recipient. One of her compositions, "scored for stepladder and various cleaning tools that made appropriate noises," made a spectacular impression at a festival sponsored by the Intercollegiate Music Guild of America.[44]

After graduating from Bennington in 1940, she was Virgil Thomson's amanuensis in his fabled Chelsea Hotel suite. Thomson credited her copying and editing work with helping to launch his composing career, describing her as "a curly-haired blonde" who "could copy music, speak French, and play the double bass."[45]

She returned to the conference in 1951, where she is described in the conference brochure as a "noted copyist and autographer." Because xerographic photocopying was not commercially introduced by Xerox until 1959, Wallner and other skilled copyists (including the composer Chou Wen-chung) were indispensable in copying musical scores, making corrections, and extracting parts for rehearsal and performance, all on a very tight schedule. Wallner later married staff oboist Robert Bloom—perhaps the first of many conference romances?—and, as Mrs. Bloom, returned as the conference's music librarian for 1972 and 1973.

the wealthy founding families, early supporters, and educational leaders who inspired the college's founding. The college houses framed the Commons lawn, with its "end of the world" view over the Walloomsac River valley to Mount Anthony and the Bennington Battle Monument to the southeast. As new conference participants arrived on campus each year for the sixty-seven years that the conference was at Bennington, their experience was probably much like that of Alan Arkin, who arrived in 1954 as a student in the college's theater studio, feeling, as he walked past the "pristine New England cottages," as though he were "an extra in a Judy Garland movie."[46]

All through the years of the conference's residence at Bennington, the Jennings music building and the Carriage Barn were the center of the conference's activities, more than a quarter-mile north of Commons and the college houses. When Laura Hall Jennings donated her 140-acre estate to create the campus, her daughter Elsie Jennings Franklin continued living in the imposing forty-room family mansion, which had been built of local Vermont granite for the Jennings family in 1903. Franklin, one of the college founders and leader of campus construction projects during its early years, continued to live in the family mansion, then called "Fairview," until 1939, when it, along with the Carriage Barn, was turned over to the college. The Jennings building is thought by some to be the inspiration for North Bennington novelist Shirley Jackson's *The Haunting of Hill House*.

The mansion was quickly taken over for the exclusive use of the music program, and "Jennings Hall" became the Jennings music building. Conference attendees were housed in the college houses and had a twice or thrice daily walk to and from Jennings and the Carriage Barn.

The move from Middlebury to Bennington College has been attributed to the conference's increasing popularity. The conference, after five years, had simply outgrown the facilities—or so the story goes.[47] The *New York Times* reported in early 1951 that the relocation had been caused by a fire at Middlebury,[48] which may have been the cause of the college's inability to accommodate the conference. The story of the fire, however, seems questionable; the relevant digitized newspaper and magazine database contains no report of a fire on the Middlebury campus during that period.

What seems like the real impetus for the move emerged in a brief history of the conference, written in 1964 by Alan Carter. There, Carter offered an entirely different reason: the Middlebury administration had notified him that the operation of the conference was a "continuing financial loss to the college and it would be necessary to discontinue it." Rather than accept the demise of the conference, Carter took it to Bennington College.

An Auspicious Beginning

The conference's first decades at Bennington College were exceptionally eventful. The organization began to grow, attracting and retaining a staff roster of top-notch players who were at ease with the challenges presented by the number of new works routinely read and performed. Dozens of young composers, many of whom would go on to attain prominence as creative artists and teachers—and many of whom would return in later years—extended the conference's reputation as a testing ground for new musical creativity. Conference composers began innovative experiments with electronic music, while at the same time, the conference launched a New York City concert series as a way of sharing with a broader audience the new music created at the conference. There truly seemed to be no bounds on the conference's ambitions.

The conference kept its original model from Middlebury College: composer residencies—essentially, mentoring opportunities for younger composers—with a population of amateur players who brought their own enthusiasm for making music. This separation of the roles of amateurs from composers was in keeping with the broader cultural trend, well established by the mid-twentieth century, in which new music had become almost exclusively the purview of professionals, in terms of both creation and performance. The amateur repertory, in contrast, was largely if not exclusively the chamber music works of the distant past. And yet, as we will see, what makes this period in the conference's history so noteworthy is that this model was almost immediately questioned and put to the test. All this went on while in the background, the conference, now managed as an independent nonprofit operation, faced ongoing challenges to fiscal stability and perhaps even its existence.

The conference's arrival for its first summer at Bennington College in 1951 must have seemed to all involved to be a very promising start. With financial support from the Alice M. Ditson Fund, the conference announced five public concerts during the two-week schedule.

The conference seemed eager to prove itself in its new setting, and presented not five, but six, concerts in the Carriage Barn. Included on these concerts were six first performances of works by composers-in-residence that summer—Esther Williamson Ballou, James Dalgleish, Roger Goeb, Otto Luening, John McLennan, and Norma Wendelburg—in addition to many other contemporary works.

The Alice M. Ditson Fund

The Alice M. Ditson Fund, established in 1940 at Columbia University by the widow of Boston music publisher Oliver Ditson, would prove to be a stalwart supporter of the conference on an ongoing basis, making grants to the conference for virtually all of its seventy-five years. The fund's initial advisory committee's focus on contemporary music, and an emphasis on support for performances of music by emerging composers—a priority of the fund to the present, as stated on its website—made the conference a perfect fit with the fund's priorities.

Luening continued to head the composition side of the conference, but he was now joined by several composers who were to make significant contributions to the conference over the years. Bennington faculty member and conference incorporator Lionel Nowak was among them. Nowak was a gifted pianist (he made his formal debut with the Cleveland Orchestra at thirteen) and composer. Nowak would later serve on the conference's board and guided the organization through some of its most difficult times over almost four decades.

The composer Frank Wigglesworth, "whose music was an important part of New York's new-music landscape in the 1950's,"[49] also joined the conference composition staff at Bennington. Wigglesworth, a former student of Luening, among others, taught composition at Columbia University beginning in 1947, and later

Two composers who had long-term roles at the conference: Lionel Nowak, right, and Frank Wigglesworth, in the Jennings music building lobby, 1984.

Photo by Alice Berman

In an undated photo from the conference's 1958 brochure, Alan Carter is leading the "Center orchestra" in a reading of a new work by Frank Wigglesworth. Because conference staff musicians alone would not have made up an orchestra of this size, they were joined by amateurs from the Chamber Music Center side of the conference.

Courtesy of Chou Wen-chung

taught at Queens College and the New School for Social Research. In 1954 he was named a fellow of the American Academy in Rome. From 1951 until shortly before his death in 1996, he served on the conference's board or as an advisor to the board.

Composer Roger Goeb took on the important yet time-consuming role of screening composer applications and distributing scholarship support. Goeb, "a composer whose works were

admired for their deft coloration and inherent lyricism,"[50] was a former private composition student of Otto Luening. He received two Guggenheim fellowships (1950 and 1951) and was a prolific and frequently performed composer of chamber works during the 1950s and 1960s. His Third Symphony was premiered in a live radio broadcast and later recorded by the CBS Symphony under Leopold Stokowski in 1952.

Theodore Strongin was also on the composition staff. Strongin, who was also a journalist and music critic, would go on to write several articles about the conference in the 1950s that give us an insider's perspective and must have done much to boost the conference's visibility.

The composer Esther Williamson Ballou also returned that summer of 1951, as did the music critic Alfred Frankenstein.[51] Alexander Broude's place as the representative of the music publishing world was taken by Milton Feist of Mercury Music.

New Organization, Same Musicians

Despite the familiar faces on the composition staff, in one important sense, the conference was starting anew at Bennington College in 1951. Instead of being offered as a summer program of the college, as it had been at Middlebury for the previous five years, the conference was an independent organization, now named *Bennington Composers' Conference and Chamber Music Center, Inc.*

The new organization was not formally incorporated as a Vermont nonprofit corporation until 1953, and the articles of association stated that the organization's purpose was "encouraging young and unknown composers of ability and furthering the knowledge of established composers by instruction, criticizing, and playing their untried works." No mention of amateur

Theodore Strongin

Theodore Strongin, composer, flutist, and music critic.

Courtesy of Michael Finckel

Theodore Strongin first attended the conference at Middlebury College in 1948 as a member of the composition staff, but he also brought his music critic's perspective to the conference. He had studied at Harvard and Bard, later attended Juilliard and Columbia, and for a time, taught composition at Bennington and Dartmouth. He was a prominent music critic, starting as a reviewer for the *New York Herald Tribune* and later working at the *New York Times*, where he often championed new music. In addition, he had a reputation as a highly skilled entomologist, having identified several species of rare beetles for the American Museum of Natural History.[52] His Sonata for Solo Cello was written for conference cellist George Finckel, who often performed it on tour throughout the United States.

involvement in the "Chamber Music Center" was included; the composer-centric focus of the "Composers' Conference" was apparently foremost in the minds of the incorporators. For at the outset of the conference's life as an independent nonprofit corporation, the leadership of the conference was clearly in the hands of the professionals: two performing musicians, three composers, two Bennington College staff members—and no amateur musicians.

The seven incorporators, who had legal authority to appoint the first board of trustees (in this case, as was typical, they appointed themselves), were Alan Carter, Otto Luening, Theodore Strongin, Lionel Nowak, George Finckel, Thomas Brockway, and Joseph Parry.

To be expected, the two good friends, Carter, the original founder of the program at Middlebury College, and Luening, the leading composer involved in the conference's founding, were incorporators. Strongin had also been a staff composer for several years when the conference was at Middlebury. Nowak was then on the faculty of Bennington College, and was an obvious choice for the conference's staff and board of trustees. Carter, Luening, Strongin, and Nowak were joined by Finckel, the conference's staff cellist since the first year at Middlebury.

The two remaining incorporators, Brockway and Parry, were likely music lovers, but neither was an active musician—amateur or professional. Their involvement, however, ensured that the conference would be closely connected to the college. Brockway was a professor of history, dean (1952–61), and three-time acting president of Bennington College. He soon assumed the position of vice president of the conference's board of trustees. A close friend of cellist George Finckel, Brockway was to serve in various leadership roles with the conference's board for the next twenty years. Brockway's daughter, Joan Brockway Esch, a professional cellist, was on the conference staff in 1963 and 1964.

Perhaps even more important on a day-to-day functional level, Parry, head of food services at the college, was an incorporator and was soon serving as the conference's treasurer, a post he would hold for the next seventeen years until his resignation in 1970. Parry had responsibility for receiving and processing application fees and tuition payments, thus taking on a major administrative chore, as well as assisting Carter with foundation grant proposals. In addition to his financial reporting duties at board meetings, he also fielded complaints about the college's food service, as he did at the 1969 annual meeting of the trustees. At that meeting, he offered a "good help is hard to find" defense to a complaint about the quality of the food, and he promised—one can only wonder with what degree of sincerity—that he would "look into the feasibility" of having the tables "bussed next year rather than each individual returning his dishes and tray to the kitchen."

Some Notable Newcomers

As it settled in at Bennington in the early 1950s, the conference began to attract a talented roster of performing musicians whose involvement would significantly influence the conference's direction and operations. The first of them, Max Pollikoff, arrived in 1952, the conference's second summer at Bennington.

Pollikoff was among the conference's most high-profile and charismatic performers. A prominent New York City–based violinist and indefatigable advocate for new music, he, like Carter, had studied violin with Leopold Auer in New York City and had also studied in Europe. Staff composer Mario

Davidovsky recalled Pollikoff as "a good violin player in the Mischa Elman style, very schmaltzy . . . he would play some Purcell dances and he made it sound like Tzigane music."[53] Pollikoff's philosophy was that "music belongs to the moment we are living in, and somebody writing for today can't write for 50 years ago. Contemporary music is only avant-garde because it takes us so long to catch up with it." Noted for his wit, perhaps his most memorable comment was that "death does not enhance" contemporary composers, "only possibly their music."[54]

Today, Pollikoff is remembered primarily for his *Music in Our Time* concert series in New York City, but his role at the conference was a leading one, too, as he returned for more than twenty years, playing in numerous first performances of chamber and solo works, serving as the chamber orchestra's concertmaster, and taking on increasing leadership responsibilities over time. In 1962, he was listed in the conference directory as co-director; by 1963, he was responsible for hiring string staff members; by 1964, he was responsible for hiring all staff members; and in 1970, he was named associate director.

Left to right: Alan Carter, Robert Bloom, and Max Pollikoff in the Carriage Barn during the 1962 conference.

Pollikoff was also of a potentially difficult artistic temperament and ego. On one occasion, Davidovsky was seen going into a campus building for a meeting with Pollikoff. A few minutes later, Davidovsky emerged, clearly unsatisfied with the outcome of their conversation. As a composer whose thoughts routinely turned pitch series in inversion, retrograde, or similar permutations, Davidovsky turned to the onlookers and asked in exasperation, "Do you know what Pollikoff is spelled backwards?!"

The second of these newcomers—arriving in 1953, the summer after Pollikoff—would have a similarly outsized role at the conference: George Grossman. Grossman was a Juilliard-trained violist who, before coming to the conference in 1953, had played in the Baltimore Symphony and NBC Symphony, as well as in the Guilet Quartet. Later, he joined the faculty of Carnegie Mellon University in Pittsburgh. Grossman was responsible for recruiting staff members and participants from the Pittsburgh area, giving rise to teasing references to the "Pittsburgh mafia" at the conference.

For almost twenty-five years at the conference, Grossman had a primary role in shaping the amateur experience. In the 1970s, he was referred to in the conference brochure as the "chief coach," and in 1976 he became the music director. Conducting works

Staff violist George Grossman directing participants to their seats in 1968 in the Jennings music building, perhaps for one of his massed readings of string quartets. Later, he recalled being immersed in "playing and teaching endless hours every day" upon his arrival at the conference in 1953, yet he "couldn't wait to get back the next summer." The violist, lower right, is Hassler Whitney.

Courtesy of UVM Special Collections

written for string quartet as string orchestra pieces was his way of introducing string players en masse to the string quartet literature, although some amateurs shunned these sessions as going against the one-on-a-part chamber music concept. A demanding but quirky coach, he could be expected to admonish amateur ensembles that they were "too loud!" even before they began playing. His penchant for interrupting earned him the nickname "twelve-bar Grossman," since twelve bars was about how far he would let an amateur ensemble play before stopping them.

One Organization, Two Programs

During the first two decades at Bennington College, 1951 to 1971, and even beyond, the conference was two separate programs: the amateur "Chamber Music Center," on the one hand, and the "Composers' Conference" on the other.

For the conference's second year at Bennington, 1952, we have for the first time a full listing of attendees as well as a financial report allowing us to piece together how the organization was run. The conference's roster lists sixty-six individuals. Twelve were core staff members (including director Alan Carter) who each received "professional fees" of $40 for their two weeks at the conference. Among the paid staff were five composers—Esther Williamson Ballou, Roger Goeb, Otto Luening, Lionel Nowak, and Theodore Strongin. Nineteen other composers attended, receiving varying amounts of scholarship support. Although the roster does not indicate whether conferees were amateur participants or professional staff, there appear to be about twenty amateurs—roughly a third of the conferees and equal to the number of scholarship composers attending.

To avoid confusion about these two programs, in 1954 the conference developed separate brochures for each. In a letter sent to previous conference attendees, including composers Ezra Laderman and Chou Wen-chung (whose help Carter sought in recruiting new composer applicants), Carter explained that in prior years, when only one brochure had been circulated, "chamber players when reading the combined circular would be given the impression that they would be playing nothing but contemporary music hot off the pen." By "chamber players," Carter clearly meant the amateurs attending the Chamber Music Center. Through the early years, the conference sought to differentiate these programs explicitly. Six years later, for example, in staff meeting notes from 1960, Max Pollikoff is quoted to the effect that "future advertising would make clear that the Chamber Music Center and Composers' Conference are separate entities."

Despite the promotion of this image of two "separate entities," there were clear signs that the dichotomy between amateurs and professionals was never complete. An example of the blurred distinction was violinist and violist Ellen Loeb, who first attended in 1954. She was certainly an accomplished player, having graduated from the American Conservatory of Music in Chicago. She later performed with the Adirondack Players, a chamber ensemble in Saranac Lake, New York, where she resided with her husband, James Loeb, the owner and publisher of the *Adirondack Daily Enterprise*. James Loeb was a politically involved activist on a range of liberal causes, resulting in his appointment by President Kennedy to an ambassadorship to Peru and later to Guinea. During her husband's ambassadorship to Peru, Loeb played in the viola section of the National Symphony Orchestra of Peru.

Ellen Loeb was an amateur player only in the sense, perhaps, that she did not make music her livelihood. A conference musician's status as either amateur or professional staff is not indicated—that in and of itself seems remarkable—on the conference directories during the 1950s. She is simply listed in 1954, for example, as "Loeb, Mrs. James (Ellen)" without identification even of her instrument. Loeb and Elizabeth deBlasiis Karrick, a professional-level amateur cellist, were among the first amateurs to serve on the conference board of trustees. Both Loeb and Karrick—highly accomplished musicians, who apparently chose, for whatever reason, not to pursue professional careers—would have defined "amateur" within the culture of the conference, making it clear that "amateur" need not mean "unskilled."

George Grossman was clearly concerned about the split between the composers and the amateurs. In a letter to Carter in June 1954 he offered his own, apparently unsolicited view: "Suggestion: I think the chamber players interest may be aroused and increased by presenting on each <u>concert</u> <u>one</u> work which they have studied. Also composers should be urged to write music <u>for</u> amateur players – perhaps to be studied <u>and</u> performed by them right <u>in</u> Bennington. Bring composers and amateurs together, O.K.?" Grossman's suggestion seems to have prevailed, at least to some extent.

Reporting from the conference in 1956 in the *New York Times*, Theodore Strongin noted that "a new facet, one that began quietly a few seasons ago, became an official part of the conference routine. It had to happen sooner or later." Strongin went on to describe the amateurs' reactions when they "volunteer to play music by the composers they live with for two weeks."

> Two objections were very common: technical difficulty and harshness of sound. Amateurs felt that

they played for pleasure and saw no reason to extend
themselves. But all said they understood better the
piece given in concert after having played it the night
before. A few said they liked it. Five asked for more
chances at their new friends' works—and wanted
to hear them done by experts later. Several asked
for contemporary works for the chamber orchestra,
where they play alongside staff.

Ultimately, as Strongin described it, "very few amateurs discovered a new and abounding love for contemporary music," but
nevertheless "by far the commonest reaction of all to playing
music by Bennington friends was: 'I'm willing to try.'" The
composers, on the other hand, "were impressed by the extra
skill needed to write easy but still expressive music. 'It's much
harder than writing for virtuosi' was one comment."[55]
But whether the conference should support a closer relationship between the composer and amateur sides of the conference,
or whether it should foster an even more distinct and separate
relationship, continued to be an open question throughout the
conference's first two decades at Bennington. At a board executive
committee meeting in December 1966, the committee (Carter,
Loeb, and Pollikoff) took up the question of whether the organization should change its name, since *Bennington Composers'
Conference and Chamber Music Center, Inc.*, was thought by all
members of the committee to be "too long and unwieldy and too
connected by association of names with Bennington College."
This was among the first of several discussions on the board
level about what the conference should be called.
The discussion, however, immediately shifted—probably
at the prodding of Carter—to whether the renaming should

involve *two* names for *two* reorganized, separate entities. Loeb is recorded as responding that the two-entity proposal would "negate one of the unique features of the conference in that it makes players (amateur) aware of what is going on and, although this may not always be pleasant and it may have its abrasive qualities, it is a process of learning."

Next, none other than Pollikoff, a champion of new music who had just six years earlier emphasized to the board of trustees that the conference and center were "two separate entities," immediately agreed with Loeb. "We must get across to the amateurs," he is recorded as stating, "that Chamber Music is also Contemporary Music and that the Chamber Music Center is a marriage between the player and the composer." Thus, in Pollikoff's view, "the Chamber Music Center is a necessary adjunct to the Composers' Conference by having the players be a part of the composing area." The composers, on the other hand, "should be made to realize that music is not being done alone (that is to say, just composed for the sake of composing it), it is also going to be performed." Pollikoff went on to recommend that the amateurs should have an opportunity to study a contemporary work. "Contemporary music must be gotten out of the cliques; we need to get it back to the audiences." Then, in a surprising statement from an such an advocate of new music, Pollikoff even suggested that "we might also attempt to reach the Composers by having them write in 4/4 time so that the players can read the music and then let them worry about [how] they are going to read something in 7/16 meter." Thus, ten years after Theodore Strongin described amateurs playing their composer friends' music at the conference, the amateur-composer relationship continued to be debated by the conference's leadership.

On the question of a new name, "it was requested that anyone having a suggestion for a new name or names submit it to the Executive Committee for consideration." None appears to have been forthcoming. But the idea of splitting the conference into two separate organizations was abandoned—at least for the time being.

New Composers

Throughout the 1950s, the conference was attracting what today might be called "emerging" composers—young and talented, with great potential but not yet established professionally. Many of these composers would go on to successful and influential careers, thus extending even further the reach and reputation of the conference.

During the conference's early years, afternoons were when staff musicians read through new works by the conference composers. Here, in 1954, George Grossman, viola, and George Finckel, cello, play through a new work while the composer, Margaret Buechner, listens.

Photo by John F. Smith Jr., courtesy of Middlebury College Special Collections

Among the 1952 attendees was composer George Rochberg, then in his twelve-tone compositional period—he integrated tonal elements into his music roughly a decade later. He attended the conference on the cusp of his prominence as a composer, as his *Night Music* was to be premiered by the New York Philharmonic within the year. Rochberg was teaching composition at the Curtis Institute of Music at the time, as well as serving as editor at the Theodore Presser Company.[56]

Another young composer at the conference in 1952 was Ezra Laderman, another Luening student, who had just finished his master of arts degree in music at Columbia University. Later, as a professor at the State University of New York, Binghamton, he returned to the conference as a resident composer in 1967 and 1968. This well-connected composer went on to teach at the Yale School of Music, where for six years he served as dean. Among his many other leadership roles in the arts, he served from 1979 to 1982 as director of the music program at the National Endowment for the Arts, which was an important source of funding for the conference. He also served as president of the American Academy of Arts and Letters. Like Rochberg, Laderman found a way to incorporate tonal music in his work: "When I was very young, everything I wrote was tonal; and after that, atonal; and then serial. Finally, I've come back to tonality—but in a synthesized form, with the freedom to call upon all techniques."[57]

In 1953 and 1954, composer Chou Wen-chung was in attendance and provided assistance with copying music. Chou had emigrated from China seven years earlier, and, when he first attended the conference, he was studying with Luening at Columbia and privately with Edgard Varèse. Chou is credited with being the first composer who effectively worked authentic Asian musical elements into compositions that were predominantly Western in style and instrumentation. His early orchestral work *Landscapes* was premiered by the San Francisco Symphony conducted by Leopold Stokowski in 1953, and is often cited as independent of either Western or Eastern musical grammar. The premiere was given a positive review by the conference's own Alfred Frankenstein ("adroit and imaginative use of ancient Chinese tunes"). Chou returned to the conference again as a staff composer in 1963 and 1964.

In 1954, the teenaged Frederic Rzewski—recommended for a composition scholarship by Lionel Nowak—was at the conference. Rzewski went on to earn degrees from Harvard and Yale, and to establish a reputation as virtuoso pianist and an iconoclastic, stylistically versatile composer of works with overt political themes, such as his thirty-six variations for piano on *The People United Will Never Be Defeated!* (1975). Commenting on his time at Bennington, Rzewski explained:

I have vivid memories of the Bennington conference in the summer of 1954, when I was 16. I was tired of a job serving ice cream at Howard Johnson's in Provincetown and wanted something different. I remember hearing Webern's Piano Variations for the first time played by Lionel Nowak, an idiosyncratic cellist named George Finckel, and a drunken Roger Goeb saying "How can I explain Hegel's dialectic to you?" (The next year I took a course in Hegel at Harvard.)

I guess it started me on a path that I have followed since. . . .

Although these composers and many others had distinguished professional careers, other composers at the conference pursued musical composition without aiming to make it their livelihood—they were, in effect, composers by avocation. Among these was Elsa Golbin, a composer and pianist of Swiss-German descent, who attended for several years in the 1950s. Her *Sketch for Orchestra* was first read and recorded by the conference chamber orchestra in 1955, and the Vermont State Symphony Orchestra, conducted by Carter, gave its first public performance that October in Bennington. Golbin and her adult daughter, Vivian, who was a musician as well as a dancer, found the artistic and cultural community of North Bennington so attractive that they decided to settle there permanently. In 1953 Elsa had the noted architect Bernard Kessler, who was then on the College's faculty, design a home for her and her daughter to be built on College Avenue with such features as a living room constructed to a perfect fit for their grand piano,[58] an 1899 Blüthner that Elsa had brought from Leipzig. Subsequently, the Golbin house was acquired by conference faculty cellist Maxine Neuman and her husband, attorney and conference recording engineer Reinhard Humburg.

The Conference as Recording Studio

From its first year at Bennington College in 1951, the conference continued the practice, started at Middlebury College, of documenting through professional recordings the readings and performances at the conference.

The conference was an opportunity for musicians to make connections. It brought the recording engineer Stanley Tonkel together with the eclectically versatile composer, performer (primarily on alto saxophone), and recording producer Attilio "Teo" Macero, a recent composition graduate from Juilliard,

Moses Kligsberg

Courtesy of YIVO Institute for Jewish Research

Among the "amateur" composers during this period, one deserves special attention for attending every year for more than twenty years beginning in 1953. After immigrating to the United States from Poland in 1941 to continue his work as an archivist for the YIVO Institute for Jewish Research, Moses Kligsberg studied music history, composition and orchestration, and violin and piano at the Teachers College of Columbia University, while he continued his archival and publicity work at YIVO.[59] As an archivist, whose work involved documenting the lives of those who perished during the Holocaust, he left an extensive personal archive, including his correspondence with musicians at the conference as well as some of the only recordings to survive from this early period in the conference's history. Kligsberg's works were frequently included on the conference's public concerts.

His personal life was marked by tragedy. With the outbreak of war in 1939, Kligsberg was forced to leave his wife and infant daughter in Warsaw. His efforts to bring them to the United States were unsuccessful, and they perished in the Holocaust.

In 1968—this would have been Kligsberg's sixteenth summer—for a proposed radio broadcast of a conference recording of his *Fantasy for Cello and Seven Instruments*, Kligsberg provided this modest autobiography:

I came from Warsaw, Poland. I studied composition here with Professors Otto Luening and Chou Wen-chung and for a number of years have been participating in the Bennington Composers' Conference. In my work I frequently use elements and idioms of East European Jewish folk music—not actual folksongs or chants, though—and try to present them in a western musical framework.

When the conference prepared to move from Bennington to Johnson State College in 1972, Alan Carter was pleased to confirm by letter that Kligsberg would again be in attendance: "Look forward to having you as the Conference would not be the same without you."

who attended in 1955 and 1956—the first of several jazz-conversant composers at the conference. Among his many accomplishments, Macero was the producer or co-producer of the Miles Davis Columbia recordings, including the famous *Bitches Brew*, on which he collaborated with Tonkel as one of the recording engineers.

The conference recordings of live performances or readings often had a "field recording" sonic aura to them, as there was nothing close to a professional recording studio available. Before his arrival at the conference in 1972, composer Larry Bell recalls listening to the Fourth String Quartet of his teacher, Gregory Kosteck, on a 1971 conference tape recording that "included a dog barking in the background." The sounds of crickets and squeaking chairs also found their way uninvited onto many conference recordings.

Stanley Tonkel

Stanley Tonkel was listed in the 1951 conference brochure as the staff "recording expert"—the first of many such technicians on the staff over the years. Tonkel also contributed works as a composer and arranger for conference concerts. He returned to the conference for eight more years and had a prominent career in the recording industry, starting with Columbia Records in 1959. At Columbia, he edited legendary recordings for classical and jazz artists, receiving two Grammy Award nominations, first in 1974 for the first recording of the original chamber orchestra version of Copland's *Appalachian Spring*, with the composer conducting, and again in 1982 for Glenn Gould's second recording of Bach's *Goldberg Variations*.

During Tonkel's years at the conference and for many years to come, one drawback of the reel-to-reel technology then in use was the lack of ease, compared with current digital recording technology, in making copies, although the conference did offer acetate disk copies of recordings for a "nominal fee." The magnetic tape original recording "masters," however, were far from durable, and as a result only a handful of historic conference recordings still exist.

It was not until 2003 that digital recording was introduced at the conference, thus making it far easier to copy, distribute, and preserve conference recordings.

Stanley Tonkel, "recording expert," as featured in the conference's 1958 brochure.

The Vocalists

The conference programming was by no means limited to purely instrumental works; on the contrary, composers at the conference had a strong interest in writing for voice, sometimes with piano accompaniment, but just as often in a chamber ensemble. The exceptionally talented soprano Helen Laird attended in 1946 at Middlebury on a composition scholarship, but it is difficult to imagine that a singer of her caliber was not also enlisted as a performer. At Bennington in 1951, soprano Stephanie Turash performed in many works, including Luening's *Nine Songs to Poems of Emily Dickinson*, which she also presented at her Carnegie Recital Hall debut that fall.

The gifted soprano Ethel Codd Luening, whose husband was Otto Luening, although they had separated in 1944 and divorced in 1959, performed in 1951 in works by Frank Wigglesworth.

In 1954, the conference added Earl Rogers to its staff, and he returned often as the regular staff vocalist. Rogers was a New York-based tenor, who performed in notable premieres and first recordings of works by composers such as Vivian Fine, who taught composition at Bennington College from 1964 to 1987.

The vocalist component continued on into the next decade and beyond. In 1963 the soprano Antonia Lavanne joined the staff, apparently gratis, as a vocal coach. Active in New York City, and affiliated with Mannes School of Music, Lavanne brought several of her voice students to the conference each summer. In 1969, an entire concert of vocal music by four of Lavanne's students was presented at the conference, including a Handel aria with violin obbligato by staff violinist Joel

Berman, and the Spohr *Sechs Deutsche Lieder*, opus 103, in which Norman Abrams, a long-time conference amateur clarinetist, also performed.

Noteworthy Early Staff Members

In addition to the newcomers Max Pollikoff and George Grossman, several more musicians soon joined the staff during the first decade at Bennington. They held important roles for roughly the next five decades, both in musical collaboration with each other and in shaping the conference's direction and growth.

The first of the string players to attend—eventually, they would form a string quartet—was Paul Wolfe, who joined the staff in 1956, playing violin and conducting the chamber orchestra, although he was also a professional-level oboist and pianist. He continued on the faculty for fifty years, for a time serving as music director, before he retired from the conference in 2006. The distinguished Russian-born cellist Alexander Kouguell, who was on the faculty of Queens College, joined the conference staff two years later, attending almost every summer for fifty years. In 1959, Joseph Schor, violinist and future conference music director, joined the staff. Violist Jacob "Jack" Glick, yet another long-term faculty member, who also later served as music director, first attended as a staff violist in 1961.

Wolfe, Kouguell, Schor, and Glick made up the Silvermine Quartet, which was formed in 1959 as the resident quartet at the Silvermine Guild Arts Center in New Canaan, Connecticut. The members often performed together as a quartet during their years at the conference and returned as the conference's quartet-in-residence in 1998. The original members were Wolfe

Joseph Schor leads a coaching session in 1994.

Photo by Claire Stefani

and Schor, violins; Melvin Berger, viola; and Kouguell, cello. In 1961, Glick replaced Berger, who continued his very active career as a professional violist, and was also a prolific writer—mostly of children's books, frequently in collaboration with his wife, Gilda Shulman Berger, and often on scientific and musical topics.[60] Among his titles for adults is the often-reprinted *Guide to Chamber Music*, originally published in 1985, and in 2018, translated into Chinese.

On the wind instrument side of the staff, the oboist Melvin Kaplan, another longtime staff member who joined the conference in 1958, had for many years the responsibility, along with Robert Bloom, of organizing the wind staff. In later years, the clarinetist Charles Russo also assisted with wind staff selection. Kaplan, who taught at Juilliard for twenty-five years, was a founding member of both the New York Chamber Soloists and the Festival Winds. In 1974 he co-founded the Vermont Mozart Festival. His New Art Wind Quintet was in residence at the conference.

In 1952, the conference announced that it would focus more attention on winds, with oboist Bloom, who had joined the staff in 1949 at Middlebury, heading up a distinguished group of wind staff, denominated as "Associate Faculty" on the conference flyer, including Bernard Garfield, bassoon, and Robert Nagel Jr., trumpet.[61] The conference's wind quintet was made up of Bloom and Garfield, plus Wallace Shapiro, clarinet (Shapiro was the longtime concertmaster of the New York City–based Goldman Band); Albert Richman, horn (an active New York City freelancer, with many recording credits); and Richard Giese, flute (from the Baltimore Symphony Orchestra, where he played the 1952–53 seasons).

Luening, Ussachevsky, and the Birth of Electronic Music

From its beginning the conference was a fertile ground for musical experimentation. The conference's first year at Bennington College, 1951, was noteworthy for the arrival of composer Vladimir Ussachevsky, a Columbia University faculty member who was in the process of abandoning his neo-romantic compositional style and looking to the future. He was soon collaborating with Luening at the conference in experiments in electronic music. Later, the two composers established what was to become the Columbia-Princeton Electronic Music Center[62] (today, the Computer Music Center). Luening explained how his "experiments" in electronic music started at the conference in August of 1952:

I persuaded Ussachevsky to transport the laboratory from New York to Bennington where we could, individually and together, investigate the possibilities of the strange new medium. We set up a small, primitive studio in a corner of the rebuilt Carriage Barn.... Violin and clarinet interested us, but we decided to concentrate on our own instruments—flute and piano. We were both fluent improvisers and both of us sang, after a fashion. . . .

For a composers' party at Bennington we were asked to prepare several short compositions. Our "works"—*City Nocturne, Country Nocturne,* and *Insect Nocturne*—were all based on flute sounds. After we played them, the other composers, astonished by our discoveries in the world of sound, countered with much applause and some grumbling. Lionel Nowak and Roger Goeb were fully aware that we were working with very primitive means but were generous and almost solemn as they congratulated us. Other composers came around and said, in effect, "This is it"—"it" meaning the music of the future. Ussachevsky and I were rather surprised at such a response. We had performed the compositions as entertainment for the party and had not expected a profound reaction.[63]

Two months later, on October 28, 1952, at the Museum of Modern Art in New York City, Luening and Ussachevsky presented the first U.S. public concert of tape recorder music, including Luening's now-famous *Fantasy in Space*, under the auspices of Leopold Stokowski, who introduced this historic occasion with the remarkable opening line, "I am often asked: 'What is tape music, and how is it made?'"[64]

The next summer, Luening and Ussachevsky tried out their new Louisville Symphony commission, *Rhapsodic Variations for Tape Recorder and Orchestra*, with the chamber orchestra at the conference and received "little reaction." The Louisville Symphony premiered the work in 1954 in what is believed to be the first performance of tape recorder music with symphony orchestra.[65]

Electronic music continued to be a feature of the conference over the years. In 1962, Ussachevsky presented a lecture on the topic, followed by performances of works created at the Columbia-Princeton Electronic Music Center, including Luening's *Gargoyles for Solo Violin and Improvised Sound*, with Max Pollikoff performing the solo violin part. In 1970, Robert Moog, who, also working at the Electronic Music Center, had recently invented the electronic synthesizer that bears his name, was a guest lecturer.

The Conference at the 92nd Street Y

Among the notable attendees listed in the conference's 1952 directory is William Kolodney, education director of New York City's well-known 92nd Street Y, known at the time as the Young Men's and Young Women's Hebrew Association. Kolodney apparently attended as a guest, and the conference underwrote at least part of his travel expense to Bennington. Kolodney's keen interest in contemporary arts made the Y, beginning in the mid-1930s, a cultural and performing arts center.[66] Kolodney must have liked what he heard at Bennington, because later that year, the conference and the Y launched the first of three seasons of a jointly sponsored contemporary music series.

The Y concerts, which showcased the conference's role in the creation and performance of new music, make it clear that the conference did not see itself confined to its two weeks on the Bennington campus. Just as Carter had brought the Vermont State Symphony Orchestra to a New York City venue in 1939, the conference was now bringing its summer music programming to another New York City venue, and a prominent one at that.

Harold Schonberg, a critic not known for warm enthusiasm for new music, reviewed the opening concert in the first year's Y series in the *New York Times*, and he could not have been more positive: "All of the music on the program was of a thoroughly professional character and some of it was more than merely promising. If this is a representative example of the work going on each summer at Bennington, the Composers Conference is building better than it knows. Or than most people know, for that matter."[67] Later that first season at the Y, Tonkel's Suite for Brass Quintet (Schonberg's review: "This was an amusing, irreverent piece that Mr. Tonkel managed to keep interesting all the way through") was among the featured works.[68]

Schonberg found Nowak's Quartet the "most impressive" work on the program, describing it as:

> a composition with several interesting ideas handled in a concise manner. There was something highly personal about the quartet, something that breathed a joy in making music and also a certain amount of wit—qualities by no means common among today's younger composers.

The Y Concert Program

The concert program that earned plaudits from Harold Schonberg in the *New York Times* in 1952:

Robert Nagel, Trio for Brass ("short, cleanly composed, objective")

İlhan Usmanbaş, Music for Cello and Piano No. 2 ("free, improvisatory, exotic")

George Rochberg, Twelve Bagatelles for Piano ("dissonant, percussive")

James Dalgleish, Trio for wind instruments ("gentle, lyrical")

Marshall Bialosky, Sonata for Solo Violin ("skillfully composed, spirited")

Lionel Nowak, Quartet for Oboe and Strings ("most impressive")

The next season, Schonberg's review of the first of the conference's series of concerts, although expressing reservations about some of the works, was again quite positive overall, singling out Louis Calabro's Trio for violin, cello, and piano for its "excitement, conviction, belief, personality."[69] The performances by conference staff and guest musicians, including Pollikoff, Grossman, Finckel, and pianist Abba Bogin, led Schonberg to conclude: "they did a first-class job." Two years later, Calabro joined the faculty of Bennington College, where he remained for thirty-six years and often attended the conference. Bogin, a 1947 Naumberg award winner, did not join the conference faculty until 1986, despite this very successful outing more than thirty years earlier.

Taking over from the conference's new music series, which ended after the second season in 1954, Pollikoff launched his own *Music in Our Time* series at the Y in 1956. Pollikoff's programming for his concerts (an eight-concert series for $5) in New York City was largely based on the new music he was getting acquainted with the previous summer at the conference.[70] Among the composers featured on the Y programs was Charles Wuorinen, who first attended the conference the same year that Pollikoff started his series.

Coming of Age at the Conference: Charles Wuorinen

In 1956, into this quirky mix of ongoing experiments in electronic music and amateurs trying out their friends' new compositions, Wuorinen, then eighteen, arrived at the conference for the first time. He was to come back for eight more summers, when, during his student years at Columbia University, he was finding his own individual voice as a composer. In 1957, the conference chamber orchestra premiered his *Concertante for Violin and Strings*, with Pollikoff on violin and Carter conducting.

In 1961, Wuorinen served as the recording engineer for the conference. In a *New York Times* photo, he is seen controlling the dials of a tape recorder, while clarinetist Charles Russo plays and composer Charles Whittenberg supervises the try-out of "a new work fusing live music and electronic sound."[71]

Wuorinen's 1961 composition *Evolutio Transcripta* for chamber orchestra—an early work still in his catalog—was premiered at the conference, under the baton of Paul Wolfe. In his *New York Times* review, Eric Salzman noted that it was "the most extraordinary new work" on the program, describing Wuorinen as "a prolific, if an undisciplined, young composer and no composer of 23 ever sowed such wild oats."[72] Salzman went on to proclaim, ever so presciently, that "there is a talent here and a genuine search for an original and expressive means of communication." He also singled out the "excellent" conducting by Wolfe, noting that the chamber orchestra, "with its limited rehearsal time, just about managed to get through the exceptional difficulties of the work."

By 1963, Wuorinen had joined the conference's composition staff; by 1964 he and Otto Luening were, in effect, co-directors of the composition program, selecting the composers for the conference's staff. Wuorinen also served on the conference's board of trustees through 1966. In 1970 Wuorinen won the Pulitzer Prize—at the time, the youngest person to be so honored—for his entirely electronic work, *Time's Encomium*.

Exactly as intended by Carter when he founded it, the conference provided a setting for the exchange of ideas among performing musicians and composers. Staff violist Melvin

Berger—the original Silvermine Quartet violist—recalls being approached by Wuorinen, then in his teens, with questions about how he might transition from playing violin to playing viola. Violist and composer discussed the matter, and years later, Berger wrote his own *Basic Viola Technique*, and included a supplement "for the violinist changing to viola," written with Wuorinen's questions from a decade earlier in mind.

A Cooperative Effort

The complex and sometimes vexing relationship between the "two separate entities" of the conference, the composer and amateur player wings, had yet another wrinkle to it—the issue of money. Although the conference was growing very successfully on several levels through the 1950s and 1960s, when it came to its finances, the organization wobbled considerably from year to year. At times, it appears, it was on the brink of collapse.

As Luening recalled, even during the Middlebury years (1946 to 1950), "financing was a problem," with the conference run on a "cooperative" basis: "the staff divided up the balance of the income from tuition after paying all the bills."[73] And even then, they were "regularly bailed out" by the Alice M. Ditson Fund and the Rockefeller Foundation, as well as by contributions from amateurs, both past and current attendees.

In his 1983 memoir, staff violist George Grossman echoed Luening's view: at the end of his first two-week session in the summer of 1953, he wrote, "I was astonished to learn that there was no money for me because the conference had not made any money. It was only then I realized that this was a cooperative effort."[74] Grossman obviously had no regrets—he returned for twenty years—recalling, "So my first year [1953] at Bennington was a financial loss but a musical gain. After that, I began earning some money there, but not a lot; I did, however, have lots of pleasure."

That the conference struggled financially through these early years should come as no surprise, since scholarship awards appear to be the rule, not the exception. In 1952, only thirteen of the sixty-six attendees were recorded as having paid full fee ($160 for the two weeks), although many others paid some portion. Nine instrumentalists participated as additional staff, receiving room and board subsidies, but no additional compensation. Nevertheless, the conference managed to break even: having carried over a fund balance of $54 from 1951, the conference moved on to 1953 with a fund balance of $60.

The conference was truly run on a shoestring, to borrow one of Carter's frequently used metaphors. When the expenses, including scholarships, exceeded income from fees, contributions and grants made up the difference. In 1952, for example, ten donors were listed, including the Alice M. Ditson Fund; the Ditson grant of $1,000 made up 80 percent of the donations and about 20 percent of the conference's total income that year.

The conference operated on a fairly straightforward model: on the expense side of the ledger were the costs for publicity and communication, payments to Bennington College for everyone's room and board, and staff compensation. On the income side were the fees paid by participating composers and amateur players, donations in excess of fees, and grants from corporations and foundations. Although the conference board could reduce costs to some extent (e.g., by reducing the number of compensated staff) or increase income to some extent (e.g., by increasing fees), in reality, while it was not so difficult to project the next summer's costs, it was not always possible to project accurately the conference's income. As a result, making it to the end of the conference session each year without a deficit was a hit-or-miss proposition. The result of missing the break-even target raised questions about the conference's viability.

By 1954, perhaps given the significant expansion of the staff, the conference was on especially shaky financial footing and questions came up about whether it would take place again that summer. Carter apparently put out an urgent call for help in raising funds and received responses expressing worry in return.

Reflecting the concern about whether the conference would continue in 1954, then-student composer Joseph Castaldo wrote in a postscript to Carter that "if there's a Bennington next year, count me in!" Castaldo had attended the previous summer and would return that year and the next. As he explained to Carter in 1954, he had "begged, cajoled, and beseeched" for donations to the conference, but without any luck. His final plan was to approach Philadelphia businessman and philan-thropist Edwin Fleisher, founder of the vast Fleisher Chamber Music Collection, now at the Free Library of Philadelphia, for a major donation, but with the warning to Carter that "I don't know if I can get it, but it is probably worth a try—even though I have been advised that he is very 'tight.'" Whether Fleisher was tight with his money or not, Castaldo apparently had no success.

Luening provided Carter with a report on his own fundrais-ing efforts: "I saw one lady who was interested and said if we got in a jam she would help some." Expressing his personal commitment to the conference, however, Luening offered to "cough up 50 bucks if I have to, but I would just as soon not; I really can't afford it." Luening's offer might not seem all that generous, but in fact he would be giving back his entire pay, plus some, for two weeks at the conference as a staff composer.

Amateur cellist Elizabeth Karrick sent a donation to Carter, noting in her cover letter that "if the Conference needs to skip a year (we won't say 'fold')," the check might then be used for the Vermont State Symphony Orchestra instead—an indication of how the conference and the Symphony were viewed as almost one entity. Karrick went on to write, obviously tongue-in-cheek since her sister, Virginia deBlasiis, was one of the staff violinists:

> Do think, that after all these years, it is rather pre-
> sumptuous of the Staff to expect any compensation!
> Shows a complete lack of the proper spiritual quality
> necessary for music. Their minds have dropped to
> their stomachs again! Then again, I do feel that the
> shock of receiving any remuneration might prove
> fatal to some of them. Do hope you will give these
> thoughts the proper consideration.

Tjalling Koopmans, a Dutch-born mathematician and econ-omist (with a 1975 Nobel Prize), had attended the conference as a violist in 1953 (and would attend as a composer in 1961). As he reported to Carter in 1954, he had spoken to the highly successful wine merchant and philanthropist Paul Fromm in Chicago about funding the conference. "I found Mr. Fromm a man of considerable musical erudition and judgment, and bubbling over with enthusiasm for helping young composers get established," he wrote to Carter. He urged Carter to invite the Fromms to the conference.

Grants from the Fromm Music Foundation do not seem to have been forthcoming, but later in the spring of 1954, the conference was once again "bailed out," this time, apparently through the efforts of Luening, by a multi-year grant from the Rockefeller Foundation. The conference was held once again at Bennington College.

IV. The Next Decade: Toward Maturity, 1960 to 1971

Would you like to play the xylophone? You never played one before? Well, now you'll learn how.

—Eric Salzman, quoting conference composer Henry Brant, "Performers Aid Creators on Mountain," *New York Times*, August 27, 1961

A S THE CONFERENCE ENTERED its second decade at Bennington College, the funding struggles continued. Board meeting minutes for 1961, the first year for which we have minutes, provide an inside look at the challenges the board and staff faced in keeping the conference going. That year, at the conclusion of the conference's two-week session, the treasurer, Joseph Parry, reported at the annual board meeting that "the treasury will contain about $400.00 after all . . . expenses have been paid." Those funds, combined with $1,400 in a "Sponsors' Fund," made it possible for Parry to recommend that each staff member—there were about a dozen staff members that year—be paid $100; it was so

Zita Carno and Warren Smith in 1970 in rehearsal in the Carriage Barn. During this period, the conference orchestra expanded to provide a broad range of options for composers, including the many percussion instruments used here.

moved by Theodore Strongin, then approved unanimously by the board. The conference was still operating on what Luening had called the "cooperative" model, with the staff dividing up whatever funds were left over after paying expenses.

The board then turned its attention to "the necessity of being able to guarantee such salaries in the future." After reviewing a variety of fundraising options, the board agreed, with a view toward enhancing staff retention, that "those who are responsible for recruiting staff members shall be able to guarantee such prospective staff members $80.00 minimum for the two-week session."

The board's commitment was difficult to keep. During the 1964 conference, a preliminary treasurer's report projected a deficit of about $1,500, forcing Carter to urge that the conference immediately take out a loan from a local bank, which it did. Carter, Luening, and others redoubled their efforts to bring in additional funds, particularly from organizations, such as the Rockefeller Foundation, the Alice M. Ditson Fund, ASCAP (American Society of Composers, Authors, and Publishers), Broadcast Music, Inc., and Music Performance (Recording Industries) Trust Fund.

When the board of trustees met in August 1964, the minutes of that meeting note, in a concerned tone, that the amateur population was down to sixteen players. At that 1964 meeting, the board declined to re-elect William Osgood Morgan and William Sunderman Sr., both amateur violinists, due to their poor attendance at meetings. In their place, George Grossman joined the board, along with participant Hassler Whitney. Whitney had earned an undergraduate degree in physics at Yale and then stayed on for an additional year to complete a degree in music. Keith Kendig, his friend, biographer, and fellow conference participant, described Whitney as a giant of twentieth-century mathematics who was keenly interested in the math-music connection.[75] Whitney, who played piano, violin, and viola, was also an accomplished mountaineer.

At that same meeting, Milton Babbitt was elected to the board. While having such a prominent composer and teacher on the board added prestige to the conference's reputation for new music, there is no evidence of his presence at any meetings, so his attendance record was no better than that of the two amateurs who were replaced. The board created an "executive committee" consisting of "the members present" (Carter, Pollikoff, Luening, Wuorinen, and deBlasiis) to "carry on the affairs of the Corporation between its annual meetings." The conference finished the summer $800 in debt.

The board adopted plans to expand fundraising, and Carter reported on his meeting with representatives of the Rockefeller Foundation. Luening urged that the conference apply for $50,000 per year for the next five years. But if the conference in fact pursued that lead, there is no record that the Rockefeller Foundation responded favorably.

Looking to the next summer of 1965, Carter proposed cutting back on staff in an attempt to balance the budget. His proposed staff comprised two string quartets; one double bassist; a wind quintet; two trumpet players, one trombonist; one pianist; one percussionist; three staff composers; one recording technician; one director (Carter); and one secretary. But when the board met again three months later, Carter had trimmed the staff down even further.

This proposal was opposed by Charles Wuorinen, who is recorded as stating that "from the viewpoint of composition, the session could hardly do without percussion and brass," and that composition staff should be paid, "except for those donating salaries, *e.g.*, Mr. Chou and [Mr. Wuorinen]."

Despite these efforts to economize, at the end of the next summer, while able to repay its debt to the bank, the conference had expenses of $560 in excess of income and had to rely on the "generous cooperation" of Bennington College in carrying the debt until the conference was able to pay. By 1966, things were looking better, as the redoubled fundraising efforts seem to have paid off, particularly in regard to a $2,500 grant from the Martha Baird Rockefeller Foundation. The conference finished the year with a $1,105 fund balance.

Additional funding was soon to come from the National Endowment for the Arts. Created by an Act of Congress that was signed into law by President Lyndon Johnson in 1965, the NEA began funding arts organizations in 1966, and the next summer the conference received a very generous grant of $13,000—the first of many from the NEA. The Vermont Arts Council was also established in 1965 to receive funds from the NEA and engage in local grant making. The conference received its first Vermont Arts Council grant in 1966. Both these funders would continue to support the conference for many years and into the present, often underwriting some of the expenses relating to the composer side of the conference.

Return to Middlebury?

In what now seems like a surprising turnaround, in 1966 Carter reported on his discussions with Middlebury College administrators about the possibility of having the conference back for 1966. Perhaps more than anything, this episode demonstrated Carter's frustration with trying year after year to keep the conference financially afloat. His willingness to entertain the idea of moving the conference also demonstrates his belief that the conference's identity existed independent of its host site.

In a report prepared for the board of trustees, Carter recommended that the conference corporation be dissolved, with both the composers' conference and the chamber music center returning as programs of Middlebury College, and with the college taking over all fiscal and administrative responsibilities. The origins of this idea are not explained in Carter's proposal. But having Middlebury manage the administrative side of the conference must have seemed very attractive, and there were hopes that the college would underwrite conference expenses, thus relieving Carter and his board from the annual headache of trying to balance the budget. The availability of Middlebury's 400-seat Wright Memorial Theatre, which opened in 1958, must also have been a plus, along with the anticipated opening of a new Music and Fine Arts Center.

In his report, Carter pointed out that Middlebury allowed for a "more closely coordinated operation as living and working would take place in the same locale," in contrast to Bennington College, where living and working areas were, in Carter's somewhat exaggerated sense of geography, "a mile apart." But from Carter's discussions with Middlebury, it was unclear whether Middlebury would "assume financial responsibility" for the conference once the conference's Rockefeller grant ended. At least initially, Middlebury administrators seem to have been willing to entertain this proposal, but ultimately, it seems to have been quietly dropped. Middlebury College, having kicked the conference out as a money-losing program fifteen years before, was apparently not willing to risk a similar outcome. This would not be the last time that Middlebury College played a role in the conference's site-selection story, as we will see when it comes to the conference's planned relocation in 2020 to Colgate University.

Two Entities or One?

The crux of the relationship between the conference's "two separate entities"—the composer and amateur wings—was financial. Throughout the first two decades of the new organization's life at Bennington College, leaders of the conference acknowledged the reality of the fiscal relationship between the "Composers' Conference" and the "Chamber Music Center." While often referred to as "two entities," in reality, as Carter put it, "the Chamber Music Center financially makes both sessions possible as all amateurs pay the full price and receive no scholarships, which is [not] the case with the composers" (many of whom *did* receive scholarships, full or partial). At an executive committee meeting in 1966, Ellen Loeb shared her views—with blunt honesty—on the amateurs' role in the functioning of the conference:

> As it is quite evident that the composing program is subsidized by the amateur players, we must ask the amateurs for more money. However, the amateurs should not be told to what uses the money will be put, only that they can play quartets, be coached, etc.

Finally, in 1967, George Todd, who had taken over as the conference's "executive secretary" in the mid-1960s, proposed a major reorganization. Todd was a composer who had studied with, among others, Milton Babbitt in graduate school at Princeton. He joined the music faculty of Middlebury College, where he succeeded Carter as chair of the music department in 1971. Throughout his career he focused on electronic music, but he also held a master's degree in business administration from Stanford University.

As might be expected from a composer with an MBA, Todd set about solving the conference's financial and programmatic woes. He identified what he believed was the conference's central problem: instrumental staff who were at ease reading and performing the composers' new music were not necessarily adept at coaching amateurs—and staff who were effective coaches might not have a strong interest in or adequate comfort level with new music. Indeed, not all conference staff were meeting the challenges posed by the amateur ensembles, to judge by Loeb's comment during a previous board meeting that "some of the Staff [during morning coaching sessions] had their groups just reading through something rather than actually working on it."

Todd's proposed solution for 1968 was to schedule these different activities at separate times by adding a third week to the two-week schedule. The first two weeks would be exclusively for amateur coaching by skilled coaching staff, with the third week exclusively for the composers and staffed by new music performance specialists. The conference would truly be two separate entities. The board did not fully accept Todd's recommendation, but instead split the conference over the usual two weeks; the first week was exclusively for the amateur chamber players, while the second week focused on composers "with provision for continued coaching for those Chamber Music Center participants who wished to remain."

As an indication of the growth of the amateur coaching program, Grossman requested of the board that he be excused

The proposed 1968 schedule included expanded, afternoon coaching:

9:00–11:00 AM
Coaching for one-half of participants

11:30–12:30 PM
Seminar

2:15–3:15 PM
Chamber orchestra

3:45–5:45 PM
Coaching for other half of participants

Evenings
Concerts by the staff and by the string/wind orchestra

from the afternoon reading sessions of the composers' new works so that he could "work in Jennings [music building] with different groups of winds and strings combined during the afternoons."

The 1968 conference, which used the new "two one-week sessions" plan, finished with a projected loss for the year of $1,100 despite the attendance by a record-breaking sixty-three amateurs during the first week, although there were considerably fewer staying for the second week. Seventeen composers were in attendance, and thirty-one new works were performed.

The board ruled out asking Bennington College to help with the projected loss, as Joseph Parry, the treasurer and college employee, reported that the college was "already operating at a deficit." Returning to the cooperative model, Todd then recommended that several members of the staff, including himself and Carter, "should either not be paid at the present time or that their fees should be cut." Carter's counterproposal was that he and three other staff members should receive half their salaries, thus making it possible to pay the others their full amount. Pollikoff is recorded as asking "how it was possible for the Center to have more money and yet pay the Staff less." At the same time, the conference received substantial support from the NEA and the Vermont Arts Council, making up 22 percent of the conference's income.

The Composers' Conference at Maturity

Even as the challenge of making ends meet continued through the 1960s, the music went on as intensely as before. By 1960, composers at the conference had been writing for diverse groups of instruments, beyond the traditional chamber music ensembles of strings, winds, piano, and combinations thereof. The "Composers' Conference," it should be recalled, was not a "Composers' *Chamber Music* Conference." The only limits on a composer's imagination were perhaps the conference's budget and the performance space available in the Carriage Barn. Although brass instruments had been included even during the first years at Bennington, by 1960, the question of creating permanent staff positions

Part of the score of a work by Moses Kligsberg, who attended the conference for more than twenty years starting in 1953 and wrote music in his spare time.

Courtesy of Chou Wen-chung

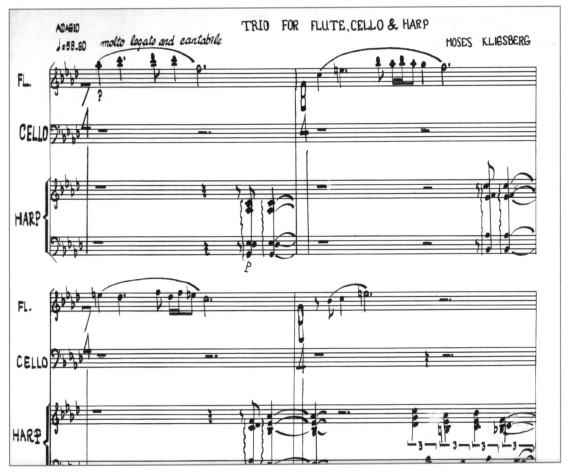

for trumpet, trombone, and percussion was broached. In fact, works for percussion instruments, including xylophone, were now being routinely programmed. The conference's archive contains photos of percussionist Warren Smith, who first attended in 1967, moving a xylophone into the Carriage Barn, and of Smith and Zita Carno in rehearsal, on temple bells and marimba, respectively, and with vibraphone and timpani close at hand.

In 1961, the composer Harvey Sollberger attended the conference. The next year, Sollberger, along with Wuorinen and cellist Joel Krosnick, founded the groundbreaking Group for Contemporary Music, which was based at Columbia University. The Group for Contemporary Music was "one of the most influential and foremost contemporary ensembles in New York,"[76] and its founders extended their adventurous approach to new music to the conference. Later, in 1967 and 1968, Krosnick was a conference staff cellist. Sollberger, who was a virtuoso flutist as well as a composer, returned again in 1963 and 1964 with his wife, Sophie Sollberger, also a professional flutist. As one might guess, the 1963 conference concluded with the *Brandenburg* Concerto no. 4, with the Sollbergers on flute, joined by Pollikoff on violin.

Composers such as Wuorinen and Sollberger had a zeal for new music in live performances that included the composer as performer. The idea that composers should also be capable performers who could participate in their own works was espoused by Otto Luening, who often performed on flute in his own compositions as well as in those of his colleagues at the conference. The conference was a setting where that ideal could be actualized. The conference concert on August 19, 1964, for example, included Sollberger's Music for Flute and Piano (1964), performed by the composer, with Wuorinen at the piano.

In 1961, Henry Brant brought another innovation to the composition staff. Brant had joined the Bennington College faculty in 1957, having previously taught at Columbia University and Juilliard. He was frequently at the conference until his retirement from Bennington College in 1980.

Brant's signature compositional feature was the spatial place-ment of performers and instruments as a fundamental element of musical expression—a technique inspired in part by the music of Charles Ives, in particular his *Unanswered Question*. In 2002, Brant was awarded a Pulitzer Prize for his work *Ice Field*, which was evocative of "his experience, as a 12-year-old in 1926, of crossing the Atlantic by ship, which navigated care-fully through a large field of icebergs in the North Atlantic."[77] An apparently typical Brant musical experiment at the con-ference is documented in another of Eric Salzman's *New York Times* reports, this time on how Brant constructed one of his "free-style pieces," pressing instrumentalists, composers, "and even visitors into service."[78]

> Now trumpets, play something marcato style for eight bars. Try it out. That's right, alternate. Now keep playing for two bars while the percussion comes in. Pianos play octaves. Anything. No, that's too thin; fill the octaves in, any note will do. Say, we need a xylophone. Would you like to play the xylophone? You never played one before? Well, now you'll learn how.

A Xylophone Goes Missing

In 1962, the College's percussion collection lacked a xylophone, but composer Henry Brant hap-pened to have one, borrowed from a Bennington colleague, in his house on campus. Brant was away, so what was a resourceful new music performer at the con-ference to do when a xylophone was needed?

As Brant later reported in a letter to Carter, "one of the con-ference instrumentalists under-took to break into my locked house during my absence." As if being burgled were not enough, Brant went on to com-plain that "the xylophone was not even returned to me after the Conference; I found it on the floor of the Carriage Barn in a damaged condition with some parts missing." Moreover, Brant learned of these actions from "the person involved who expressed polite regret and some surprise that I found the incident discon-certing." With his letter of com-plaint, Brant submitted a bill for the rental of the instrument ($10) and a repair bill ($15). The con-ference promptly paid.

The "visitor" in this case was likely Salzman himself, who was also a composer.

Green Mountain Fiddlers

In 1963, Alan Carter introduced an entirely new, third population at the conference, in addition to the chamber players and composers. This was the crowd of kindergarten through twelfth grade string instrument students attending the Green Mountain Fiddlers summer camp. With Carter's encouragement, this string instruction program was started in Connecticut in 1957 (where they were called the "Red Barn Fiddlers") by Stanley Eukers, who specialized in teaching young string players. The program was expanded by Carter to Vermont in 1959 with the support of the Vermont State Symphony Orchestra.[79] The Fiddlers summer camp was sited on the Bennington campus alongside the conference for more than a decade.[80] With the Fiddlers campers sharing meals with the adult conferees in the Commons dining hall, and attending conference concerts and other events, they were viewed as part of the conference itself, even to the point that when the conference looked to balance its budget at the end of a summer session, they called on funds from the Green Mountain Fiddlers to do so.

On August 28, 1971, the *Bennington Banner* published a photo of Carter about to begin a Center Chamber Orchestra concert in the Carriage Barn. He is looking up to the balcony, his finger raised to his lips as he indicates "quiet!" to a group of exuberant youngsters who are leaning over the railing or sitting with their legs hanging down underneath it. Among them that evening was very likely Eric Bartlett, who, as a fourteen-year-old cellist, was attending his sixth summer at the Green Mountain Fiddlers summer camp. Bartlett was a cello student of George Finckel, and he returned to the camp each summer until 1973 when he attended the conference as a non-staff cellist, but was able to rehearse and play new works with the professionals.

Bartlett's subsequent career was largely in the contemporary music scene in New York City, with a long association with one of the city's leading new music groups, Speculum Musicae, as well as with the Orpheus Chamber Orchestra. He joined the New York Philharmonic in 1997. On the Philharmonic's website biography page, Bartlett summed up his formative experiences, which included those at the conference:

Max Pollikoff, left, with cellist Michael Finckel in the Carriage Barn in 1970.

Courtesy of UVM Special Collections

As a teenager I was exposed to contemporary and experimental music and was taught to listen with an open mind. It's interesting, challenging, and it makes earlier styles easier to play by stretching one's ability to hear complex music.

Recalling the violinist Max Pollikoff at the conference more than fifty years ago, Bartlett still remembers a solo violin performance in the Carriage Barn. With no opportunity for turning pages, Bartlett recalled, "they set up fourteen music stands—Max just kept playing while walking slowly to his right."

The 1960s' Stellar Composer Roster

Although the leaders were still struggling to manage the conference's finances and tweak its program, the roster of staff and scholarship composers during the same period is indeed impressive. Staff composers from previous years who were familiar with the conference often returned, giving continuity to the program, while notable and prominent composers were frequently among the newcomers.

In 1960, for example, the staff composers were Roger Goeb and Theodore Strongin, both of whom had been at the conference during the previous decade and were highly involved in the conference. The next year, Goeb returned, now joined by Hugh Aitken and Henry Brant. Joan Tower, Bennington College class of 1961, was among the scholarship composers that year. Within decades, she would go on to achieve prominence as a Grammy-winning composer, and as a pianist and conductor.

In 1962, Vladimir Ussachevsky, who had not been at the conference since 1954, joined Goeb, Aitken, and Ralph Shapey

Opposite: A page from Chou Wen-chung's photo album. Clockwise from upper left: Edgard Varèse, left, congratulates conductor Arthur Bloom after a performance of Varèse's Ionisation; *Varèse acknowledging applause; Chou Wen-chung, left, and Charles Wuorinen; Chou Wen-chung, Charles Wuorinen (piano), and Sophie Sollberger (flute) following a performance of Chou's* Cursive.

Courtesy of Chou Wen-chung

Bennington Bros, August 1964.

· AUG · 64

· AUG · 64

Varèse and Art Bloom

· AUG · 64

· AUG · 64

After Cursive
Charles Wuorinen
Sophie Sollberger

for Shapey's first year at the conference. Ursula Mamlok was a scholarship composer for the first of three consecutive years.

In 1963, Chou Wen-chung returned after a ten-year absence, joined by Charles Wuorinen (in his eighth summer) and Earl Zindars, a versatile musician successful in both the jazz and classical music worlds. Barney Childs was among the scholarship composers. That year also had four "Visiting Lecturers": Ussachevsky, who had a long association with the conference at this point; Lester Trimble, who had first attended in 1956, and who was now the executive director of the American Music Center; James Tenney, the composer and music theorist, whose influential 1961 master's thesis, which applied cognitive science and Gestalt psychology to musical analysis, was soon to be published; and Peter Westergaard, a composer and theorist who was then on the Columbia University faculty.

Chou Wen-chung returned again in 1964, the same year he began his long career teaching at Columbia University, joined by his former teacher, Edgard Varèse, who, at age 80, was finally receiving, as Nicolas Slonimsky put it, "long-delayed recognition of his music as a major stimulus of modern art."[81] As a composer who did not write works of chamber music (his *Ionisation* for thirteen percussionists comes as close as any of his works to a chamber ensemble piece), his presence at the conference may have seemed odd; but again recall that it was a composers' conference, not a chamber music composers' conference. That same year, the composer Robert Stewart first attended, and Wuorinen was back for what was to be his final year as a staff composer. Scholarship composers included John Harbison, winner of the 1986 Pulitzer Prize.

In 1965, staff composers were a set of notable newcomers: Morton Feldman, James Randall, and Stefan Wolpe, and with Lester Trimble returning. In 1966, Feldman and Randall returned, now joined by Mel Powell and Arthur Berger.

The Wuorinen Controversy

For the board meeting on the Friday afternoon of the conference's second and final week in 1966, a quorum of eight board members was in attendance, although the three composers on the board (Milton Babbitt, Otto Luening, and Charles Wuorinen) were absent. The conference board's agenda included a very unusual item: Carter had received a telegram from Wuorinen the day before. Wuorinen, who was on the board, expressed his regrets about not being able to attend the meeting in person. Wuorinen went on:

> I would like to bring to the Board's attention the
> fact that this year's Conference is being illegally held.
> The Executive Committee meeting of February 5,
> 1966, concluded with a unanimous vote to postpone
> the Conference for one year. I would appreciate the
> Board's reaction and the Director's explanation.

As reflected in the meeting minutes, the board's immediate reaction was to call in Philip W. Lowry, attorney-at-law—presumably the same Philip W. Lowry who was attending that summer as a composer. Lowry explained that given the wording of the articles of association, the previous board of thirteen members had been duly constituted "by custom rather than by requirement." Thus, having tidied up that matter, Lowry went on to explain that having a minimum of three trustees was the only requirement the conference needed to meet. The board then approved a motion limiting the board membership to eleven trustees for the next year, and, after Lowry left the meeting, he was elected to the board, while Wuorinen was not re-elected. Only two composers, Babbitt and Luening, remained on the board.

The board also passed a resolution, very likely drawn up with Lowry's assistance—given its lawyerly verbiage—that rendered the executive committee's action in postponing the conference "hereby cancelled and rendered null, void and of no effect *nunc pro tunc*." No other documents survive to enlighten us about the issues—why did the executive committee vote to cancel the 1966 conference?—underlying this dispute. Very likely it was Wuorinen's view that it would be better to postpone the session for a year if funding were not adequate to provide for full brass and percussion instrumentation.

In sum, the conference had lost a board member who was among the most prominent composers of his generation, while the board members at the meeting, none of whom were composers, prevailed. The number of composers on the board was now reduced to two, and one of them, Babbitt, appears to have been inactive. The composer role in the leadership of the conference was weaker than it had ever been. This was not the last time there would be a failure of the non-composer leadership of the conference to see eye to eye with the composers, and the next time such a conflict arose, it would have a far more significant impact on the conference.

Davidovsky and Other Notable Newcomers

Additional players also joined the faculty during this period, including Allen Blustine, clarinet, in 1965. Blustine recalls the significant workload faced by conference faculty in preparing so many new compositions for first readings and performances—during one two-week session, he had twenty-one new works assigned to him. "[The flutist Karl] 'Fritz' Kraber and I used to compete to see who had more," he recalls.

Staff pianist and percussionist Zita Carno also began with the conference in 1967. Remembering Carno's formidable skills at the keyboard, faculty member and later Assistant Music Director Joel Berman recalled, still with astonishment, "you could put the score in front of her upside down, sideways, open to the wrong page, it didn't matter! She'd start from the beginning and play every note, she could play anything!"

Efrain Guigui, who had emigrated from Argentina in 1960, was recruited by Carter to assist with conducting the VSO as well as taking on conducting duties at the conference in 1969. Guigui's special expertise was in conducting contemporary works, and he later succeeded Carter at the VSO.

The 1969 conference also marked the arrival of the Argentinian-born Mario Davidovsky as a staff composer. Davidovsky, a childhood friend of the conductor Efrain Guigui who came to the conference that same year, emigrated to the United States in 1960 at the urging of Aaron Copland. When he first came to the conference, he was teaching at the Manhattan School of Music, and, through his work with Babbitt, had worked at the Columbia-Princeton Electronic Music Center, which he was later to direct. He is perhaps best known for his long-term project of composing *Synchronisms*—a series of works started in 1963 that feature virtuosic solo or ensemble live instruments combined with pre-recorded electronic sounds. To date, there are twelve *Synchronisms*, the most recent composed in 2006.

That summer of 1969, Davidovsky was joined by Donald Erb, and they both remained as staff composers for the next six years. They were joined by others, such as Stefan Wolpe, who returned as "visiting composer," and Joseph Ott, who was a staff composer in 1970 and again in 1971. Luening also returned in 1971 as "visiting composer," as well as composer and critic Virgil Thomson, who, now in his mid-seventies, was given the position "senior composer in residence," the first time such a title had been bestowed on a composer at the conference.

Carter had struck up a friendship with Thomson, at least since Thomson's attendance as a speaker at the Green Mountain Arts Festival in 1941. Writing to his friend in March 1971, Carter confirmed Thomson's attendance that summer at the conference where, Carter confessed, "much musical nonsense takes place."

> Perhaps I am a bit hard sometimes on the place as once in a great while something does manage to come through.... We will have a small housekeeping apartment for you so you can cook something when you feel like it as you will not be at all charmed with the fare at Commons, to which you of course [are] welcome. As we can not pay you a fee we at least can make it as comfortable as possible for you.

Thomson replied, confirming that he would be there and explaining, "I had not expected there would be a fee, but it would be in every way convenient if someone coming from New York would offer to drive me there and back."

Although the pianist Marya Sielska gave her New York Town Hall debut recital in 1968, she began attending the conference in 1969 as a chamber player, not a staff pianist. She returned each year on scholarship until 1972 when the board acted on Grossman's recommendation and paid her an honorarium for her services as a coach and then appointed her as a staff pianist for the next year. A much beloved chamber music pedagogue, she remained on the conference faculty until 1998. When she died in 2008, she left the conference a substantial legacy. The conference used this gift to establish a fund in her memory to support a piano faculty chair position each year.

Altogether in 1969, twenty-four composers attended, and forty-nine new works were read. Of these, during the four concerts of the conference, twenty-five new works were performed.

The Amateur Experience

The experience of the amateurs attending the Chamber Music Center had not changed much during those first two decades from 1951 on at Bennington. Throughout this period, the conference offered a wealth of playing opportunities—as well as exposure to new music for those who wanted it—although exposure to it would have been difficult to avoid. During this period, the conference seems to have avoided labeling these musicians as "amateurs," but instead referred to those attending the Chamber Music Center as the "chamber music players"; the term "participant" came into use later.

At the same time, the conference seems to have had a casual attitude toward the amateurs, despite the essential role they played in keeping the organization solvent. The leadership in the early years was drawn from the professional musician side of the conference, with only a few amateurs gradually added over the years to the board of trustees, where they might influence the conference's operations.

The conference typically began with a Sunday concert by staff on the first day, immediately after everyone's arrival. The unplanned (not to say *unrehearsed*) quality of this first concert was taken up at a staff meeting in 1960—nine years of winging it was perhaps too much for some staff members—resulting in a recommendation that the "first Sunday concert could be arranged the previous evening during the first staff meeting, making for a less haphazard event than is usually the case." Wednesday and Saturday evening concerts (planned and rehearsed) were presented each of the two weeks.

Except for that first year of 1951, the four-concert evening schedule (Wednesday and Saturday, both weeks) was maintained for at least the first two decades at Bennington, as was the concert format, which primarily consisted of modern chamber works, including those written for or at the conference. The concert then concluded, often without an intermission, with a work for chamber orchestra, combining staff professionals and amateur players and conducted by Alan Carter. Referred to as "dessert" or, by those less than enthusiastic about the new music portion of the program, as "mouthwash," the chamber orchestra works were typically familiar baroque-period warhorses, such the Bach *Brandenburg* concerti. A typical day for amateurs consisted of a two-hour morning coaching session followed by a late morning, hour-long rehearsal, typically led by Carter, of the Center Chamber Orchestra. After lunch, the amateurs were on their own (the staff musicians were busy trying out new works by the composers), free to continue rehearsing their morning assignments or reading other works. Evenings were also available for reading sessions or attending concerts or rehearsals. Not everyone liked having coaching sessions limited to the morning. As late as 1969, Hassler Whitney, for one, was urging at a board meeting that the conference should add coaching sessions and focus more attention to the quality of coaching, because the coaching during the second week that summer was "worse than ever."

By 1954, a formal coaching schedule had been put in place, directed, perhaps through default, by staff violist George Grossman. Writing to Carter before that summer's conference, Grossman scheduled each conference week into two sessions (three and four days each) and then listed standard works for string quartet (Haydn, Mozart, Beethoven, Borodin, Dvořák, and Debussy) and piano quartets or quintets (Mozart, Dvořák, Fauré, and Franck), along with works including oboe (the Mozart quartet, plus the only modern work on the schedule— Robert McBride's 1937 oboe quintet) and clarinet (the Mozart and Brahms quintets).

Grossman made a point of including one work with piano in each session, noting that the previous summer, "pianists were shunted around rather like poor relations." Grossman also suggested that "an additional no. of works could be added consisting perhaps of Trios (with piano) and Sonatas—and possibly to be handled by [staff cellist] George Finckel. About how it happened last summer."

The schedule and assigned works, however, were not communicated to the amateur players in advance of their arrival, as is apparent from the recommendation, from a 1960 staff meeting, that "the morning groups should be set up for the entire next week on Sunday." The idea was that "everyone who would be expected to be on hand during the week could be given ample notice ahead of time." But advance scheduling does not seem to have caught on, and players had little if any

Participant oboist Marty Lipnick in 1992. Lipnick first attended the conference in 1964 and returned for roughly fifty years, making him one of the amateur musicians with the longest history of attendance.

Photo by Claire Stefani

time to prepare. Three years later, in 1963, staff meeting notes reflect the need to include adequate time at staff meetings on Saturday and Wednesday "for scheduling of the chamber music groups." Amateur oboist Marty Lipnick, who first attended in 1964, recalls how in his early years at the conference all wind players would have a "day-one lineup" along the wall in Room 136 of the Jennings music building, with the coaches then picking out players for each group.

As late as 1967, amateur violinist and violist Ellen Loeb suggested at a board meeting that "participants be given their music ahead of time." Another decade would pass, however, before the conference would be able to implement that idea.

Another significant innovation was offering performance opportunities for the conference's amateur musicians. According to the 1960 staff meeting notes: "It was thought advisable for the chamber music players to present one concert each week." And because it was apparently believed that this performing opportunity would appeal to amateurs, it was also recommended that "mention of it be included in the description in the brochure." (The passive voice construction provides no identification of the staff person who was the source of this idea.) Another recommendation—one can only wonder why it took a decade at Bennington for anyone to have this idea—was to "have coffee served mid-morning at Jennings for the chamber music players."

As the decade came to a close with the 1969 conference, a total of forty-three amateurs, including Antonia Lavanne's voice students, were in attendance over the two weeks, although the first week of the conference was far more popular with an attendance of forty, as compared to only twenty-seven during the second (the Composers' Conference) week.

Who Were the Amateurs?

Who were the amateur players who attended the Chamber Music Center during the early Bennington years? Then as now, they came from diverse backgrounds, with a love of music making, often shared with family members. At least some were highly accomplished players, such as the cellist Elizabeth deBlasiis Karrick and the violinist and violist Ellen Loeb, both of whom were conservatory-trained.

The father and son violinists and physicians, F. William Sunderman and F. William Sunderman Jr., were in attendance in 1957 with their Stradivarius instruments. The senior Sunderman was later to publish his *Musical Notes of a Physician 1980–1982*, called by one music historian "a fanciful, undocumented, out-of-date, incorrect volume that is enjoyable reading."[82]

Another amateur from this period was cellist John Yang, who attended in 1952. He was then an undergraduate at Harvard and had studied cello with George Finckel. Later, Yang had a career as an architect and landscape photographer in New York City. Yang's son, professional violist David Yang, is artistic director of the Newburyport Chamber Music Festival; Yang's daughter, Naomi Yang, played electric bass in the band Galaxie 500. And Yang's granddaughter, Eliana Razzino Yang, is pursuing a career as a cellist.

On some pieces, such as a Mozart wind divertimento, professional-level amateur players such as oboist Woodford "Bill" Garrigus, a 1949 graduate of Middlebury College, performed alongside the professionals. During his graduate studies in geography at Clark University, Garrigus, who was the principal oboist of the Vermont State Symphony Orchestra, returned to the conference for the summers of 1954, 1956, and 1957.

Composer Frederic Rzewski and amateur pianist Sophie Kary posed for this photo in 1954 as the youngest and oldest conference members; it was published the next summer in Vermont Life *to accompany an article by Theodore Strongin.*

Photo by John F. Smith Jr., courtesy of Middlebury College Special Collections

Most of the conference's amateurs, however, were not professional musicians in the making. During the early years, Alan Carter appears to have personally handled all correspondence with potential participants. Often, interested musicians would send written inquiries to Carter, who would reply with an application form. He would then confirm attendance upon receiving the application.

In late spring of 1954, Carter received a brief inquiry from an amateur pianist in Miami, interested in a "musical vacation" at the conference: "I am an elderly lady, but I love music and I am a very experienced chamber music player. Would my age be a hindrance in taking part at the musical performances?"

Carter replied, "We would be delighted to have you," adding, "I feel quite certain you will fit into the musical picture well and that you will find congenial people with whom to work and live."

This pianist, Sophie Kary—she was well into her teens when Brahms died—expanded on her background in her application: "I play piano since 50 years. Most of the time I played chamber music classics, all the trios and quartets of Mozart, Beethoven, Brahms, Dvořák, Schubert, Mendelssohn etc. Also I know most of the violin-piano sonatas."

During her summer vacation at the conference, she was, as the oldest participant, invited to pose for a *Vermont Life* photograph—Carter was literally right about her fitting into the "musical picture"—with the youngest participant, the composer Frederic Rzewski.

Seated outdoors, the youthful Rzewski, holding a pen and a score, seems to about to make some serious point about music, while Kary, with her hands folded across the purse in her lap, looks somewhat bemused. They are not quite making eye contact. The photo captures perfectly the two ongoing yet not quite fully connected sides of the conference. The composer side had its mostly young composers striving to create the music of the future in the present, while many of the chamber music players were focused primarily on a tradition rooted in the past. The wide range of ages is a feature of conference participants, composers, and faculty to this day.

About a month after Kary's letter arrived, another inquiry landed on Carter's desk, this time from a prospective horn player. In his detailed four-page handwritten letter, this self-described "medium skilled horn player" wondered if "you have enough work for horns in the Chamber Orchestra and various ensemble groups to make my presence worthwhile."

After reviewing the somewhat limited options for horn in the chamber music repertory, the potential applicant surmised that if Robert Bloom was planning wind quintets then "naturally there would be enough to do in the small sessions."

But musical concerns were not the only, or even pre-eminent, items on this amateur's agenda. He continued, explaining that he would be using a "precious two week vacation to attend the Center" with the result that "naturally I would like have a good time as well as play music." Finally, he got to the point: "Do you normally get the kind of people at the Center who would be congenial for a lively, 29 year old bachelor, or are they more elderly, sedentary types?" Having gotten "favorable reports" on the conference when it was at Middlebury, he expressed concern that the conference's "character" had changed since moving to Bennington. One wonders if Carter was still reading on page four, when the hornist asked him "to estimate in advance the number who will be attending this year."

Carter's prompt reply started off positively enough, noting that "you would have a good time socially and to a certain extent musically," but then veered suddenly to the conclusion that "the Center is not for you." Ignoring the idea that there might be adequate opportunities to play wind quintets coached by Bloom, Carter explained that "we have a first class professional woodwind quintet on the staff and there is hardly ever anything we do in which we use more than one horn."

Carter promised to keep the prospective applicant on the mailing list, concluding that "perhaps another year we will be large enough to have two horns." But that two-horn year came quickly—and without the lively bachelor—when the next summer Bennington College student and hornist Carita Richardson attended the conference, joining staff hornist Albert Richman.

The Conference at Twenty-Five

When a *New York Times* reporter asked Carter on the eve of the conference in 1970 how he was planning to celebrate its twenty-fifth anniversary that year, Carter replied, "Why, I don't know, we hadn't realized it was here."[83] Although Carter ventured that "we'll probably play works associated with the conference in its early years," it is not clear that even that happened. That year, like all those before it, held a full two-week schedule, with the usual worries about keeping the conference on budget.

The conference continued to be closely linked with the Vermont Symphony Orchestra. Joseph Parry, treasurer since the conference first arrived at Bennington, resigned, and was replaced by Phyllis Heywood Franze, a violinist who also had administrative duties with the VSO. Another VSO player, cellist Dane Anderson, a recent Middlebury College graduate, came as a conference staff factotum in 1970, and was responsible for everything from sitting in with the professional or amateur groups, as needed, to setting or breaking down the concert stage, to serving as a chauffeur to Albany for Senior Composer-in-Residence Virgil Thomson.

For Anderson, these weeks at the conference were life-changing: "In two summers, I learned all the Brahms chamber works [with cello]," he recalled, thinking of those exalted moments of first discovering music that one comes back to again and again for the rest of one's playing career. Anderson went on to study cello with William Stokking, principal cellist in the Philadelphia Orchestra, then played cello professionally and established himself as a leading luthier in the Philadelphia area.

As the conference finished its twenty-fifth year in 1970 and was poised to start its third decade at Bennington College, the only changes on campus were the addition of the American Institute of Architecture award-winning Crossett Library in 1959, and the Fels, Noyes, and Sawtell college houses, which were built in 1968 and 1969. (These would later come to be known as the "old-new dorms" when the Kyu Sung Woo Architects–designed Perkins, Merck, and Paris-Borden college houses supplanted them as the "new dorms" in 2001.)

But during this same period, the conference itself had gone through striking changes and developments. The conference's leaders—Alan Carter in particular—should have been immensely proud of what they had accomplished. If they had taken the time to look back at the past twenty-five years, they could have counted hundreds of composers and amateur musicians who had been part of the conference experience, surely a life-changing one for more than just a few. Very likely no one at the conference, however, would have sensed the dramatic changes that would occur in the decade to come.

The Nineteen Seventy-Two

COMPOSERS' CONFERENCE

AT JOHNSON STATE COLLEGE · JOHNSON, VERMONT
(formerly at Bennington)

ANNOUNCES

Fifteen Tuition Scholarships

AUGUST 13-27, 1972

❀ Composers' works will be rehearsed, performed, and taped in stereo by an ensemble of professional instrumentalists selected for their experience in performance of Contemporary works.

❀ Staff Composers, Mario Davidovsky and Donald Erb will oversee rehearsals and be available for private consultation. Seminars in electronic music, multimedia and other specialized fields will be given.

❀ Applicants may submit works for any combination of the following: flute, oboe, clarinet, bassoon, french horn, trumpet, trombone, piano, harpsichord, double percussion, double string quartet, contrabass, and soprano. A professional conductor will be in residence.

SCORES SHOULD BE
SUBMITTED TO:

ALAN CARTER, DIRECTOR
COMPOSERS' CONFERENCE
BOX 271
MIDDLEBURY, VERMONT 05753

DEADLINE, JUNE 15TH ■ AWARDS WILL BE ANNOUNCED IN EARLY JULY

Past Staff Composers

HUGH AITKIN · ARTHUR BERGER · HENRY BRANT · INGOLF DAHL
MORTON FELDMAN · ROGER GOEB · EZRA LADERMAN · OTTO LUENING
HALL OVERTON · MEL POWELL · J. K. RANDELL · CHOU WEN-CHUNG
HALSEY STEVENS · LESTER TRIMBLE · EDGARD VARESE · RALPH SHAPEY
STEFAN WOLPE · CHARLES WUORINEN.

V. A Change of Name— and Location

We simply outgrew Bennington last summer. Johnson is a new campus with excellent facilities for music making etc.

—Alan Carter, letter to Moses Kligsberg, July 5, 1972

A S THE CONFERENCE WAS WRAPPING UP its two weeks on the Bennington campus in August 1971— in fact, the day before the concert featured in the *Bennington Banner* photos of Alan Carter indicating "quiet!" to the Green Mountain Fiddlers in the Carriage Barn—the conference board approved an amendment to the corporation's articles of association. The word "Bennington" was dropped from the conference's name, and it would now be known simply as the *Composers' Conference & Chamber Music Center, Inc.* The reason was that the conference, after twenty years on the Bennington campus, was moving in 1972 to Johnson State College (today, part of Northern Vermont University) in Johnson, Vermont, its location for the foreseeable future.

Why Johnson State College?

Although the board approved the organizational name change at the end of the 1971 session, thus freeing the conference from

A poster advertising composer tuition scholarships for the conference in 1972, the first year it was held at Johnson State College.

Bennington's name and supporting the move to Johnson, we have no documents that record the board's consideration and approval of the move. But it does seem likely that either Bennington College's proposed room and board fees had risen too high or that Johnson had simply offered a better deal. There were also rumors that Bennington College might not be financially viable; after all, the college was operating at a deficit, as had been reported at a conference board meeting just three years earlier.

Yet another factor might have been the possibility that the Vermont Symphony Orchestra would be in residence at Johnson. At the 1973 meeting, the board was informed that the VSO might be at Johnson three days before the start of the conference to read and record orchestral works written by conference composers.

Or, as Carter stated in his letter to Moses Kligsberg several weeks before the start of the first Johnson session, the conference simply may have outgrown Bennington College. More participants were attending than ever before.

Johnson may have lacked the seemingly unchanging old–New England charm of Bennington's Colonial Revival campus, but it did offer modern facilities. Johnson's Dibden Center for the Arts, a "striking late modernist building, whose sculptural roofline echoes the contours of the Sterling Mountain Range—its backdrop to the south,"[84] contained a 500-seat auditorium and was the brand-new center of the conference's activities, having been built in 1971. The 1972 conference brochure described the "air conditioned" Dibden Auditorium as "acoustically the best in Vermont."

Dibden Auditorium must have been attractive to the composition side of the conference. The possibility of having a full orchestra, such as the Vermont Symphony Orchestra, in residence at Johnson would have appealed to the composers, as well as to Carter, and it was an option that Bennington, with its much smaller Carriage Barn performance space, could not provide. Bennington's Greenwall Auditorium did not yet exist.

But on the chamber music player side, without the many rooms of Bennington's Jennings music building, conditions at Johnson were cramped, resulting in "coaching sessions . . . set up in the anterooms of lavatories, in hallways, and on stairway landings, not to mention outdoors in the shade of a tree, or even on the lawn in the sunlight."[85] But as cellist Dane Anderson, who spent three of his four summers on the conference's staff at Johnson, explained, any inconveniences were soon overshadowed by the musical experience: "after all, what really matters is the playing, it doesn't matter so much where you put your head at night."

An undated photo from the Johnson State College years shows the diverse wind instrumentation used by conference composers in works performed by staff musicians. Karl Kraber, piccolo; Neil Boyer, English horn; Allen Blustine, bass clarinet; Lester Cantor, bassoon.

Photo by Clemens Kalischer, courtesy of Allen Blustine

During the three years at Johnson, the conference's two-week amateur coaching program was highly popular, despite the additional three-plus hours added to the drive for anyone south of Bennington. In 1972, the first year at Johnson, there were 100 amateur chamber players, including singers coached by Antonia Lavanne; in 1973, there were eighty-nine amateurs (despite the board's decision the year before to limit the chamber players to seventy-eight—no doubt reflecting concerns that space was tight); in 1974, there were ninety-eight amateurs. The conference's growth in amateur population was remarkable.

Chamber Music Conference by the Numbers: Selected Statistics over the Decades[*]

			Number of composers[†]	Number of participants[‡]	Number of faculty[§]
1946	1st year	2 weeks	2	Unknown	5
1952	7th year	2 weeks	¶	66	¶
1955	10th year	2 weeks	23	53	¶
1965	20th year	2 weeks	19	16	24
1970	25th year	2 weeks	21	80	35
1975	30th year	2 weeks	3	156	18
1985	40th year	3 weeks	2	250	36
1995	50th year	4 weeks	4	241	41
2000	55th year	4 weeks	7	262	49
2005	60th year	4 weeks	8	258	44
2010	65th year	4 weeks	7	285	43
2015	70th year	4 weeks	7	275	52
2019	74th year	4 weeks	7	293	54

[*] This information has been derived from conference archival materials, and some records are incomplete or difficult to verify.

[†] This includes all types of "composers": in the early years, there were "staff composers"; more recently the conference has added "composition fellows." The senior composer-in-residence is also included in the composer numbers from 2005 onward. And while composers also serve as faculty and are listed as such in conference directories, they are not included in the faculty numbers on this table.

[‡] Includes auditors.

[§] For some of the early conference years, the term "staff" was used for the professional musicians who coached, conducted, and taught seminars. Many staff members are also participants; they have been included in the participant numbers and not the staff numbers. Faculty numbers exclude visiting and guest faculty.

[¶] 1952 is the first year for which we have a "directory," which is just a list of sixty-six names, and does not indicate who was a participant, composer, or staff member. Similarly, the 1955 directory does not separately identify participants and faculty.

Ten years earlier, there had been only fifteen amateur chamber players in attendance. For 1973, the board also limited scholarship composers to fifteen, plus three alternates, since there were too many in 1972.

The Amateur Admission Process

Given the growth in the number of amateur players, by 1972 George Grossman was voicing his concerns to the board that new applicants needed to be screened more carefully in regard to playing ability. Various approaches were discussed: asking for more information on the application itself, requesting that new applicants provide references, or undertaking "short auditions held when players arrive," suggesting that the issue was not with admission standards, but with forming groups of compatible players. The 1973 conference application form, apparently for the first time, included questions intended to address this issue ("How many years have you played? Do you sight read easily? Presently associated with a musical group? What Chamber music pieces are you currently playing?"). The 1974 application form added an additional yes-or-no question about "present or recent study," with a blank for the teacher's name for those responding "yes," along with self-rating categories, "pro" and "A" through "D."

The Davidovsky and Erb Years

In a significant break with conference tradition, Mario Davidovsky and Donald Erb continued as staff composers during the Johnson State College years, having already held those positions for three consecutive years. This was the first time in the conference's recent history that two staff composers returned for so many seasons. The year before the two composers joined the conference in 1969, the board had discussed continuity in composer staffing, with George Todd pointing out that "it had been our policy not to have any particular name or composer attached to the conference." Pollikoff affirmed this, saying he would "rather see a completely different composing staff" every two years. But the fact that Davidovsky won the Pulitzer Prize in 1971 for his *Synchronisms no. 6* may have secured his ongoing role at the conference; 1974 was then his sixth consecutive year on the staff.

The conference was an enthralling musical environment during these years. When the pianist Robert Miller, whom Allen Blustine describes as an "extraordinary force in contemporary music," brought Davidovsky's *Synchronisms no. 6* to a conference concert in the Carriage Barn, the first note, played by the solo piano but immediately transformed and extended by the electronic soundtrack, was a shock. At that moment Blustine, and surely other audience members as well, knew they were hearing for the first time an electronic medium that was as of yet unexplored.

At Johnson, Davidovsky and Erb were joined by other composers, often denominated as visiting composers (at a meeting in 1970, the board defined a "visiting composer" as a "non-teaching, composer-emeritus of the conference").

In 1972, they were joined by Otto Luening and David Raksin, a former composition student of Arnold Schoenberg who was already a prolific and well-established film composer, widely known for his immensely popular score to the 1944 movie *Laura*.[86]

In 1973, Normand Lockwood, who had been at the conference in 1948 and 1950, was a visiting composer, as was Frank

Wigglesworth, who had also been closely associated with the conference from the beginning. In 1974, Davidovsky and Erb were joined by John Eaton, another composer with a strong interest in electronic music as well as in microtonal music.

For young composers, the conference offered profound immersion in a supportive and inspiring creative community. Twenty-one-year-old Larry Bell first arrived at the conference at Johnson in 1972 bringing with him his latest, as yet untried, compositions. The conference afforded him contact with musicians like violinist Joel Berman, pianist Robert Miller—who had premiered Davidovsky's *Synchronisms no. 6* only a few years earlier—and pianist and percussionist Zita Carno.

At Johnson State College in 1974, composer Mario Davidovsky strikes a mock-theatrical pose for the photographer. That summer, the conference split into two organizations, with Davidovsky staying on at Johnson State, while Alan Carter returned to Bennington College in 1975.

Photo by Alice Berman

Bell returned to the conference as a composer-in-residence at Bennington in 1991, has taught at the New England Conservatory and Berklee College of Music, and is the recipient of numerous prizes, including a Charles Ives Award from the American Academy of Arts and Letters. In 2019, he reflected on his experience at the conference:

> It is difficult to impress upon anyone now how amazingly sophisticated these musicians and composers were. There was a tremendous excitement about everything challenging to execute. These were some of the best freelance new music performers in New York. It was quite a heady experience for me coming from a small town in North Carolina. Also, I was only a sophomore in college when I arrived and most of the other composers were in graduate school or working professionally in connection with a university.

Bell worked directly with Davidovsky and Erb, both of whom were supportive of the younger composer. Erb, who had an "adventurous sense of sound," suggested, for example, that Bell use the high-pitched E-flat clarinet in *Continuum*, one of his new works first performed at the conference (later published as his opus 3), if he "wanted it to be out of tune" and a B-flat clarinet if he "wanted it to be in tune." At the time, Erb seemed "far out" and had notions that whatever sounds the player made could be used in a piece. Davidovsky urged Bell to explore a wider range of rhythmic possibilities. Bell's reminiscences touch on how changing musical aesthetics and trends—in particular the 1960s "Downtown music"—began to arrive at the conference:

> The big debate in '72 was about the role of *alea* or chance. Since [the conference] was a real uptown place there was very little patience for anything bordering on the aleatoric.* One female composer had a graphic score with no real music on it but a lot of instructions and diagrams. I recall [staff pianist] Robert Miller being enraged about this piece and he said, "who is responsible for this!" Of course, this was the essence of the problem. No one was responsible for it.

Although Carter continued as the director of the conference and president of the board, in 1972 Grossman was appointed associate director of the Chamber Music Center—and chief coach. Paul Ross, a violinist with the Pittsburgh Symphony Orchestra, was designated as assistant coach.

The newly created position of executive director was held by Ernest "Ernie" Stires Jr. beginning in 1972. Previously, he had been an administrator for the VSO, so like other VSO staff members, he took on a similar role with the conference. He came from a musical family—his grandmother had a career as a mezzo-soprano at the Metropolitan Opera, and Samuel Barber was a cousin—and he was a composer as well, known for "jazz-based classical music" and later as a formative compositional influence on another Vermonter, Trey Anastasio of

---

* Bell is referring to aleatory music ("alea" is Latin for "dice"), in which an element of composition is determined by chance or in which the performers are to determine, typically at random, how the work will be performed. The composer Pierre Boulez is credited with popularizing the term.

the band Phish. As executive director, Stires was joined by his wife, Judith, who served as secretary for the Chamber Music Center, and also by his son Ernest Stires III, who in 1972 was awarded an honorarium for his efforts as stage manager.

That same year, on the composition side of the conference, Reynold Weidenaar filled a newly created conference coordinator position. Weidenaar had a strong interest in electronic music, having founded, with Robert Moog in 1965, the Independent Electronic Music Center, and he was finishing up his bachelor's degree in music.[87] In a significant change in leadership at the board level, an opening on the board was filled by the conference staff conductor, Efrain Guigui.

The Composer-Amateur Player Conundrum

The board continued its discussions about integrating the amateur players and the composers. Trustee Norman Reiss, an amateur double bassist, commented that "many of the chamber players would like to have more contemporary music included in the coaching sessions." Pollikoff responded favorably, stating that "when a composer is accepted to the conference, he should be asked to bring any of his music that is accessible to amateur players." Grossman then recommended that a commission be offered through a competition to choose the best work of the year. Grossman also recommended that "we as an organization should commission a work each year by an established composer, thereby drawing more attention to the activities of the Conference."

If the conference's three years at Johnson held any lesson, it was that the site had only a small impact on whether the conference could achieve its mission as both a composer residency and an amateur musician program. All that was needed was a site that provided basic amenities and, perhaps most important, adequate playing and performance spaces. As it would turn out, however, the conference was about to face its biggest challenge—one that had little to do with location, but instead with whether it would reexamine and perhaps abandon its original mission.

Play Chamber Music . . . for two glorious weeks
August 12-26, 1979

A CONFERENCE DAY

7:45 a.m. – 8:45 a.m.	Breakfast
9:00 a.m. – 11:00 a.m.	Assigned coached ensembles
11:00 a.m. – 11:30 a.m.	Coffee break
11:30 a.m. – 12:30 p.m.	Orchestra (Mon.-Fri.)
12:30 p.m. – 1:30 p.m.	Lunch
2:00 p.m. – 3:30 p.m.	Assigned coached ensembles
3:30 p.m. – 5:30 p.m.	Free time
6:00 p.m. – 7:00 p.m.	Dinner

Evenings: Concerts by faculty and participants; open
rehearsals; seminars on technique; informal
ensemble sessions; etc.

A BACH'S LUNCH AND SQUARE DANCE
Sunday, August 17, 1980

From noon until 4 p.m., Master Chef Jack
Glick will cook up a special gourmet musical
offering for the playing and listening delecta-
tion of all Conference members. The menu
will include J.S., J.C., C.P.E. and P.D.Q.
Box lunches will be provided.

In the evening, following a picnic on the Great
Lawn, there will be a square dance with the
Pumpkin Hook Old Time Orchestra.

Conference Fees

Participants

Two weeks	$495
One week	$275

Includes tuition, room and board, use of all facilities, and
admission to all concerts.

Auditors

Two weeks	$345
One week	$195

Includes room and board, use of all facilities, and admission
to all concerts. Coaching not included.

Accompanying Family Members

Two weeks	$270
One week	$145

Special arrangements for children 2-16 years of age. Includes
room and board, use of recreational facilities, and admission
to all concerts.

Special problems such as diet, or stair-climbing, will be accommodated upon advance notice.

Why play by yourself when you can play with us?

VI. The Great Schism and Return to Bennington

THE COMPOSERS' CONFERENCE: A Seminar of young composers takes place at Johnson concurrent with the Chamber Music Center. Center members are encouraged to attend their readings, rehearsals, concerts and lectures. Members of both communities share the beautiful campus and dine together.

—Chamber Music Center brochure, 1974

T HE THIRD SUMMER at Johnson State College, in 1974, was a momentous one for the conference, as it split into two separate organizations. The fault lines in the organization's structure, already visible a decade earlier when Charles Wuorinen unsuccessfully challenged the leadership about the need to postpone the conference for a year, had now resulted in a complete rupture.

The original corporate entity, the Composers' Conference and Chamber Music Center, Inc., remained at Johnson State College,*

---

* The Composers Conference remained at Johnson State College for the next two years and then in 1977 moved to Wellesley College (Wellesley, Massachusetts). In 2018, it moved to Brandeis University (Waltham, Massachusetts).

under the leadership of Mario Davidovsky, who continued as its director until his death in 2019, with Efrain Guigui also staying on as the music director. Carter, Grossman, and many of the conference staff and trustees returned to Bennington College the next summer, in 1975.

Despite the importance of this remarkable development in the organization's history, we have no documentation concerning how it occurred. The central question of who would be in charge, and how the two "communities"—as the conference brochure of 1974 referred to the composers and amateur chamber players—would be combined or not, had now been answered, at least for those remaining at Johnson. The Composers' Conference at Johnson would now be led by a composer, and although it preserved a place for amateur players, going forward the amateurs and composers continued as separate communities. The musicians returning to Bennington College now faced the challenge of resolving that issue for themselves.

Three weeks before the start of the 1975 session at Bennington College, Carter was feeling very pleased. He sent a copy of the conference treasurer's handwritten budget for the summer to Lionel Nowak, commenting, "we hope you will feel as encouraged as we do at the present time." After a detailed listing of projected income and expenses, the budget showed a profit of more than $1,000. If the organizational division that occurred the year before had disrupted the conference's functioning, there was no sign of it.

The budget, drawn up by Treasurer Valtin "Val" Lust, projected a significant increase in the number of participants over the number attending at Johnson. Lust was perhaps the only local community member and non-musician ever to serve on the board. Lust had sold his ballpoint pen manufacturing business in 1961 and moved to Vermont, where he supported, as a volunteer and high-end donor, a variety of civic and community organizations including the conference, whose board he had joined in 1970.

A New Nonprofit—In Name

A few days after forwarding the budget to Nowak, Alan Carter, along with Grossman and Lust, incorporated a new organization, *The Chamber Music Conference and Composers' Forum of the East, Inc.*, with the stated purpose of "encouraging, advancing and assisting musical amateur[s] and professional composers." In naming the new nonprofit, Carter seems to have forgotten that in 1966 he had concurred with the view that the organization's equally lengthy name at the time—*Bennington Composers' Conference and Chamber Music Center*—was "too long and unwieldy." The new name flipped the positions of the organizational components: now, it is the Chamber Music (and not the Composers') Conference. The reference to "composers," formerly first, is now second. The emphasis endures in the conference's latest short-form name, the Chamber Music Conference, and the often-used initials CMC.

At the same time, the incorporators appointed the initial board of nine directors. Five of the nine (Carter, Grossman, Nowak, Bloom, and Luening) had longstanding connections with the conference, going back twenty years or more. Joining them were violinist Joel Berman and two amateur double bassists, Norman Reiss (who had joined the board in 1970) and Robert Sharon (who started attending the conference in 1971). Lust, the local community member and philanthropist,

What's in a Name?

What we refer to in this history as the "Chamber Music Conference" (or simply "the conference") is both an event—a coming together of chamber music enthusiasts—and a legal entity. When it was started by Alan Carter in 1946, however, it was the *Composers' Conference and Chamber Music Center*, a summer program of Middlebury College. For its first five years, it continued as a Middlebury program, but when the conference moved to Bennington College in 1951, it was incorporated as an independent tax-exempt nonprofit organization, *The Bennington Composers' Conference and Chamber Music Center, Inc.* For the next twenty years, despite some grumbling from some members of the community that the name was too long and cumbersome, it seems to have served the organization well.

In the summer of 1971, in anticipation of a move the next year to what was then Johnson State College, the conference dropped "Bennington" from its name, becoming simply *Composers' Conference & Chamber Music Center, Inc.* In 1974, while still at Johnson State College, the organization split in two, with one group, focused on the composer side of the program and led by Mario Davidovsky, staying on at Johnson and retaining the corporate entity and name. The conference's founder, Alan Carter, along with many of his staff members, returned to Bennington College in 1975, continuing the conference activities under a newly incorporated nonprofit organization, *The Chamber Music Conference and Composers' Forum of the East, Inc.* The seemingly odd geographical reference in the name, "of the East," was included because Carter—never lacking in ambition—had also started an affiliated conference, "of the

West," based in Santa Fe, New Mexico. The western affiliate, however, was soon abandoned, and the conference continues to this day as *The Chamber Music Conference and Composers' Forum of the East, Inc.*

From 1975 through 2019, the conference was sited at Bennington College. Given the close association of location with identity, in 2013, the conference began using *Bennington Chamber Music Conference*, often in abbreviation as "BCMC," as its official short-form name. In 2019, as part of its relocation to Colgate University, the conference again had to remove "Bennington" from its name, becoming simply *Chamber Music Conference*, and in 2020, a new logo was developed.

In early 2020, the conference adopted a new logo designed by Nancy Skolos, a graphic design professor at the Rhode Island School of Design and clarinet participant since 2012.

Depending on how you count them, the conference has had six names throughout its history. The conference's mission, however, while tweaked at times over the years, has remained essentially unchanged.

also continued to serve. The corporate officers were Carter, Grossman, Nowak, and Lust. So while the CMC was a new nonprofit corporate entity—at least in name—it was still under the original leadership from the Middlebury College years and its earliest years at Bennington College.

Pleased to be Back Again

That first summer back at Bennington College in 1975 was a great success. In his budget Lust had projected, as of six weeks before the session's start, a participant population of 116. But a record-setting 156 participants attended.

Because facilities at Johnson State College were inadequate for even a smaller number of amateur participants, splitting into two organizations, separately located on two campuses, certainly made sense. The CMC participant population now had additional space to grow at Bennington. Additionally, the amateur participants were not competing for space with the thirty or so composers who typically attended each summer. Nor did the amateurs need to compete with the composers for time with the professional coaching staff, as the CMC's 1975 brochure announced, making it abundantly clear that the focus was on the amateur community: "The teaching staff will give its full time to the participants and it will not be divided between composers and amateurs as heretofore, with the exception of the preparation of five public concerts."

Along with the increased amateur attendance, the CMC now had a reduced staff compared to previous years, which also contributed to financial stability. Gone were the brass and percussion players. There was no longer a sizeable group of composers attending on scholarship with their new and expansively scored works to be read and performed. The 1975 conference had only eighteen staff musicians: Carter and Grossman, in their administrative roles, plus nine string players (two string quartets and one double bassist), a wind quintet, and two pianists.

On the composition side, there were only three, not thirty, composers, whose payment for attending included a commission for a new work for the amateurs to play, much as Grossman had proposed years earlier. These important changes are easy to mark. The brochure for the 1974 conference at Johnson State College noted that the amateurs were "encouraged to attend [the composers'] readings, rehearsals, concerts and lectures." That brochure went on to describe the interaction of the composer and amateur communities—they "share the beautiful campus and dine together." But the next year, for the conference's return to Bennington in 1975, the brochure now described an entirely different scene:

> On the contemporary side, we are commissioning several chamber works for various chamber combinations for the amateur participants. Many of you have requested that contemporary works be made available to you at your performance level. Composers will be in residence during the periods of the readings, and rehearsals for suggestions and explanations of their works.

Carter's selection of composers seems highly significant, in both looking back to the conference's past and realigning it as a far more amateur-oriented, and less composer-centric, organization.

Two of the composers were conference old-timers: Normand Lockwood—this would be his third summer at the conference over as many decades—and Frank Wigglesworth. Lockwood's commission for the CMC was his Symphony for String Orchestra, which was premiered by the "Chamber Music Conference String Orchestra," conducted by Grossman. Wigglesworth's commission resulted in his Woodwind Quintet, which premiered with a new faculty clarinetist, Michael Dumouchel.

The third composer, Robert Baksa, was new to the CMC. Baksa's selection as a staff composer seems intentional, given the CMC's repositioning in relation to the composers who stayed on at Johnson State College. Baksa's music goes completely against the aesthetic grain of what most if not all composers under the tutelage of Davidovsky and Erb had been doing at Johnson. It is not only wholly, exclusively tonal, but of a very traditional melodic style and structure.

The new work he composed for the CMC, his Nonet in F Major, is identified even in its title as a tonal work, and indeed a major key, and a one-flat one, at that. As Baksa himself put it, "I have tried to compose (with great delight, I might add) memorable melodies with attractive tonal harmonies and interesting counterpoints and an overall architectural integrity, qualities I cherish in the composers I admire."[88]

The contrast with the stylistic trends of previous conference composers could not be more striking. At about this same time, Wuorinen, as a youthful "radical progressive" composer, was to write that "while the tonal system, in an atrophied or vestigial form, is still used today in popular and commercial music, and even occasionally in the works of backward-looking serious composers, it is no longer employed by serious composers of the mainstream. It has been replaced or succeeded by the 12-tone system."[89]

Perhaps one of the greatest ironies of the CMC's history is that the "experiments" in electronic musical composition undertaken by Luening and Ussachevsky in the Carriage Barn, and the early works of composers like Wuorinen, were of a musical world that had no place for amateurs, except perhaps as listeners. This fact, more than anything, may account for the conference's schism in 1974. Not only was the new music of the time intellectually and emotionally forbidding to amateur players; it also presented technical demands far beyond their skills. Even the highly accomplished professional clarinetist and new music specialist Allen Blustine conceded the extreme difficulty of many of these works, which required him to put in hour upon hour of preparation and practice. The Baksa Nonet in F Major, however, presented none of these challenges.

About two weeks before what was to be the first meeting of the new CMC board in 1975, Alan Carter wrote to the directors, bringing them up to date on the incorporation of the new organization and enclosing the new articles of association and bylaws.

Carter's letter also clears up, to a point, one of the mysteries surrounding the CMC's new name. If it was "*of the East*," was there also an affiliated organization "*of the West*"? Indeed there was. In his letter, Carter explains that he had previously incorporated a "*Composer's [sic] Conference and Chamber Music Center of the West, Inc.*," in Santa Fe, New Mexico. That organization was granted tax-exempt status by the Internal Revenue Service in May 1974, so it was likely incorporated sometime in 1973. Carter also applied to the Vermont secretary of state for the New Mexico corporation to do business in Vermont. But once the new CMC was incorporated in Vermont, there was no need for the New Mexico corporation to continue any activities there, and Carter obtained a "Cessation Certificate" for it from the Vermont secretary of state.

The Tragedy of Alan Carter

Having now updated the directors on these esoteric legal matters, Carter concluded his letter, "I look forward to seeing you in New York on September 26th." But five days before the meeting, on September 21, 1975, Carter died by suicide by carbon monoxide poisoning, parked in his car off a country road outside of Middlebury.[90]

Carter's death was a profound loss, not just for the CMC, but for his family—he left a widow and six children—as well as the wider musical community of Vermont and beyond. In addition to his college teaching career of thirty years, he was a founder and leader of two music organizations—the conference and the VSO—both of which continue to thrive to this day, with a reach far beyond Vermont.

Irwin Shainman, a music professor at Williams College, who had been a trumpet player at the conference from 1952 to 1954 ("a satisfied alumnus of that conference, where I toiled in the orchestra for three summer sessions"), published a brief encomium on Carter two years before he died, concluding, in what now seems to be an understatement, that "the state of Vermont is a much richer place because of his efforts."[91]

When the board met on September 26, they noted "the sudden and unexpected passing of our founder and president," and indeed news of Carter's death earlier that week must have been a shock. News of his suicide must have been met, as is so often the case, with disbelief, guilt, shame, and even anger. As is also so often the case, the cause of Carter's despair will never be known. He may have suffered from depression for years before 1975, as some have speculated. He was said to have been diagnosed with cancer, which would have been consistent with his cigarette chain-smoking habit (having attended a party at Carter's home in the 1960s, longtime participant oboist Ralph Kirmser recalls only the overwhelming smell of cigarette smoke). His beloved Vermont Symphony Orchestra had recently suffered financial problems, and he was replaced as principal conductor in 1974 by the younger, highly skilled, and charismatic Efrain Guigui. He may have despaired over the conference's 1974 split, but there is no evidence of it.

The CMC did not seem to know how to respond to the loss of its founder. It fell to Nowak, apparently on his own initiative, to compose a brief work for strings, *Elegy in Memory of Alan Carter*, featuring a solo viola, which was first performed by the VSO during its 1975–1976 season; the CMC premiere was during the 1977 session, with Paul Wolfe conducting.

The CMC without its Founder

The September board meeting in 1975, the first without Carter, took place at the home of Harold "Hal" Laufman, who was just then joining the board. The board, disoriented by Carter's unexpected death, appointed only an interim set of directors until they met again in October. They then appointed a full board and officers that reflected a sea change in leadership.

The new board included three professionals with long-term ties to the conference: Luening and Bloom, plus Grossman. But five amateur players joined the board, in addition to Laufman: David Arons, a flutist who had first attended in 1973, and who was working in advertising, graphic arts, and printing; William Horowitz, a physician and violinist; Muriel "Petie" Palmer, a professional-level pianist who was then running the historic Park-McCullough House in North Bennington; the remarkable polymath Norman Pickering, violist, acoustic engineer, and inventor of the famous eponymous phonograph cartridge; and Norman Reiss, double bassist and physician.

For the officer positions, naturally enough, Grossman was appointed to succeed Carter as president-director; Berman was vice president, taking the place vacated by Grossman; Nowak continued on as secretary; and Robert Sharon, a New York City attorney and double bassist, took over from Lust as treasurer.

Whether anyone at that meeting in 1975 realized it is not clear, but the CMC had reached a tipping point—for the first time in the organization's history, professional musicians were outnumbered by amateur players in the organization's governing body.

Grossman's Conference Directorship

The next year, 1976—Grossman's first as conference president—was again a successful one. That fall, the CMC had more than $3,500 in the bank to begin preparing for the next summer's program. On campus, in addition to the Carriage Barn, CMC now had access to the new 125,000-square-foot Visual and Performing Arts Center (VAPA), including Greenwall Auditorium, for rehearsal and performances.

The "participant musicale" was apparently introduced that summer, yet another sign of the increased attention given the amateur experience. The first surviving program to bear that "musicale" title is for a concert on August 27, 1976, at 4:30 PM, in Jennings Room 136. On this historic occasion, thirteen participants, in various combinations, presented six works for piano four-hands and piano with winds. The piano four-hands works reflected "master class" coaching sessions specifically for that literature, taught initially by Marya Sielska, who was later joined by Cynthia Adler.

The next summer, participants presented a "Meet the Composer" program featuring the three composers for the session: Michael Finckel (later, a long-term staff cellist), Louis Calabro, and John Heiss. As the program explained:

These compositions have been written during the composers' residency at the Conference and for these particular performers. Each composer will introduce the new work with respect to the special circumstances of its composition.

While the new CMC was successful on artistic and financial levels under Grossman's leadership, the college's hosting services were less than five-star. As Nowak later put it with characteristic diplomacy, the college's "vagaries of management" resulted in "an unusual degree of irritation among conference participants." CMC staff prepared a four-page report chronicling the deficiencies, and one need read no further than the subtitle to get the idea: "A Saga of Confusion, Un-Cooperativeness, and Broken Promises." Although no one seems to have anticipated it, these facility problems of 1976 had a significant impact on the CMC's next summer at Bennington.

But even before the 1977 session, conflict between professional staff and participant leadership emerged. That spring, the board's finance committee, which had been appointed the previous fall, suddenly came to life and made several fiscal responsibility recommendations. Not surprisingly, the committee was composed of significant donors, and they felt they had every right to attend to how the CMC's funds were spent. Among its other points, the committee opined that the CMC should cease commissioning composers with its own funds and instead rely exclusively on grant funding restricted to that purpose. Instead of commissions, they explicitly recommended that "every effort should be made to direct funds to support the basic needs of the Conference as a first priority." In effect, it was the committee's wish that the CMC would no longer directly support composers and include their new music in its programming. Moreover, the finance committee report was overtly critical of Grossman for acting on his own and not obtaining board approval when he made decisions such as paying additional salary bonuses to certain staff members.

Grossman and Luening must have been alarmed by the idea that new music was not a basic need of an organization with "Composers' Forum" in its name. In June, Grossman wrote to Luening, enclosing a copy of the CMC articles of association, and quoting from the organizational purpose clause: "there is absolutely no doubt about the 'aiding, advancing, and assisting . . . professional composers'" (underline in original).

Grossman—not shy about pushing back against the two pairs of doctors and lawyers who had signed off on the finance committee report—responded, with copies to the entire board, in a single-spaced, four-page letter. He reminded the board that "the Composers' Forum is an integral part of our structure and is in our Articles of Association," a point he likely relished making to the lawyers on the finance committee. And he pointed out that what he had done with the staff bonuses was "exactly the same procedure followed the previous year by Alan Carter." But apparently lost on Grossman was that although he had been with the organization for almost twenty-five years, he lacked the autonomy that Carter, as founder, had enjoyed with a very different board of directors.

The board's response, when it met in August 1977, was to add to the agenda the exploration of "the possibility of changing our charter to exclude the composers' program." This idea was to provoke a strong rebuke from Otto Luening later that fall.

More than a few participants who during the 1976 session had endured, among other discomforts and inconveniences, untuned or missing pianos, incorrect room keys, and "Turkish bath" conditions in the new VAPA studios—the air conditioning was reportedly turned off to save money—did not come back in 1977. Attendance was down to 123 participants and two auditors, compared to 154 participants and 22 auditors the year before. Staffing expenses remained the same, and as initially reported to the board as the session was drawing to a close, the CMC would suffer a significant deficit, estimated at $8,000—precisely the situation that Laufman and his finance committee had sought to avoid.

As if attempting to resolve the deficit issue were not enough, the board also charged Maxwell Lehman, an amateur violist who had joined the board that year, with restructuring the CMC. Lehman, an expert in municipal administration—as a city administrator for New York City, he had been integrally involved in revising its charter[92]—was certainly up to the task. His basic charge, as he was to put it, was that "policy-making and operations should be separated."

Although hardly to blame for the CMC's fiscal woes, Grossman—who, in addition to being in conflict with board members, was in ill health—retired from the CMC as director and president after the 1977 season. During his twenty-four years at the conference, no one had done more to consistently support the amateur music side, while remaining true to the original mission of supporting composers and new music. In his subsequently published memoir, Grossman fondly recalled the challenges and rewards of coaching and playing:

> The first minute I got there [in 1953] I was rushed down to the Carriage Barn and thrown into the middle of the chamber music wars, playing and

teaching endless hours every day. At the end of the
first week I collapsed and was carried out and put
to bed. The second week I was again thrown into
the cauldron, so to speak, but I rapidly found myself
acclimated to this furious pace and although I felt
that I had been through two weeks of utter misery,
I couldn't wait to get back the next summer.[93]

For the next two years after his retirement, Grossman was
acknowledged as the CMC's "president emeritus."

The board moved ahead, with Laufman now taking on a
significant role, including hosting board meetings, when they
were not held during the conference at Bennington, at his
Upper East Side Manhattan apartment. Laufman, originally
from Chicago, had excelled at his violin studies—as a teenager,
he soloed with the Chicago Symphony Orchestra. He was
sixty when he first attended the conference at Johnson State
College in 1972, and he already had an illustrious career as a
vascular surgeon (he made a national reputation for himself
in 1951 by reviving a woman from a "frozen coma" caused by
an accidental exposure to sub-zero temperatures),[94] an author
of numerous articles and books, and a medical illustrator.
Although he was something of a newcomer to the conference
at the time, he joined the board at a crucial point, just as
the organization was coping with the loss of Alan Carter.
He was to serve in various leadership capacities for the next
fifteen years. One of his daughters, Laurien Laufman, became
a professional cellist and attended the conference as a faculty
member in 1982 and 1984.

Laufman's letter confirming the September 1977 board
meeting and announcing an eight-point agenda set a very

business-like tone: "Please be punctual. Brunch will be served at 12:30 PM sharp and the meeting will begin promptly at 1:00 PM." In fact, brunch apparently detained the board for only fifteen minutes, and the meeting began at 12:45 PM. A little over four and a half hours later, the board had approved broad changes in how the conference would be managed.

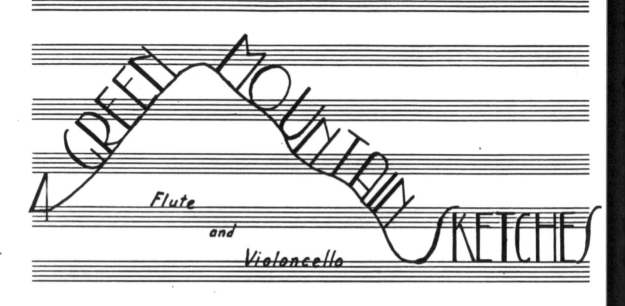

GREEN MOUNTAIN SKETCHES

Flute

and

Violoncello

written for ARDITH BONDI

LIONEL NOWAK

November, 1980

MUSIC MASTERS

No. '88

VII. A Fundamental Restructuring

I cannot help remarking on the measure of enthusiasm, efficiency and cooperation among the officers and trustees. The Conference is alive and well.

—Lionel Nowak, chairman of the board of trustees, writing to his co-trustees, January 4, 1978

WITH MAXWELL LEHMAN'S restructuring plan before them in the fall of 1977, the Chamber Music Conference board was preoccupied with defining staff assignments and functions. They did not directly address the deficit—estimated at $8,000 at the August board meeting—but awareness of it certainly focused their attention on their management responsibilities. Lehman's proposal—complete with organizational charts and job descriptions—was quite straightforward, and the board initially adopted it in its entirety. In doing so, the board took its first steps to define the CMC's organizational structure as it is known today.

The title page of Lionel Nowak's Four Green Mountain Sketches, *commissioned by Ardith Bondi, a conference participant.*

Courtesy of American Composers Edition (BMI)

Lehman's Redesign

Perhaps the most significant change set forth in Lehman's proposal was the splitting of artistic and administrative duties. What had previously been the role of the "president-director" (that is, a combination "president-music director" position)— as held previously by Carter and then briefly by Grossman— was now divided into two separate positions. The "president" (essentially, the role of "executive director" in many nonprofits) had overall staff management responsibilities and reported directly to the board of trustees. At the same time, the chairman of the trustees (Lionel Nowak) was responsible for managing the board of trustees, but presumably had no additional management responsibilities, since those were vested with the president. The organization thus had both a "chairman of the trustees" and a "president of the conference."

In retrospect, this bifurcated arrangement of officers seems unnecessarily cumbersome. Indeed, six years later, board meeting minutes reflect "considerable confusion regarding the relationship between Officers of the Corporation and Officers of the Board of Trustees," requiring the appointment of a committee to "clarify this matter and see that the letterhead is fixed up properly." The next year, the committee, chaired by Haskell Edelstein, recommended renaming Laufman's "president" title to that of "executive director," a staff position that Laufman filled on an unpaid, volunteer basis.

Reporting to the president, in turn, were the music director, the conference coordinator, and an administrative director. The music director had overall artistic leadership, supported by the conference coordinator, while the administrative director had responsibility for scheduling participant coaching sessions, handling communications with participants, and managing campus housing arrangements.

The composition of the board also changed significantly, with Laufman suggesting that paid conference staff should not have voting rights on the board. Laufman was concerned with the obvious conflict of interest posed by the scenario where staff would be voting on their own compensation or other matters that might directly affect them. Most importantly, a motion was unanimously passed for a bylaw amendment that the board "shall consist of participants and others interested, together with such staff members as the board may wish to elect, but who shall not have a vote."

At the time this change was made, conference director George Grossman and violinists Joel Berman and Paul Wolfe were the only staff members on the board. For the next several years, staff members were invited "guests" at board meetings. These changes ensured that the organization would be governed on a consumer-driven model, and we can see the effect of this almost immediately. But banning the staff from having a voice in the conference's management was to prove controversial—and, as we shall see, short-lived. As early as 1979, Music Director Paul Wolfe was reporting to the board that the faculty wanted to be represented at board meetings.

The board also formulated an array of committees, reflecting the functional needs of the organization: finances, fundraising and grants, public relations and recruiting, and advance planning. The officers of the board were typical: that of chairman (not to be confused with the conference president), vice chairman, secretary, and treasurer. One might quibble with some features of the reorganization, but overall it reflected a new level of organizational maturity. The various staff roles and responsibilities were more clearly defined, resulting in higher levels of accountability and coordination, and volunteer and paid functions were separated.

Laufman and others were clearly proud of these organizational changes, which they saw as distinguishing the CMC from other chamber music workshops or programs that were run by "an entrepreneur or professional person or group of persons." The change was indeed profound for the organization. Consider that in the summer of 1977, the board was led by two professional musicians, George Grossman, president and director of the conference, and Joel Berman, vice president. There were seven amateur participants on the board. A year later, in 1978, Grossman was gone from the organization, and his position as president of the conference, previously held only by Alan Carter, was modified and taken over by participant Harold Laufman. Other staff leadership roles were that of musical director (Paul Wolfe), conference coordinator (Joel Berman), participants' ensembles coordinator (Myron Levite), and administrative director (Judith Ensign). Lionel Nowak continued to chair the board, which now included eight amateur participants, along with professionals Robert Bloom and Otto Luening. Amateur musicians were the overwhelming majority on the board of directors, and an amateur also headed up the staff.

During this period, we also see a change in the way conferees were classified, indicating a larger organizational shift. In the 1976 directory, for the first time, the amateur players are referred to as "participants" rather than "chamber players"—reflecting the more active role they were taking on in organizational leadership. Two years later, in the 1978 directory, there is an even more significant change. Now, for the first time,

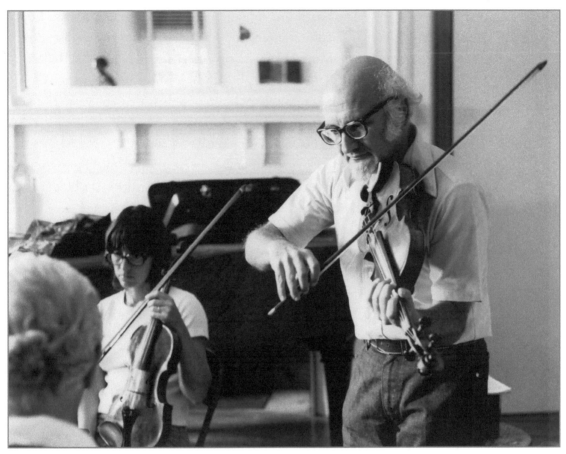

the professional musicians on staff are referred to as "faculty," reflecting the importance of their teaching role as coaches. The term "staff" continued to be used, but exclusively for administrative roles. This nomenclature of participants, faculty, and staff has continued to the present.

While control of the organization had clearly shifted, the reorganization was by no means a total housecleaning. Luening remained on the board, as did Nowak, who continued to chair the board. The new music director, Paul Wolfe, was hardly new to the conference, having first attended in 1956.

Paul Wolfe, who served as music director for four years beginning in 1978, demonstrates a musical point during a coaching session in 1980. The violist is Judy Silverman.

Photo by Alice Berman

The board did appoint a relative newcomer, Myron Levite, who had first attended as a staff violinist and violist in 1977, as coordinator of participants' ensembles for 1978. Reflecting some of the necessary but unsuccessful experimentation during this period, that appointment only lasted one year. The next year, Norman Pickering took over orchestra conducting duties and was listed as staff violist.

Two new board members were Rufus Smith, a passionate amateur cellist who after nearly three decades in the U.S. Foreign Service had recently retired as a deputy assistant secretary of state,[95] and Gerald "Gerry" Carp, an amateur oboist and New York City attorney, specializing in estate litigation and probate matters—with an interest in nonprofit legal issues as well. Carp is listed as the organization's "counsel" to the present day—in recent years, the title has been largely honorary, but he has remained available for consultation when needed. For many years he was responsible for negotiating the contract with Bennington College.

Judith Ensign, Administrative Director

The appointment of Judith Ensign as the CMC's first administrative director in 1978 was an important step forward. Whether it reflected astute judgment or a lucky circumstance, or both, it ensured successful functioning of the CMC on a day-to-day basis as it went through this transition period.

Ensign was a highly accomplished violinist when she first attended in 1970. She came on the recommendation of her violin teacher, the great virtuoso and pedagogue Oscar Shumsky, who urged her to play chamber music because, as she recalls him saying, "it makes you a musician, more sensitive and less arrogant." One of Ensign's personal traditions every summer was organizing a Mendelssohn Octet reading on the second

Opposite page: In 1982, in front of the Bennington College Commons building, participant violist Maurice Kouguell, left, with Administrative Director Judith Ensign, and Stephen Reid, treasurer and later chair of the board.

Photos by Alice Berman

Saturday night, after the staff concert, to close out the two weeks. Knowing, as Ensign put it, "we had to wait another fifty weeks to come back," opportunities to join this wistful reading session were much sought after.

Ensign's seven years as a violinist participant gave her an ideal perspective on the participant experience, particularly the need to introduce newcomers into the community. She also had an interest in nonprofit organizational and fundraising matters. She was the first to recommend (in 1980) that the board have a "planning retreat," and she authored a six-page memo on organizational issues for the board to consider. She had joined the board in 1976, and during the 1977 session, she was volunteering to take on administrative chores. With the reorganization in 1977, she assumed the role of administrative director in 1978—the CMC's only paid administrator—with an honorarium of $1,000.

After the 1978 session, Wolfe, the music director, praised her excellent participant recruiting skills. At the board's meeting during the 1979 session, the minutes reference Nowak's comments that "the conference appears to be going extremely well, and he lauded Judith Ensign for the superb job she has done." After these two years, Ensign resigned (she was succeeded in that role by Marilyn Bell), immediately rejoined the board in 1980, and then became deputy executive director in 1983.

The Start of the "Buddy System"

Several of the CMC's lasting features were developed during Ensign's time on staff or on the board. As early as 1978, she introduced a "buddy system" as a means of welcoming newcomers and reducing their bewilderment upon arrival on campus. "Old-timer" participants would be assigned newcomers from their dorms and encouraged to welcome the newcomers, accompany them to dinner Sunday night, answer questions, and make them feel a part of the conference. This was among the first attempts to integrate newcomers to the conference, and it evolved over time to include pre-arrival communications between newcomers and experienced participant "buddies" about how to prepare for an optimal experience at the conference. The buddy system is a feature of the CMC to this day.

The First Winter Reunion

Another of Ensign's innovations was the first CMC winter reunion in 1982 at the State University of New York (Purchase) Guest House. Often combined in the early years with a CMC fundraising event, the conference's winter reunion has been held on the Presidents' Day weekend—the winter midpoint between summer conferences—every February almost without fail.

As conceived, the reunion provided not just an opportunity for friends from the summer to come together for a winter weekend of music, although that was certainly its original purpose. The reunion would also be a recruiting opportunity, allowing potential newcomers to meet and play with the CMC crowd, just before the due date for applications for the next summer session. In typical years, the early reunions were expected to draw as many as ninety participants.

After its first two years at Purchase, in 1984 the reunion moved to Wainwright House—a mansion thought by many to have an uncanny resemblance to Bennington's Jennings music building—in Rye, New York, where it continued for another thirty years. In recent decades the reunion has been managed by Louise Lerner, CMC participant violist and later summer staff member.

The reunion relocated in 2014 to the Graymoor Spiritual Life Center (Garrison, New York), in the hills just east of the Hudson River, about an hour's drive from Manhattan. In 2017, it moved to the Stony Point Center (Stony Point, New York).

Saving the Composers

As part of the 1977 reorganization, the board also confronted the question of what to do with the composers. Withdrawing support for composer participation in the CMC was an attractive and potentially viable option for at least some board members. Recall the finance committee report in the spring of 1977 that recommended not underwriting composer participation with CMC funds, but instead relying exclusively on whatever foundation or government funding might be available. The board's August 1977 meeting included the future agenda item that "the possibility of changing our charter to exclude the composers' program be explored." (At least some board members may have been thinking, if not saying out loud, that since most of the composers had decided to remain at Johnson State College in 1975, they should stay there!) Lehman's reorganization report also touched on this question, almost as an aside in a discussion of the design of the brochure for the next year, and betrays the view that among amateurs, interest in new music was nil:

> The COMPOSERS' FORUM, if it is to be continued, should be minimized in the brochure. This is a valuable activity of the Conference in terms of public relations and grant possibilities, but not in the minds of the paying customers the brochure is designed to attract.

Naturally enough, board member Otto Luening, then seventy-seven—a composer with a history at the CMC going back three decades to its founding in 1946—spoke up about the importance of having composers. He submitted a seven-point memo to the board in which he argued that if the CMC were to continue as an "educational and cultural" federal tax-exempt nonprofit, inclusion of composers was a necessary element. A conference exclusively devoted to amateur music making, or as he put it, "fun and games," was not, in his view, deserving of tax-exempt status:

> I for one would not see the merit of having fun and
> games tax-free. I think that the educational part of
> this kind of contract can best be met by playing
> some new music; that is a cultural contribution even
> if every piece is not a hit.

Luening went on to suggest several options for including that "new music." The musical staff and librarian "could simply see to it that a good percentage of the works studied would be by American composers." Another option would be "to pay a composer the same fee that the coaching staff is getting." Or, the CMC could commission only Vermont composers (perhaps here Luening was thinking of obtaining support from the Vermont Arts Council or other local funders).

Luening was certainly wrong—factually and legally—if he thought that an organization devoted only to supporting amateur study of chamber music masterworks was not an activity eligible for nonprofit, tax-exempt status. But he did not leave any doubt about the strength of his views on the matter: he abstained from a subsequent vote ratifying the organizational restructuring, and then tendered his resignation from the board.

A Newcomer's Perspective

One participant's account of musical life at the CMC in the late 1970s is included in correspondence with George Grossman about his experience. As an earnest adult student of the clarinet, Stephen Poppel was studying with a member of the Philadelphia Orchestra, and engaging in a number of local chamber music playing opportunities. After attending the second week of the conference in 1977, Poppel was hooked—the program was "unimaginably delightful," and he returned off and on for the next forty years.

As Poppel related, there was quite a bit of variety: "wind quintet in the morning, Schubert Octet in the afternoon; winds together and also mixed with piano and strings;

Joseph Schor, who later served as music director, coaching the Brahms Clarinet Quintet in 1980 on the notoriously hot third floor in the Jennings music building. Stephen Poppel, clarinet; Bonnie Maky and Frances Kaplan, violins; Jean Block, viola; and Nina Malkevitch, cello.

Photo by Alice Berman

scheduled activity with ample free time to arrange other groups; exposure to a range of different coaches; a fixed wind quintet for six mornings to allow for group cohesion; but also exposure in other sessions to groups with other players; modern music and 'classical.'"

The staff's playing level was inspirational. "As a clarinetist I would say that I have never heard the Mozart concerto played so musically, engagingly and intelligently," Poppel wrote, "as Michael Dumouchel's performance."

He got his way—and remained on the board. The board did not drop the composition component. Instead, it was continued as one of the options Luening had proposed. Writing to Grossman a few months later, Nowak explained how things stood: "We are thinking particularly of grounding the relationship between participants and visiting composers more securely by having the composers more active in the daily schedule." That approach has continued to the present day.

At a subsequent meeting of the board, Luening's resignation was "unanimously rejected on the grounds that his forthright, intelligent points-of-view constituted a worthy and necessary kind of loyal opposition, and that his continuing service on the board would be invaluable." Luening was to continue as a board member for the next seven years, ultimately giving the conference almost forty years of service. When he left the board at the end of the 1984 session (he was succeeded on the board by composer and Bennington College faculty member Vivian Fine), the board noted that "he will always be a valued friend of the Conference." Indeed, he continued to advise the board informally, and he returned in 1988 as composer-in-residence. For the conference's fiftieth anniversary in 1995, a year before his death, Luening's Sextet was recorded by conference faculty, conducted by James Yannatos, and the resulting CD was presented to him. Luening's persevering leadership ensured that the conference remained true to its foundational concept of being a place for both composers and amateur musicians. Had it not been for him, the conference of today would very likely not have its new music component.

Program Fine-Tuning

The board continued to make changes to the schedule and program, at times eliminating longstanding activities. Beginning

Violinist Joel Berman coaching in 1968. Berman first attended the conference in 1967 and later served in several leadership roles, including vice president of the board and conference coordinator.

Courtesy of UVM Special Collections

with the 1978 session, as indicated in board meeting minutes, the participant schedule was modified to drop piano and wind coaching sessions in the evening.

Similarly, the first (Sunday) night faculty concert, seemingly always somewhat hit-or-miss (participant clarinetist Stephen Poppel referred to it in 1977 as an "informal quintet concert"), was eliminated, apparently to everyone's relief. Joel Berman described his first experience with the Sunday night concert: immediately after his arrival on campus for the first time in 1967, Max Pollikoff took him aside and said, "Listen, after dinner, we're going to George [Finckel]'s to rehearse tonight, for tomorrow's concert." The rehearsal was for the Ravel String Quartet, a work that Berman—in a state of astonishment—was playing for the first time.

The staff orchestra, once an indispensable ensemble for performing and recording the composers' new works, was also eliminated; concert programs were shortened.

As a sign of the new sensitivity to participant concerns, the CMC undertook a participant questionnaire during the 1977 season. When asked whether the assigned groups "were basically compatible in level of playing ability," 67 percent said "yes;" 13 percent, "no," with an additional 20 percent giving a mixed "50-50" (neither "yes" nor "no") response. Participants expressed a preference for performing in informal "musicales," with another 22 percent of respondents saying "maybe." Three days of coaching with the same group was overwhelmingly preferred to two days with an optional third day.

Solving the Scheduling Puzzle

A little more than a month before his arrival on campus in 1977, a new participant asked in a letter to Music Director Grossman, as probably many newcomers did at the time, "if you can let me know in advance what pieces my groups will be playing, I might be able to look at them ahead of time." "At this time I can't tell you what to prepare," Grossman wrote back, "just keep practicing!"

But there was a clear need for advance scheduling for the serious amateurs, ardent in their ambition to better themselves musically, that the CMC was increasingly attracting. As far back as 1967, violist and board member Ellen Loeb had identified the need for advance assignments in her comments to the board. There had to be a better system than having the music director sorting index cards with participant names and instruments, but no other information, into piles on the floor in order to make group assignments. Nor did anyone seem in favor of having participants standing around in the Jennings music building lobby just before 9:00 AM, when their group assignment was posted on the wall, at which point they'd run to the music library to select a work, ideally by consensus, for coaching. It was not much of an improvement when all participants in an ensemble assembled on Sunday night to decide what they would begin working on the next morning. Then, as stated in CMC brochures in the early 1970s, "chief coach" Grossman "reassigns players every three days to a new coach and group"—but again without notice to the players in advance.

When Marilyn Bell first arrived as a participant pianist in 1975, her piano teacher, Marya Sielska, who was a piano coach at the conference at the time, arranged for her to be coached on two works Bell had prepared at home. (At the time, pianists were coached in four-hand piano literature in the morning, and chamber works with other instruments in the afternoon.) But when Bell returned the next year, upon arrival, she was assigned the Brahms Piano Quintet—which she had never played before. In a panic, she quickly had to find another pianist as her substitute.

Hugh Rosenbaum also experienced the vagaries of on-the-fly coaching assignments in 1978, the first year he and his wife, Rowena, a violinist and violist, attended the conference. Rosenbaum recalled that although he was "fairly new to the bassoon," he was accepted to the conference on participant oboist Ed Bowe's recommendation ("he can read anything!"). The conference did ask on its application form for references—"either a former participant, teacher or someone able to evaluate your playing ability."

"I barely knew the fingerings for the E-major scale," Rosenbaum recalled, yet there in front of him for his first coaching session was the Nielsen Wind Quintet and its famous—but not to Rosenbaum, who had never heard the piece—opening E-major bassoon solo. Despite being "thrown into the deep end," both Hugh and Rowena are still devotees of the conference forty-one years later. As Hugh put it, "the community kept pushing me," and two years after his inauspicious debut coaching session, he played that same movement of the Nielsen quintet—"with an extraordinary sense of accomplishment!"—in a participant recital.

Lehman's reorganization plan in 1977 had already hinted at a solution to the problem of players not having assignments in advance with its reference to the administrative director's

Participant bassoonist Hugh Rosenbaum leads a madrigal session in front of the Bennington College Commons building in 1982, with a group that includes his wife, Rowena, far right. Informal part-song and madrigal singing is a regular activity at the conference to this day.

Photo by Alice Berman

first-listed responsibility: "Schedules participants' sessions after computer programming."

Among Grossman's many contributions to the CMC, and in some ways his most lasting and important, was his collaboration with Eve Cohen, then a graduate student in mathematics who first attended as a viola participant in 1976. Cohen had studied viola with Grossman at Carnegie Mellon some years before, although amateur flutist David Arons—who happened to be Grossman's landlord and downstairs neighbor—deserves the credit for finally getting Cohen, along with violinist and violist Bonnie Maky, to attend. As Cohen was to put it later, "David badgered us mercilessly over several years, and we finally somewhat reluctantly acquiesced and then never looked back." Looking at the scheduling problem from a computer programmer's perspective, Cohen's approach was to prove transformative.

Working with Grossman for the first time for the 1977 session, Cohen was able to develop personal schedules for arriving participants. Because participant pianists—Marilyn Bell was one of them—reacted "with horror" (in Cohen's words) when faced with the assignments that many would have to sight-read in their coaching sessions the next day, they were the first to receive their assignments in advance. But as Cohen was later to explain:

> The pianists, however, were still not satisfied (can you believe it?): it seems that now they were arriving prepared, but the other people in their groups were still sight-reading. The desirability of making advance assignments for everyone had become obvious, so we started doing it.

Paul Ross coaches Eve Cohen, viola, and Millicent Fairhurst, violin, on a string quartet in 1980.

Photo by Alice Berman

In 1978, the CMC brochure announced—with little fanfare, given the significance of the change—a deadline of June 15 for coaching requests, noting that "all scheduling is done prior to the opening date of the Conference." The conference began on August 13, giving Cohen only two months to complete the assignments.

In 1980, when Bell became the conference's administrative director, she went to Pittsburgh to spend a weekend working with Cohen "to provide more pre-assignments for all instruments." The scheduling that took place for the 1980 session, according to Marilyn Bell's report as administrative director, "seemed to work well and was met with enthusiastic responses." If anything, participants indicated—very likely to no one's surprise—that "they would like to see more of it." The scheduling was expanded in stages, with string quartets and wind quintets still meeting for some years on Sunday night of the conference to select their pieces. The advance scheduling increased year by year until the early 1990s, when virtually all assignments were pre-scheduled and announced to participants. Perhaps one of the last "unassigned" coaching sessions took place in 1993 when an ambitious string quartet coached by Jacob Glick chose—on the spot—Beethoven's opus 59, no. 2 quartet for its afternoon coaching session. This advance scheduling innovation, a hallmark of the conference, was to effect a profound change in the CMC, as participants could now accomplish far more in their sessions than would be the case if they came unprepared. Pre-session preparation was to become a CMC norm, and one not to be transgressed.

Cohen designed and wrote her own computer program (in LISP, a high-level programming language, used in artificial intelligence applications at the time) that would support the scheduling process—what Susie Ikeda, who later served on the scheduling team before taking over as executive director in late 2018, describes as "fitting puzzle pieces together." The task is indeed a daunting one: during just one week there may be more than 100 participants, and each must be placed in a group, with no one left out. But each participant must be placed not just in *one* group—but in as many groups as there are coaching sessions (typically, four per week). And, of course, each participant must be placed not just randomly into *any* group, but only into *compatible* groups. Each participant was also to have a varied mix of groups, in terms of instrumentation or size of ensemble, coach, and the other players.

Cohen's computer program facilitated this process by immediately flagging errors, such as assigning a flutist to a string quartet or attempting to double-book the same participant into two groups at the same time. Other parameters were, for example, not assigning a work that had been assigned to that participant within the preceding five years, or assigning a group to an appropriate room in the music building—an ensemble that includes piano needs to be assigned to a room that has one, for instance. The basic parameters could be overridden by the scheduler when appropriate. For example, when a participant *asked* to have the same assignment within five years of previously having it, the work could be scheduled again.

Former executive director and longtime participant Bell emphasizes that what has made the CMC such an attractive and valuable experience for amateurs—resulting in an "incredible return rate"—is the "high-quality attention to coaching and assignments."

Mike Kong, who first attended in 1983 and witnessed the early development of the coaching system, concurs in this view:

> By far the most critical development in the history of the coaching program was Eve's transformation of it from something haphazard and casual (groups for the day formed by the music director with index cards the night before) into something sophisticated and serious (assignments weeks in advance, requests of various kinds, tracking of history, and many, many more features) that makes possible the level of work and learning we enjoy today. For her impact on scheduling, and for her warm and generous presence in almost every week of the conference for over thirty-five years, I consider Eve to be the most important participant in the history of the conference.

Participants Mike Kong, violin, and Phyllis Anwar, cello, during a coaching session on Beethoven's opus 74 string quartet in 1984.

Photo by Alice Berman

Before assignments are sent out, coaching schedules are reviewed and discussed in conference calls that include some or all of the following: the music director, the assistant music directors, the executive director, and the scheduling team. Participants and faculty are informed of coaching repertoire in advance—typically two months or more—for preparation. After coaching sessions, participants and faculty provide written feedback on each coaching session and can comment on the suitability of the repertoire, the compatibility of the personnel, the participants' level of preparation, and many other criteria. This feedback is reviewed by the music director and executive director, and informs the ongoing work of subsequent years.

The Ideal Coaching Experience

A goal of the scheduling process was, as Cohen put it, "for each group to consist of players well-matched in ability, playing style and personality." The board minutes during this period repeatedly reference discussions of "the question of matched groups." The CMC objective for well-matched groups was combined with the equally important objective of ensuring that participants are assigned to play with many other participants, particularly newcomers to the CMC, and not to be consistently isolated with the same players.

Cohen enjoyed recounting one of her less successful musical matchmakings. After assigning several participants to an ensemble that she thought would work just fine, she was taken aside privately by each of the participants, one by one, and, much to her chagrin, each gave precisely the same feedback: "how could you have possibly put *me* in a group with *those* people?!"

When the scheduling process resulted in an assignment that might not be quite to a participant's liking, Cohen had a ready answer, according to Ikeda, which reflected Cohen's own "truly generous spirit." "You do your part to make the group as good as it can it be—you should ask yourself what you can do to make the group better," Cohen would say. "It's not just about the group providing *you* with an optimal experience." Cohen herself would try to play with all newcomers at least once during free-time playing sessions, so that she would know them personally and have a feel for their musicianship and technical capacity, musical interests, and individual temperament.

Consistent with the participant-driven management of the CMC that was established at the same time, the scheduling process was designed to be responsive to participant requests. Perhaps one of the most important features of the scheduling system that Cohen put in place was the ability to accommodate participant requests. Participants could join together to request "pre-formed" groups, in which everyone decides in advance to request a piece for coaching with each other; or, a person could request specific works, works in a particular style, other participants they would like to be coached with, or coaches to whom they would like to be assigned. These requests could not always be honored, but when possible, they would be.

Participants could also make "negative" requests and designate specific players with whom they felt incompatibility—musical or otherwise. Cohen urged that these requests be kept "to the barest minimum," and reminded participants that "requesting not to play with a large number of your fellows is identical to having a large number of people request not to play with you, and unpopularity, even self-induced, does not particularly result in being assigned with 'better' players."

From the start, Cohen wanted to share the scheduling responsibility—it was a huge time commitment to an often thankless endeavor. She offered to alternate with someone else year by year. Keith Kendig, a cello participant and professor of mathematics (and one-time colleague of participant Hassler Whitney at the Institute for Advanced Study in Princeton), took over for 1984. Conference participants Mike Kong and Evan Dunnell also helped in the early years when coaching schedules were developed.

The computer-based assignment system had other impacts that perhaps even Cohen did not immediately foresee. First, once assignments were worked out, it was possible to print those assignments on paper for each participant, giving rise to the CMC "dance card"—an indispensable scheduling tool for both faculty and participants.

By the early 1980s, these assignment sheets were designed to be folded in half the long way, top-to-bottom, once, and then twice side-to-side, resulting in a pocket-size octavo daily schedule of activities (Sunday through Sunday, inclusive). This design was reportedly inspired by a homemade dance card invented by participant Albert Wray, and it continues in use to the present. In 1993, the contents of the dance cards were expanded to include activities specifically scheduled for the participant, optional events such as concerts and lectures, and blank "free time" periods.

Participants could fill the free-time periods with scheduled reading sessions with other participants and faculty members throughout the week, keeping track with handwritten notes on their dance cards—and most did. The zeal to make such advance bookings, leaving as little free time as possible, soon gave rise to group social interactions that became somewhat controversial at least among some participants—such as the frenetic effort of some participants to schedule groups for all of

their available free-time slots on the first night of high-atten-
dance weeks.

The computer assignment system also resulted in a searchable
archive of coaching schedules, going back to the early 1980s.
In 2015, Eve Cohen's husband, Don Cohen, a computer scientist
and a participant cellist and violist who created the conference's
administrative software, introduced a feature that allows participants to retrieve from the coaching database via email a
chronological list of all their coached groups since 1984.

*From left, violist Alice Berman, oboist
Sylvia Lipnick, clarinetist Janet Johnson,
and hornist Alan Katz consult their
dance cards in 1998. The hand-lettered
name tags seen here, with calligraphy
by Johnson, have been a feature of
the conference for many years.*

Photo by Claire Stefani

The conference also began codifying recommendations for participant behavior in coachings. The resulting document, "Coaching Etiquette: Some Do's and Don'ts," was expanded, refined, and continuously updated with participant input over the years. As compiled by Music Director Phillip Bush, it was included in materials distributed to each participant and continues in use today.

Nineteen bullet points are included in the current "Coaching Etiquette" document, ranging from recommendations that are life lessons going well beyond the context of chamber music ("remember that people don't mess up on purpose" and "beware perfectionism") to very specific directives on how to behave ("if you don't like a piece, keep it to yourself until asked"). In addition, there is a six-step process to be followed "if you find yourself in a group situation (coached session) that is less than ideal for whatever reason." Step number one, for example: "Begin by self-examination: 'Is it me?'"

The CMC Measure-Numbering Convention

If "Coaching Etiquette" represents an overview of the CMC culture as it developed over the years, one point stands out as a most fundamental norm, and indeed, it is the first-listed bullet point, stated directly, without equivocation, and in italics: *"Have your measures numbered."*

Behind this simple directive is no doubt a history of numerous instances of maddening frustration caused when the players and coach are unable to identify, or identify with reasonable efficiency, the same point in the work being rehearsed and studied.

Although western music has a uniformly accepted system of conventional notation, no such convention is accepted by composers and publishers for referencing specific measures. In older, public domain works that are issued and reissued in different editions, each edition is likely to follow a different convention: some count both first and second endings, some do not; some number variations separately, others number the entire variation movement's measures consecutively; some have no numbers at all; and so on.

Nor was it deemed acceptable for the conference to decree that only one edition of a work could be used for coaching, since participants might already own different editions, and individuals might not wish to purchase other (potentially expensive) editions.

To address these and similar problems, the CMC developed, through the efforts of Eve Cohen, its own system for numbering measures. These are the rules that faculty coaches and participants must obey, in one of the more ritualized aspects of pre-coaching preparation.

But even with the rules in hand, errors in measure counting occur, given the hundreds of bars of music in just one movement of a multi-movement work. The CMC has sought to solve that problem as well, with its *Works with Measure Number Totals by Movement*, which in its current edition, runs to nineteen single-spaced, dense pages—a compendium of the correct measure counts using the CMC rules. Now when participants and faculty receive their coaching assignments in the spring, measure number totals for each piece are included.

A Financial Crisis Averted

But what did the board do about that crushing $8,000 deficit that was estimated at the end of the 1977 session, the compelling reason for the CMC's reorganization as recommended by Max Lehman? The reports of the deficit certainly got the board's attention, but discussion of it was deferred to the next meeting in October. By then, apparently as a result of closer examination of a fuller set of financial records, the deficit had shrunk to $1,175. The solution proposed to eliminate the deficit and provide cash on hand to get the conference up and running was for several well-heeled board members to pay their 1978 fees in advance.

By February 1978, the conference's accountants at Peat, Marwick, Mitchell & Co. in Pittsburgh had issued their statement of receipts and disbursements for the year ending September 30, 1977. That statement showed that the conference's 1977 session concluded with $5,900 in the bank. Clearly, the trustees had difficulty tracking and reporting on the CMC's financial situation, and that difficulty was to end with the Lehman plan reorganization.

So when Lionel Nowak wrote to his co-trustees a month earlier in January 1978 that "the Conference is alive and well," he was more correct than he may have known.

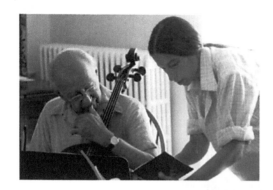

VIII. Seeking a New Prominence

"Musical Director Glick expressed his enthusiasm for the recent expansion and his hope for one day making Bennington the center of Chamber Music for the entire month of August."

—Minutes for board meeting, August 13, 1982

I

N THE EARLY 1980s, the conference emerged from its reorganization with new leadership in place. Conference participants were now the majority on the board. The conference had developed—again through collaborative participant effort—its own, unique system for advance scheduling of coaching sessions. Its commitment to composers and new music had been affirmed. With its focus on enhancing the experience of amateur musicians, the conference was set to attract new players, who, once they came, would often return for years.

Opportunities to contribute to the conference through volunteer involvement in its management, and to influence its direction, assured a high level of retention in these roles. The longevity of these volunteers was remarkable. Often they moved from one important role to another, as board members, officers of the corporation, and board committee chairs; some

A page of photographs from the conference's 50th anniversary history, entitled Fifty Vermont Summers of Chamber Music.

also served in staff roles. This small coterie of devoted chamber music enthusiasts would be responsible for expanding and consolidating many of the features of the new CMC, which is the conference as we know it today.

Chief among these important leaders was Stephen Reid, a highly accomplished amateur cellist who grew up in a musical family in Connecticut. He began his cello studies at an early age, and later played the double bass as well.

Reid first attended the conference in 1972 at Johnson State College. He recalls: "Judy Ensign was already a participant, [and] she and I came to CMC thanks to Marya Sielska with whom we began playing trios in the late 60s." By 1977, he was invited to join the board of directors and served as secretary and then as treasurer. In 1992, he succeeded Harold Laufman as the chair of the board.

Reid was chair for the next twenty-three years. His years on the board span over half the total years that the conference was at Bennington College, and his ongoing leadership provided direction for the organization's extraordinarily successful growth and consolidation. In addition to his board service, he took on significant staff duties, such as filling in as co-administrative director in 2001 and as acting executive director from 2005 until Marilyn Bell was hired in 2010.

Similar to Reid, Marilyn Bell shifted from board to staff and back again. A Bronx public school music teacher, she started attending the CMC as an advanced amateur pianist in 1975. In 1980, she was appointed administrative director, a post she held for four years. She returned to the board and was then appointed executive director in 1987 for four years. She was reappointed executive director in 2010, served until 2018, and now continues as a participant. Throughout her many years

managing the conference, Bell had a significant impact in defining its culture. Each week, for example, at the Sunday evening orientation meeting that kicked off another week of music making, she would typically conclude by sharing her deeply held sense of what the conference's "music of friends" was all about—a place where listening to others is as important as playing one's own part; where players can make their musical voices heard, but know when to step back and let others' voices emerge; where there is an eagerness for learning; and where newcomers are welcomed and feel valued. As she later

Marilyn Bell, at the piano in 1994, first attended the conference in 1975, and held a series of board and staff administrative roles over the years, serving most recently as executive director from 2010 to 2018. In the foreground is Harold Laufman, a participant violinist who first joined the board in 1975, led the conference's reorganization in 1977, and served for fifteen years in a leadership capacity.

Photo by Claire Stefani

explained, "I wanted everyone to walk out of that meeting with a sense of chamber music being so special."

The early 1980s also saw the formation of a wind quintet that would become a prominent faculty ensemble. When Lauren Goldstein (later Lauren Goldstein Stubbs) first arrived in 1982, she was the latest in a long line of distinguished professional bassoonists at the conference (these had included Jane Taylor, a founding member of the Dorian Quintet, who in later years returned as a guest faculty member). Goldstein joined the venerable CMC ensemble, which included oboist Patricia Stenberg and flutist Sue Ann Kahn (recent additions to the faculty, in 1979), hornist

Hornist Ralph Froelich was a member of the faculty wind quintet for many years. Here he leads a coaching session in the Carriage Barn in 1984.

Photo by Alice Berman

The faculty wind quintet in concert in Greenwall Auditorium: Sue Ann Kahn, flute; Patricia Stenberg, oboe; Joseph Anderer, horn (having succeeded Ralph Froelich in 1998); Lauren Goldstein Stubbs, bassoon; and Michael Dumouchel, clarinet.

Photo by Claire Stefani

Ralph Froelich (who had attended twice in the 1960s, and then returned as a regular faculty member in 1980), and clarinetist Michael Dumouchel (the most senior player, in terms of faculty membership, having attended regularly beginning in 1975). Stenberg was to be appointed assistant music director in 1986.

Another addition to the faculty in this period was the consummate cellist (and occasional crumhorn player) Maxine Neuman, who first joined the conference in 1983. Over the years, she frequently served as a faculty representative on the board and later served as an assistant music director. A highly respected coach—"with Maxine one is in the presence of musical mastery and the quest for musical integrity," one

In 1984, faculty cellist Maxine Neuman coaches a group that includes violist Marc Bastuscheck.

Photo by Alice Berman

participant was to write about being coached by her—she also has been the organizer and musical leader for two generations of youngsters from CMC families who informally concertize at the conference. Neuman's husband, Reinhard Humburg, has been the long-term conference recording engineer, a sideline from his day job as an attorney.

Scouting New Locations

But as a mere tenant of Bennington College, with nothing more than a year-to-year lease, the board was sensitive to the fact that there was no guarantee that the college would always be available as a host site. In some years there were fears that the college would fold—in August 1979, Lionel Nowak, then a college faculty member, reported to the board that the college was in "severe financial straits." Nor was it altogether clear that the CMC would necessarily *want* to return to the college, given the seemingly chronic problems with the facilities, including the lack of air conditioning. The board—and certainly not for the last time, as we will see—began considering other possible locations. Middlebury College was immediately ruled out, but Williams College seemed to have some potential. But for the time being, the board decided that moving elsewhere was neither necessary nor advantageous.

A Faculty Voice in Governance

The faculty continued to press for full representation on the board, after having lost voting rights during the 1978 reorganization. Consideration of this issue in 1979 had resulted in the adoption of a motion that the "board would welcome having issues presented to it by the faculty and having faculty members appear by invitation from time to time." This invitation was hardly what the faculty was looking for.

Meeting again at Laufman's Upper East Side Manhattan apartment in 1981, while uniformed staff served brunch, the board was confronted by long-time faculty members Joseph Schor and Ronald Oakland, who pointedly requested "two fully functioning board membership positions for the faculty." Schor and Oakland were both active in the musicians' union—early in his career, in fact, Schor had been fired from the Radio City Music Hall orchestra for organizing a strike, a pro-labor stand he remained proud of throughout his life.

They must have come away greatly disappointed, if not insulted, as they, as "guests," were asked to leave, and the board then met in "executive session" to pass a resolution "that two faculty representatives attend Board meetings, to participate without voting privileges, in all matters in which there is no conflict of interest." The faculty, represented by Schor and double bassist Lewis Paer, continued to press its case, and finally, two years later, succeeded in persuading the board. That vote, in 1983, was unanimous to amend the bylaws so that "two representatives elected by and from the staff will serve as full-fledged members of the Board with voting rights on all matters except faculty salaries." Having two faculty representatives, elected by their peers, on the board and with voting privileges is a feature of the organization to this day. But the bar against other paid staff being on the board continued, so that any staff receiving compensation, such as the executive or administrative director, would continue to attend as a "guest" without voting rights at board meetings.

The Glick Music Directorship

After having taken over from George Grossman as music director, Paul Wolfe served for four years, resigning the post in 1982, but continuing as a faculty violinist. The board immediately selected Jacob "Jack" Glick to take his place.

Glick had first attended the CMC as a faculty violist in 1961, and after joining the Bennington College faculty in 1970, he returned to the conference more frequently.

Glick was a perfect match for the CMC's needs. In terms of musicianship and musical versatility, he was unexcelled. He had performed in numerous premiere performances and recordings of new works, including the U.S. premiere of Pierre Boulez's *Le Marteau Sans Maître* and the first recording of George Crumb's *Ancient Voices of Children*, on which he played the musical saw. In addition to premiere performances as a violist in works by many composers associated with the CMC, including Otto Luening, Ursula Mamlok, George Rochberg, and John Harbison, Glick often performed baroque repertoire on the viola d'amore, and he also performed and recorded on the mandolin.

Glick was committed to sharing his knowledge, his skill, and above all, his passion for music making. For Glick, music making should not be the exclusive purview of those who make their living at it. Instead, he believed that the communal music making that took place at the CMC was indispensable in maintaining our musical culture. This theme was picked up for the conference's 50th anniversary in 1995, when board member and participant cellist Ann Franke developed a T-shirt bearing Glick's portrait and the motto "Music is too important to be left entirely to professionals" for sale to raise funds for the conference.

Glick was also known for the intensity of his focus on music, in his own playing as well as in coaching sessions. Setting up to record a faculty performance in which Glick was playing, the recording engineer Reinhard Humburg asked Glick about the quartet's seating, so he could properly position the microphones. Glick answered, "I don't play for the recording, I only play for the audience."

Despite his serious approach to music making, he also had a self-deprecating sense of humor and reveled in viola jokes. Violist Louise Lerner, who at the time was working as an attorney in the Civil Rights Division of the Department of Justice, recalls getting a phone call at home one evening during the year. It was Glick calling to ask, "What do an attorney and a violist have in common?" Glick's punch line: "Everyone is really pleased when the case is finally closed."

The Lectures: A Culture of Learning

Lectures and demonstrations by faculty and guests have always been a part of the conference's program, going back to the Middlebury College years, when Alfred Frankenstein discussed his role as a music critic and Alexander Broude held forth on publishing and intellectual property rights.

All manner of subjects have been covered: injury prevention for musicians, mechanics of cueing, score reading skills, enhanced practice techniques, Alexander Technique—the list could go on—and all evidencing the conference as a community of learners. Pete Seeger presented on folk music during the conference's first summer. In 1980, as announced in the conference brochure, daily, hour-long workshops on "Elements of Chamber Music" addressed "basic and not-so-basic problems in chamber music playing." Guest lecturer Robert Moog demonstrated his electronic synthesizer in 1970. Styra Avins, cellist and annotator-translator for the magisterial collection of Brahms correspondence, *Johannes Brahms: Life and Letters*, has been a frequent lecturer and guest faculty member.

Among the notable lecturers is faculty violinist Joel Berman, who first presented on the string quartets of Bartók

In 1970, Robert Moog lectures on his recent invention, the electronic synthesizer that bears his name, in the Carriage Barn.

Courtesy of UVM Special Collections

Faculty oboist Jacqueline Leclair presents in 2019 on "How to Practice More Efficiently Now!"

Photo by Claire Stefani

"Farewell to Bennington—Muss es sein?," a 2019 lecture and demonstration on Beethoven's opus 135 string quartet, is the most recent of Joel Berman's many presentations on the string quartet literature. Joel Berman and Mayuki Fukuhara, violins; Alice Berman, viola; and Stephen Reid, cello.

Photo by David Oei

and Beethoven in the 1980s and continued lecturing on these topics over the next forty years. His focus on the late Beethoven quartets accelerated amateur interest, encouraging study not just for the purpose of learning to play the works, but also to more deeply understand their thematic and structural design.

In 2001, Music Director Shem Guibbory invited the pianist and music historian Frank Daykin to the conference. In addition to his well-regarded work in music history—his monumental *Encyclopedia of French Art Song* was published in 2013—Daykin is also a published poet. Daykin has lectured at the conference on a wide range of subjects, often demonstrating at the piano or inviting faculty or participant ensembles to play musical illustrations. His topics frequently relate to conference programming or involve dialogues with resident composers.

Daykin describes the conference as "the anchor of my year," finding it "absolutely thrilling" to be there as participants are engaged in "pursuing beauty in their own way."

Staff violist Jacob Glick provides an instrument demonstration for young composers in front of Jennings music building in 1970.

Courtesy of UVM Special Collections

Glick often pushed, on an individual level, as well as institutionally, for inclusion of new music. Bell recalls that she, like many pianists at the CMC at the time, was shy about sight-reading. On a Monday morning, when Bell saw that she had been assigned Elliott Carter's Sonata for Flute, Oboe, Cello, and Harpsichord for a coaching session, she understandably blanched. She protested about her unfamiliarity with twentieth-century music to her coach Jack Glick, who characteristically responded, "The century is almost over, so you better start now." As it turned out, the coaching session was one of Glick's many successes in engaging with amateur players and eliciting results that the amateurs did not know they were capable of achieving.

Glick's interest in coaching was often focused on less- rather than on more-experienced participants. Previously, the board had directed him to discuss with then-Music Director Paul Wolfe a "chamber music workshop to be planned next year for less advanced participants." Early in his tenure as music director, Glick asked the board members if they were familiar with the ACMP (Associated Chamber Music Players) self-grading questionnaire, and asked "how does a 'B' rated player [as opposed to an 'A' rated player] get to play a first part?" The conference did not formally adopt these ideas, and in 1984 his proposed "Baby Chamber Music Program" was "on hold"—and with that name, one can perhaps understand why. The same idea was revisited in 1992, with the proposal of a "Participant II" experiment. Although the names for these programs left something to be desired, the commitment to amateur chamber musicians' discipline and eagerness to learn was a key feature. Inclusion of players at differing levels of ability has continued to be a concern of the conference to this day. "The truth is that the conference embraces a rather wide range of playing skill and experience," Executive Director Susie Ikeda explained in 2019, "with participants always learning from each other and from the wonderful faculty."

In early 1982, at his first board meeting in his new role as music director, Glick left little doubt about his ambitions for the conference. In his report to the board, perhaps his most important initiative was "The Experimental First Week"—a new week to be added to the existing two-week schedule, focused on string quartets, and for a smaller number of violin, viola, and cello participants; pianists and double bassists were invited to apply as auditors. This "experimental" week was to involve "informal chamber music soirees with staff and participants playing together in the living rooms of the student houses." (As a man of practicality, Glick added, parenthetically, that he would "attempt to get good floor lamps for these evenings.") This "experimental" week was referred to as "Strings Plus," and became a regular feature of the schedule from 1982 until the launch of the "intensive" week in 2000. In 1985, reflecting the growth of participation in the week, pianists were invited to apply as participants. In 1988, the Strings Plus format was tweaked further with the addition of double bass.

At that same meeting in early 1982, Glick announced that he would like to expand repertoire for participants, responding to "certain complaints from woodwind players regarding the over-frequent exposure to the same woodwind quintets" by suggesting the scheduling of mixed wind and string works, but noting the risk that such an arrangement could disrupt the string quartet groups.

Noting that "much twentieth century music has atrophied from our diet since the schism with the Composers' Conference," he asked for a survey of participants and staff to determine who would be "amenable to adding more of the music of the century we are living in." Along those lines, the conference added a checkbox for several years on application forms: "Interested in receiving coaching in a classic of the contemporary music literature." He asked if he should continue the "Mid-Week Bash" (that is, on the Sunday between the two weeks) that he had conducted for the last three years or whether another staff person should take it over. These Sunday afternoon playing opportunities under the direction of "Maestro Glick" were themed around specific composers and announced in each season's brochure—and were always followed by a picnic on the "Great Lawn" and then "an old-fashioned square dance." The 1980 brochure, for example, announced "A Bach's Lunch and Square Dance," while the next year, it was "Eine Kleine Afternoonmusik and Square Dance." If he continued it (and he did), he promised "mostly Vivaldi Concerti for Diverse Instruments with a few somber string choir pieces interjected to separate the soloists who would be chosen, once again, from volunteering participants."

Finally, he echoed an idea also articulated by board member Gerald Carp that the conference should consider commissioning past CMC composers to write memorial compositions for "deceased Conference members." His report to the board ended with the question, "How many would remember Lobkowitz if it weren't for Beethoven?" (Glick was referring to Joseph Franz Maximilian von Lobkowitz, an amateur cellist and violinist, and an aristocrat and patron of Beethoven. Beethoven dedicated important works to Lobkowitz, including his set of six string quartets, opus 18, and the opus 74 string quartet.)

That summer's newly expanded, three-week session had about the same number of participants over the three weeks as had attended during the two weeks of the 1981 session. (Week 1, 40 participants and 12 auditors; Weeks 2 and 3, each 100 participants and 22 auditors). The board minutes note that "Musical Director Glick expressed his enthusiasm for the recent expansion and his hope for one day making Bennington the center of Chamber Music for the entire month of August."

Glick shared his goals for the conference in a 1983 proposal to the board:

> At this point, I honestly believe this is the time to expand the Conference to a four week operation. It should establish itself and break even in no more than two years with wise management. At present only the prestigious Dartington Festival in England rivals our Conference.

Then, in 1986, the conference was expanded to four weeks. It had taken Glick only four years after taking over as music director to achieve his dream of making the conference the center for chamber music for the entire month of August. The new fourth week was planned to include the usual strings (violin, viola, cello, and double bass), winds (flute, oboe, clarinet, bassoon, and horn), and piano, but with the addition of trumpet, harp, and voice. New coaches were recruited for that purpose: Ronald Anderson, trumpet; Susan Jolles, harp; and Jane Bryden, soprano. The next year, 1987, the conference brochure announced that because the previous year's "addition of new instruments was so successful," the scheduling of works for voice would now be expanded to Weeks 1 through 3 and works with harp would be included in both Weeks 2 and 3. (The success of including voice and harp, however, seems to have been short-lived; by 1989, both had been dropped from the programming, although they would both make occasional reappearances in the future.) Weeks 1 and 4 were described as the "Intimate Weeks," with a "limited enrollment" of about fifty participants plus auditors. Weeks 2 and 3 were the "Full Weeks," each with a "full enrollment" of about ninety participants plus auditors. Weeks 1 through 3 included the full string and wind instrumentation, while Week 4 continued in the "Strings Plus" format, featuring string quartet instrumentation with and without piano.

During that decade, it does seem that there was a divide between wind and string players. Ruth Ellen Proudfoot reports that when she first arrived at the conference as a participant violinist in 1986, she found the bathrooms labeled for either "winds" or "strings," leaving her to wonder, she said facetiously, about the facilities for pianists. The rivalry between strings and winds extended to the campus softball field, where the annual "Blows vs. Bows" game took place. As participant oboist Marty Lipnick recalled in 2019, "One year the strings won. Don't know how they did it." With that, the annual game was discontinued.

In 1983, a faculty concert included as its only wind piece the Milhaud *Pastorale*—a trifle, running less than four minutes, compared with the more substantial string works on the program. This was perceived as a slight to the wind community and provoked a show of strong disapproval. Jane Deckoff, a participant oboist who first attended in 1981, proposed that wind players should put up a "picket line around the concert hall," but another oboist, Ed Bowe, suggested that wind octets played outside the hall before the concert would be a more appropriate form of protest.

After the faculty trio—Pat Stenberg, oboe; Michael Dumouchel, clarinet; and Lauren Goldstein, bassoon—completed their brief contribution to the concert, the wind players in the audience erupted in sustained, enthusiastic applause lasting longer than the piece itself. A week later, however, the faculty wind quintet had a more significant assignment in presenting Henry Brant's arrangement of Beethoven's opus 131 string quartet to the audience in a stifling Greenwall Auditorium.

During Glick's music directorship, a new board member, Dianne Mahany, began what would be another long period of service—thirty-plus years—that included a variety of board officer assignments. As an amateur clarinetist, Mahany first attended the conference in 1978, and has attended every year since then except one. She joined the board in 1990. In charge of strategic planning at her day job, she approached Administrative Director Beth Anderson and some board members "with great respect and awe about my worry that this wonderful Conference might go away some day" and sought to address some long-range planning projects for the conference. By 1993, she was serving as secretary to the board—her practice of adding and tracking "action items" to the board minutes introduced a level of accountability for the hands-on, yet not always consistently focused board members. Two years later, she moved to treasurer and two years after that to vice chair. After thirteen years in that office, in 2010, she returned to serving as treasurer.

One of Mahany's most important contributions was instituting a weekly "lunch with the board" event—a simple idea that offered a very effective means for two-way board-community communication during the conference. Any board members present during the week would be available to meet with participants for lunch with information-sharing and open-ended discussion. The idea was implemented in all four weeks of the conference in 1993 and has continued since then. As Mahany reported to the board after the first year's lunches, the "response was very good, and interesting ideas came out of the sessions." She went on to explain that the lunch provided an opportunity for "fundraising/financial discussions with a broad and eager audience as well as communicating that the board is open to dialogue with everyone (contrary to some earlier perceptions)." As Mahany recalled in 2019:

> Those earlier perceptions might have arisen from the Friday evening Board meeting each summer, when folded paper meeting notices were placed in Board member mailboxes and, on Meeting Night, these people were seen dressed a little more formally than usual (long pants instead of shorts, mostly) walking up to Commons carrying briefcases and notebooks. It all seemed a little lofty and aloof, and certainly not inviting to 'regular' participants.

Composers' Forum Experimentation

As the conference came into the 1980s, having decided just a few years earlier to live up to its name and keep composers as part of the program, it was still trying to figure out where they should fit in. Within the framework of what was then a two-week conference, the resident composers—typically, there were three—attended only during the second week. While their presence was not a raving success, participant feedback showed that "more participants enjoy it than not." Some of the first week participants indicated that they would like an opportunity to be involved, perhaps with a composer lecture or open rehearsal during Week 1.

From roughly 1977 until 1999, the Composers' Forum was viewed as a separate program in addition to, not part of, the regular repertoire coached and played. Various experiments were undertaken, but what differed from previous years was the idea that the composers-in-residence would be writing for participant groups, not just for the professional faculty. These experiments go back to at least 1977, when three composers-in-residence wrote, while at the conference, pieces to be performed by participants that same week. In a way, the conference had returned to the composer-participant interactions that Theodore Strongin had described forty-some years earlier.

In a reflection of the change, the 1978 brochure announced, under the rubric of what would be "different and more exciting than ever," that "for the first time . . . participants will have an opportunity, on a volunteer basis, to explore in detail a recently-written composition under the coaching supervision of its composer." This approach was inaugurated with the first performances of works by Louis Calabro and John Heiss. Another new work, by composer and faculty cellist Michael Finckel, was *Himalayan Expositions*. In that performance, Ardith Bondi—on flute, piccolo, and alto flute—was joined by oboist Marty Lipnick and pianist Paul Erfer. As the program noted, "These compositions have been written during the composers' residency at the Conference and for these particular performers."

By 1980, the conference was devoting a full concert to works of the two composers-in-residence, David Jaffe and Maurice Wright. In the first half of the program, participants performed new works both composers had written for them. As described by horn participant David Kemp, in an account published in the *New York Times*, "The audience responded with wild clapping and cheering."[96] For the second half of the concert, conference faculty performed works by the same two composers.

Beth Anderson recalls Suite of Dances, a work by 1983 Composer-in-Residence Elizabeth Lauer, written for her, flutist Ardith Bondi, and hornist (and more recently, double bassist) Lydia Newcombe. Anderson shared her recollection: "Lauer wrote into one of the movements a little bit of the Marx Brothers song, 'Lydia, the Tattooed Lady.'" In 1985, a new work written for participants by Frank Wigglesworth, *Earth Smoke and Blazing Stars*, was premiered during the participant recital. This practice of integrating resident composers' works on the participant programs—in this case, Wigglesworth was between Mozart and Ravel on the program—has continued to today.

At the board's fall meeting in 1985, Lionel Nowak, facing health issues and a need to focus more on his teaching at the college, resigned after serving as president of the board since the conference's reorganization eight years earlier. As he explained in a letter to Laufman, he had accepted the chairmanship on the basis of his "compelling desire that the Conference initiate a process for establishing a firm relationship with living composers." "In eight years, this objective has been met," he continued. "Even the earlier skeptics now recognize the value in composers and players working together." Nowak was to remain involved in the conference as its coordinator of the Composers' Forum, a role he fulfilled for the next three years, until he was succeeded by Wigglesworth.

Other aspects of the Composers' Forum had yet to be figured out. The instrumentation of works to be composed was not always communicated correctly to composers, or, composers may not have followed those directions. In 1987, two new works by Composer-in-Residence Loretta Jankowski, *Contrasts*, for clarinet, violin, and piano, and *Song for Leftovers*, for oboe, violin, cello, and piano, were given first performances. As Jankowski explained in her program notes, *Song for Leftovers* "was composed in two days for participants who had also volunteered for this premiere performance but were inadvertently excluded." Parts were often not provided to the participants until the week of the performance, and as late as 1993, the Composers' Forum rehearsals were scheduled in time slots outside of the regular coaching. A participant with four pre-assigned works would then have a fifth, new work to prepare during the week. In 1994, the conference began requiring resident composers to submit the parts for their new pieces to the participants *before* the start of the conference. Beginning in 1999, the Composers' Forum works were scheduled as regularly coached works, and one of the four assigned to the players for the week.

After Wigglesworth left the board in 1995, the conference searched for another composer to join the board and lead the Composers' Forum. Although some composers took on administrative duties—including Allen Shawn, then on the Bennington College music faculty, who had served briefly on the conference board in 1988—none was able to take the place on the board vacated by Wigglesworth. For a time, until about 1998, the Composers' Forum did not have a composer leading it.

Conference Social-Musical Culture

As a participant-led organization, the conference began to focus on concerns about social-musical integration, especially for newcomers. In the late 1970s, when the conference was a two-week program, newcomers to that first week at least had the Sunday opening-night concert to attend. But for newcomers who arrived for the second week only, there was nothing. Someone—perhaps the participant pianist Paul Erfer, a folk-dance enthusiast, had something to do with it—had this idea for the second Sunday night: square dancing. As reported in the *New York Times*:

An impromptu "blanket party" after the afternoon coaching session is accompanied by an alpenhorn ensemble in 1999. Standing, from left: David Knapp, Haskell Edelstein, James Dunne, Ira King, Virginia Anderer, and Joseph Anderer; seated: Marty Lipnick and Karen Greif.

Photo by Claire Stefani

A Sunday night square dance was a regular feature of the conference until at least 1984, when this photo was taken. The dancing partners are Albert Wray and Judy Tobey.

Photo by Alice Berman

That evening there was a square dance in the Barn with live band and caller; it seemed to put people in the mood for a week of country living. The assembled musicians showed little talent for dancing; a contradance degenerated into good-humored chaos.[97]

By the time the conference expanded to three weeks in 1983, the idea of the "buddy system," first proposed by Judith Ensign in 1978, was now being fully implemented by participant cellist and board member, Erika Phillips, who later served as deputy administrative director. Pairing newcomers with seasoned participants, even before the start of the conference, for advice and guidance about what to expect upon arrival, has been a lasting practice.

But perhaps the conference's signature piece of social (and musical) integration was the "Round Robin," held the first (Sunday) night of each week. Rowena Rosenbaum recalls that she and others were concerned that there were no activities planned for those evenings. Rosenbaum remembers that in the mid-1980s, she recommended the idea to the conference administrator, Beth Anderson, who responded by asking her to organize it. Each participant was assigned to a sequence of three rooms, each for a twenty-minute interval; there they would find other players and music for that instrumentation. As Rosenbaum explained:

> The first summer was rather messy, as I recall: not everybody took to the idea, and we had to put up signs inviting people to come and play; but although a number of participants refused to take part, it eventually became a regular Sunday-night activity. MANY people have played a major role in the organising over the years, and I'm delighted that the event has become so popular.

The current CMC website notes, somewhat modestly, that the conference is "known for its informal get-togethers held in the evenings after the day's activities are over." Indeed, the conference has a long and rich tradition of throwing parties, and no one has played a bigger role in that tradition than Albert Wray, the conference's own self-appointed, unofficial social director, or "S.D." as he liked to identify himself. A fine violinist and violist, Wray first attended the conference in

1979 and soon became an animating presence every summer for nearly three decades.

Wray's contributions were varied and not limited to his party promotion activities. He served a term on the board of directors. According to Don Cohen, Wray put up the clock in the Jennings music building lobby—keeping everyone, and himself perhaps first and foremost, on time to coaching sessions. Always attentive to conditions that create social interaction, he instituted the afternoon post-coaching cookies and juice. Wray is credited with inventing a homemade dance card, which was soon replicated for all. Wray's musical generosity was well-known, as demonstrated by his asking, incredulously, of a new cellist, "What?! You've never played a Brahms quartet?!," and immediately scheduling the next-available free-time session and finding the other players to fill out the quartet. For many years before the conference's library was assembled, he would bring his own music library in his car and set it up in the Jennings music building for all to use.

He not only organized the evening parties—M&Ms and cheese doodles were his signature party fare items—but also promoted the parties through a series of posters taped on the door to the Jennings music building for participants to read upon their arrival for morning coaching sessions. The posters announced, like a manically whimsical town crier, reports from previous festivities, such as:

Albert Wray, the conference's unofficial social director, in 1980.

Photo by Alice Berman

A Shocking Notice!
A Musical Deviant was seen at last night's party!

Which is followed by a description of said "musical deviant"—among other things, "he hums Schoenberg." Or, a breathless announcement, with unbridled yet tongue-in-cheek enthusiasm, of the next party. The butt of Wray's poster humor was frequently a wind player, and most often an oboist, although he took occasional swipes at violists, Republicans, mothers of oboists, sopranos, conductors (especially if they were also oboists), and even the president of the United States. Some posters presented mock complaints from offended participants (oboists, of course) about other posters'"insulting, demeaning, obnoxious" content, and then yet another sign would present a not-so-contrite response to the offended participant. At one point, one of Wray's signs reported on the detention of the perpetrator of the offensive posters ("he and his instrument are in a safe place"). Even after he started chemotherapy for what was to be his final illness, he became "the bald guy" whose

A typical Wray party sign, from 1999.
Photo by Claire Stefani

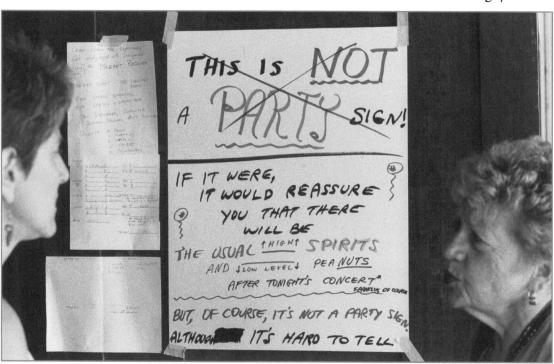

allegedly "lecherous" party behavior was duly reported on the next day's poster. Wray died in 2009, leaving his musical instruments and much of his music library to the conference, as well as instructions to use proceeds from the sale of his instruments to create a CMC Party Fund. Donations in his memory were subsequently added to the fund, which subsidized parties (and encouraged improvements to their offerings) for several years after his death.

Another important feature of conference parties has its origin in a story Roger Brooks, participant flutist, relates about how the subject of saxophones came up during mealtime conversation in the cafeteria one day. According to Brooks, clarinet participant Frank Mallory "wanted to know who would really admit that they played saxophone." "Surprisingly, about six or seven fessed up," Brooks recalls, including bassoonists Nancy Switkes and Robert Gemmell, clarinetist Dianne Mahany, and pianist and violist Kay Cynamon. A year or two later, Mallory called this group together for some "secret" sextet rehearsals of his arrangement of the Jerome Kern standard "All the Things You Are." The sextet started crashing the various evening "wind bashes"—walking in unannounced, setting up and playing "All the Things You Are," and walking out.

The group was soon playing an ever-expanding repertoire as the Casual Sax Sextet, beginning in 1987 and returning every summer for thirteen years, with Saturday night party shows during the third week of the conference. They presented Mallory's arrangements and gags, a mixture of equal parts Guckenheimer Sour Kraut Band, Spike Jones, and Mozart's *Ein Musikalischer Spass*, K. 522. His "Three-Minute Mikado" and "Poet and Peasant" arrangements were particularly popular, and so hilarious that the players themselves found them almost unplayable. In later years, Pat Stenberg, faculty oboe, joined as a guest alto sax player—borrowing Dianne Mahany's sax and taking emergency lessons the day of the party—and Maxine Neuman, faculty cellist, added her crumhorn to the mix.

Mallory's shows typically featured pseudo-educational content, with appropriate musical examples, such as his celebrated lecture "Sax Life," on the life of Adolphe Sax. Mallory, who held an appointment as W. Alton Jones Professor of Chemistry at Bryn Mawr College, did not have to go far to find the professorial persona for his lectures, delivered straight-faced and with perfect comic timing.

A spin-off group, the Enigma Ensemble (no one seems to know why it was so named), started in 1994 and included memorable performances by participant oboist-turned-soprano Karen Greif, dressed in sequins and feather boa. Yet another group, the Low Blows, featuring Mallory's arrangements of such works as Bach's Two-Part Inventions played by an assortment of bass clef wind instruments (including Kay Cynamon's trombone), performed regularly from 1995 to 2003 at the party concluding the CMC's fourth week. After Mallory's death in 2017, his widow, Sally Mallory, donated his music library, including his party music arrangements, to the conference.

During a roughly two-decade period beginning in 1982, a regular feature of the Saturday night parties was the Reading of the Limericks, most often by bassoon participant Hugh Rosenbaum, standing on a chair in one of the college house living rooms packed with partygoers. Rosenbaum would frequently organize limerick competitions, often with a conferee's name given as a "challenge rhyme"—in 1990, for example, violin coach Mayuki Fukuhara received this dubious honor. The winning limericks were read out loud, and all limericks

Frank Mallory, leading his Casual Sax Sextet in 1996, explains to partygoers that Bennington College's instrument collection lacked a suitable percussion mallet, but that an especially rainy summer made possible a more than adequate homegrown replacement.

Photo by Claire Stefani

(except perhaps the most salacious) were posted for everyone to read.

By the end of the 1980s, Rosenbaum approached the CMC board with the idea of collecting and publishing these limericks, and the result was the 1991 publication of *The Bennington Limerick Book*—an annotated collection with a "forewarning" by Music Director Glick ("the book recounts the musical history of the conference in humorous form"). Glick's forewarning was supposedly submitted in lieu of his own limerick, which began "There once was a hornist, like Tuckwell," which he claimed had been rejected by the editors. The forewarning also gave Glick an opportunity to make an arch aside to the effect that he somehow would be a better subject for a limerick if his name were "Nepomuk."

Vetted by a participant "Good Taste Committee" (fortunately, no explanation of the committee's standards was attempted), the limericks give some sense of what was on the minds of conferees during this fomenting period of the conference's history. Eve Cohen's parody contribution, "On Writing Limericks," is an example of the unusual anti-limerick limerick, inspired perhaps by W.S. Gilbert:

> *There's a genius around but I'm*
> *A week late, and it's far from sublime.*
> *   I just have no talent,*
> *   The topic's banal, and*
> *I just can't make the bloody thing scan.*

The popularity of limericks continued into the new century, then gradually waned before all but disappearing in recent years.

A Conference Pantoum

Conference versifying has not been limited to limericks. In 1996, pianist participant Richard Friedberg, who first attended the conference in 1987, was coached on the Ravel Piano Trio. One day during lunch in the college cafeteria, Friedberg wrote and recited to his tablemates his own pantoum, taking the second movement of the Ravel, "Pantoum: Assez vif," as his inspiration.

Pantoum

In case you really want to know,
    The Pantoum is a form of verse
Invented many years ago,
    Whether for better or for
    worse.
The Pantoum is a form of verse;
    It fits into a scheme so nice:
Whether for better or for worse,
    Each line must be recited twice.

It fits into a scheme so nice!
    There is no room for stress or
    storm—
Each line must be recited twice
    In this unique Malaysian form.
There is no room for stress or
    storm,
    In case you really want to know,
In this unique Malaysian form
    Invented many years ago.

The Glick Resignation

When the conference board met as usual in the Commons "Purple Dining Room" on the Friday evening of Week 2 in 1994, they started to follow the typical fourteen timed-item agenda. As reflected in the meticulously detailed minutes, kept by Dianne Mahany, secretary of the board, they approved the minutes from a special May 1994 meeting (with certain corrections regarding "historical facts"), and moved quickly through treasurer (and participant hornist) Alan Katz's brief report. The board chair, Stephen Reid, then turned the floor over to Jack Glick for his music director report.

Glick shared his observations on the usual subjects—how the orchestra and lectures were "successful so far," the participant concerts were going "more than quite well," and a Week 3 "composer emergency" had arisen due to the sudden unavailability of the scheduled composer.

Then, with no preamble or warning, Glick submitted his resignation, effective at the end of the 1994 session. The board was stunned.

Requests were made for Glick to stay on in some capacity, but he made it clear: he was "resigning, not retiring," he was resigning as "coach, performer, and Music Director," and he was "not open to negotiation." His reason: "ideological disagreements with members of the Board." Thirty-three years after he first played and coached at the conference, and after thirteen years as music director, Glick was finished with the conference.

Those "ideological disagreements" had much to do with the board's attempt to address, through a Music Advisory Committee, inter-related hot-button issues regarding the faculty, including hiring and retention issues. Two years earlier, in 1992, the committee seems to have started off on the wrong foot, with a major misstep—creating a "faculty evaluation form." This move was "not well received by the faculty," and a "brouhaha" ensued. Faculty-board relations were disturbed, and a recovery process had to begin. But the "hot-button issues" were still unresolved.

Despite some unwise attempts to address them, the board's concerns about these faculty issues were legitimate. A board discussion point was that "it may be true that changes in our participant body ('customer base') will require changes to the Conference." Ultimately, the board concluded, "we need a rational way to discuss such questions [of faculty hiring, evaluation, and retention] and effect changes if and where they seem appropriate." The "tenure policy" concerns and discussions, both within the board of directors and among faculty, were ever present, and sometimes rancorous. It would take almost another two decades until the conference would finally resolve this issue.

None of this fit with Glick's management style. As music director, he demanded complete commitment from faculty, and he offered his own ferocious loyalty in return. A CMC faculty member who accepted another gig that conflicted with their usual week at the conference, no matter how career-advancing it might be, should not expect to be invited back by Glick. The board's involvement (meddling, surely, is how Glick saw it) in any way in faculty matters—for example, the idea that a board committee might limit the number of weeks per faculty member—was anathema to him.

But behind Glick's resignation was likely another event at Bennington College earlier that summer. The college had been developing confidential plans to reinvent itself, "and with a vengeance," as one alumnus was later to write in the *New York Times Magazine*.[98] In June, twenty-five college faculty members, including Glick, Sue Ann Kahn, and Maxine Neuman, had been fired from tenured positions they had each held for more than twenty years. (Elizabeth Wright, a CMC faculty pianist, was also let go, although she did not have tenure.) Bennington College quickly landed on the American Association of University Professors censure list, where it remains to this day.[99]

Glick had been on the college faculty for twenty-four years. Now, at the age of sixty-eight, he was given five days to clear out his office, and he left exhausted—no doubt physically and emotionally. His precipitous resignation from the conference may well have reflected his anger, distrust, and profound distaste at having anything to do with Bennington College.

Fifty Years of Vermont Music Making

The Glick resignation and ongoing, unsettled faculty issues were major distractions from planning for the conference's fiftieth anniversary in 1995. Additionally, in 1994, a major board concern was whether Bennington College, after the faculty firings earlier that summer, would survive. Board members voiced their concerns about whether the conference could celebrate its anniversary at a location other than Bennington College. The site committee continued its search, just in case. But the next year, the college was again the host, and anniversary activities continued.

The primary anniversary observance was the writing and publication of *Fifty Vermont Summers of Chamber Music*. Authored by participant cellist Francis Church, a professional journalist and critic, and Laufman, the seventy-seven-page history, with four pages of photographs, was dedicated to the memory of

Alan Carter. Although its release in 1997 was two years after the fiftieth anniversary, the conference had come a long way since the twenty-fifth anniversary, when Carter, immersed in running yet another conference, admitted he had given it no thought.

MOZART
MOZART
SCHUBERT
OKTETT
PIANO QUARTETS
PIANO QUINTETS
ANO TRIOS
WINDS &
STRINGS

LOST: yellow sunglasses
Lost turquoise silver earring
DUNCAN FOLEY 249 B
Lost clarinet part to Bruch Trios #5
Sue Biniaz
MUSIC FOR ORCHESTRA
Marya
Janet
Louise
130
NIKKI
BETH
CHERYL
237
LIZ T
PAT K
JIM

IX. Experiments— and Further Consolidation

As a veteran string quartet player, I know I can reliably fill up on 18ᵗʰ and 19ᵗʰ century readings all year long, to my heart's content . . . but if I want to expand my playing of 20ᵗʰ century classics, or delve into compositions from any era that are well off the beaten path, then I focus on those few days in mid-summer Vermont when many like-minded players will be looking for the same thing.

—Stephen M. Reid, chair of the CMC board, "Foreword: I Just Wanted to Mention . . ." in *Fifty Vermont Summers of Chamber Music* (1997)

AFTER GLICK'S SUDDEN RESIGNATION, the board again turned to faculty violinist Joseph Schor— he had already served as acting music director during Glick's sabbatical five years earlier—to take over as interim music director for 1995. Schor assumed the post of music director for what was to be two more years,

Until 1995, participant Albert Wray lent his music collection to the conference, which later developed its own library through donations from conferees. Below, a chalkboard in the Jennings music building shows notes organizing free play sessions.

Photos by Claire Stefani

announcing early on that he would step down from that role after the 1997 season. The board commenced a search for a new, permanent music director, and, once again, chose an internal candidate: Shem Guibbory.

Guibbory Music Directorship

Like the four music directors (after the founding director, Alan Carter) who preceded him, Guibbory had lengthy experience at the conference, having been on the faculty for sixteen years before starting as music director in 1998. Like Glick before him, he was at ease with new music, having been a violinist with Steve Reich and Musicians, with whom he made an iconic recording of Reich's *Violin Phase*. As a teenager, Guibbory studied violin at the California Institute of the

In 1986, violinist Shem Guibbory coaching a group that included Albert Wray, viola. Guibbory would be appointed music director twelve years later.

Photo by Alice Berman

Arts and later at the Yale University School of Music. He first played with the Metropolitan Opera Orchestra when he was twenty-one.

While on a social visit to Bennington to see cellist Michael Finckel in 1980, Guibbory was invited to sit in on a string quartet reading session one evening by participant violist Maurice Kouguell, brother of the CMC faculty cellist Alexander Kouguell. They were soon "voraciously reading" string quartets in Room 214 of the Jennings music building. By the time the session ended, around one o'clock in the morning, as Guibbory recalls, "I was hooked." The next year he returned to fill a gap left by the absence of faculty violinist Eric Rosenblith. In 1982 he came back as a full-schedule faculty member. Today, Guibbory invokes Glick as a significant influence, with his "unfailing belief in the power, desire, and capacity of participants to make music together."

As a faculty representative on the board of directors in 1996, two years before he became music director, Guibbory's ambitions for the conference were already clear. He proposed a compact disc recording, designed to showcase the faculty and the composers-in-residence. The CD was to be produced on the Composers' Recordings, Inc. (CRI) label, co-founded by Otto Luening in 1954. CMC faculty were to be featured on Arnold Schoenberg's *Verklärte Nacht*, while the pieces by CMC composers—six of them—were to be recorded by participant ensembles. The selected works were by Elizabeth Brown, Lam Bun-Ching, Elliott Schwartz, Peter Susser, and Lionel Nowak. The proposal acknowledged the various hurdles that the project faced, including selection and scheduling of faculty and participants for the recording sessions. The project never reached fruition, however, since CRI soon backed out.

The Return of the Silvermine Quartet

When Glick resigned as music director over "ideological dis-agreements" with the board of directors, shocking the board at its 1994 summer meeting, board member Laufman immediately responded by making a motion, which was duly seconded and adopted, accepting Glick's resignation, but with "hope for a future association of some kind between Jack and the Conference." But for the next three summers, Glick was left sitting at his house in North Bennington, just down the hill from the Jennings music building, while the conference, led by the new music director, Joseph Schor, went on without him. Among Guibbory's self-assigned goals for his first summer as music director was to bring Glick back.

Guibbory's plan was to have the Silvermine Quartet in residence at the conference in Week 4 of the 1998 session, with that week focused on the string quartet literature, as it already was at the time. The Silvermine had concertized widely, and Guibbory remembered attending one of their concerts as a nine- or ten-year-old violin student with his parents. Guibbory still recalls their performance of the trio of the scherzo movement of Beethoven's opus 132 quartet.

Guibbory invited Glick, via handwritten letter, to rejoin his three Silvermine colleagues on the conference faculty. Glick accepted. Bringing the Silvermine together again at the conference would prove to be doubly satisfying for Guibbory. He could honor musicians who had been an early inspiration, and at the same time, the conference could try to heal the wound that had resulted from Glick's sudden resignation three years earlier. In addition to his faculty concert performances and coaching responsibilities, Glick also took a turn as a lecturer, presenting on the topic "Balancing Voices in Mixed Ensembles."

The Silvermine was in residence again in 1999, and they closed that summer's session at the last Saturday night concert with a performance of the Brahms Quartet in A Minor, opus 51, no. 2. This was to be their last performance together at the conference; Glick died less than three months later.

The next summer, each week a faculty concert included, as a memorial to Glick, works written for him or associated with him, performed by his closest colleagues and family members on the CMC faculty. These included the "Fantastic" movement from Lionel Nowak's Trio for piano, violin, and cello (1954)

In 1998, with Jacob Glick's return after having resigned as music director in 1994, the Silvermine Quartet was together again at the conference, here in rehearsal in the Carriage Barn. Paul Wolfe and Joseph Schor, violins; Jacob Glick, viola; and Alexander Kouguell, cello.

Photo by Claire Stefani

(performed by Glick's son-in-law, James Goldsworthy; his longtime colleague Joseph Schor; and cellist Maxine Neuman); and "Lento" from Vivian Fine's *Lieder for Viola and Piano* (Masako Yanagita, viola, and Stephen Manes, piano). Fine's duo was written for Glick, and Fine and Glick had given the first performance in 1980 at Bennington College.

Glick's Silvermine colleagues Kouguell and Wolfe continued at the conference for another seven years, then retired from the conference after the 2006 session. Both had been on the conference faculty for fifty years. Before his retirement, Kouguell, at age eighty-five, completed a final project that documented his elegant, refined music making, which had become such an indelible feature of the conference: Sue Ann Kahn's recording of the Mozart Flute Quartets with Kouguell and CMC faculty colleagues Eriko Sato, violin, and Ronald Carbone, viola.[100]

Wolfe retired to Sarasota, Florida, where he had been the artistic director and conductor of the Florida West Coast Symphony and co-founder of the Sarasota Music Festival.

Schor continued to attend the conference; his last year was as an "emeritus faculty" member in 2012 at age 92.

The Conference Library

On the drive back from a post-conference stay at Lake George in August 1995, participants Fan Tao and Don Cohen discussed an idea "to supplement in the short term, and possibly even to replace in the long term, Albert [Wray]'s library, with one belonging to the conference itself." Although the conference had access to the college's music library, housed in the Jennings music building, Wray had also made his personal chamber music library available to the entire conference for many years. Financial donations as well as donations of scores and parts soon came in, and the collection grew. Notable music collections were donated from the estates of Frank Mallory, Norman Pickering, Marya Sielska, Pat Stenberg, and Wray himself. Today, the library is available for free-time reading sessions at the conference, and its catalog is searchable online. Maintained by the indefatigable volunteer and violin and viola participant Fan Tao, the conference library today contains almost 1,800 works by more than 500 composers.

A Chamber Music Festival

Beginning in 1998, one of Guibbory's changes—resulting from discussion with faculty violinist Eriko Sato, and her husband,

In this 2016 faculty performance in Greenwall Auditorium, Bennington College, of Paul Moravec's Northern Lights Electric *(clockwise from left): Eriko Sato and Shem Guibbory, violins; Veronica Salas, viola; Read Gainsford, piano; Michael Finckel, cello; Armand Ambrosini, clarinet; and Conor Nelson, flute.*

Photo by Claire Stefani

pianist David Oei (a guest faculty member that year)—was to present the conference's series of faculty concerts each summer in Greenwall Auditorium under the rubric "Chamber Music Festival of the East"—a slight variation on the organization's full corporate name, but adding the key word "festival." The name was meant to reflect the high faculty performance standards as well as the cohesive programming of the concert series. There were hopes, too, that the concerts could be promoted to a larger audience beyond the conference.

Although the faculty concerts had always presented a wide range of chamber music, the conference was now presenting an award-winning four-week concert series of astonishing diversity, from familiar works of the chamber music canon to performances (often premieres) of recently written works by the composers-in-residence. Guibbory's inclusion of "Guest Faculty" members on the conference's roster made it possible to program works with unusual instrumentation.

Listeners might hear a Bach Trio Sonata followed by Stravinsky's *L'Histoire du Soldat*, narrated by actor Keir Dullea. A work by Paquito D'Rivera would follow a string quartet movement by Allen Shawn, which in turn had been preceded by a Mendelssohn piano quartet.

Listeners encountered works they very likely did not know existed: Adolph Busch's Quintet for Saxophone and Strings (with guest faculty member, Albert Regni, alto saxophone) or Arnold Black's *The Ballad of Chosen Dumpling*, with Maria Ferrante, soprano, and narration by the public radio broadcaster Robert J. Lurtsema (WGBH, Boston). And the Composers' Forum, which was expanding to include a composer-in-residence in three and sometimes all four weeks, was represented by the programming of at least one work each week by that

Double bassist Lewis Paer, who was much admired as a coach and performer, pictured here in 1982.

Photo by Alice Berman

The Double Bass Section?

At this point, an astute reader might ask, "but what about the double bass?" After all, chamber works with double bass are highly popular—Beethoven's Septet and Schubert's Trout Quintet and Octet come immediately to mind—and the conference is ideal for pulling together the players needed for such pieces. Mimi Wallner (later Bloom) received a scholarship as a composer and double bassist in 1949, but it appears that during the first two decades, there were very few—if any—amateur bassists at the conference.

Staff bassists begin to appear on the roster in 1951, the first year at Bennington College, as the conference began to grow. Over the years, the conference engaged the leading bassists of the day, musicians who often had notable careers not just as performers, but also as composers, conductors, and teachers.

From 1955 to 1958, New York Philharmonic bassist Robert Gladstone, later principal bassist of the Detroit Symphony Orchestra, was on the staff. Alvin Brehm, who was also a composer and conductor, attended for several years starting in 1960. Brehm was a member of the Chamber Music Society of Lincoln Center and served as Dean of Music at the State University of New York (Purchase). In the mid-1960s, David Walter, who was intensely committed to performing new music, was on staff, and he returned in 1979. Walter's playing spanned orchestral and jazz idioms, and he held prominent teaching posts (Juilliard and Mannes). In the 1970s and again in 1993, Bertram Turetzky—a leading proponent of new music—was on staff. Turetzky commissioned countless new works for the bass and was the author of the landmark 1974 extended technique manual *The Contemporary Contrabass*. The principal bassist of the Metropolitan Opera Orchestra, George Andre, also was on the staff in the mid-1970s. Amateur double bassists started to attend regularly around this time.

Salvatore Macchia, a prolific composer and bassist teaching at the University of Massachusetts, Amherst, joined the conference in 1992 and returned frequently over almost twenty years. In some years when he was not on the roster as a faculty bass player, he attended as a conference composer-in-residence or guest composer.

But the most significant addition to the conference's bass staffing came in 1980 with the arrival of Lewis Paer. At the time, Paer was freelancing in New York City, but he soon joined the orchestra of the American Ballet Theater and then the New York City Opera, eventually holding the post of principal bass of both orchestras. About his first summer at the conference, Paer recalls his surprise "that as soon as I arrived, [Music Director Glick] had me unpack my bass at the Carriage Barn, and play through the Schubert Octet with [guest artist and legendary Boston Symphony Orchestra concertmaster] Joseph Silverstein leading the group. At 27 years old I'm pretty sure I had a limited grasp on the repertoire, but knew enough to be awestruck." Paer would return for the next thirty-six years.

A highly popular coach and much-admired chamber music performer, Paer explained that his retirement from the conference after the 2016 session was "primarily based on the feeling that I had learned so very much from the participants, and given from my heart for so long, that they had perhaps got the best of my efforts, and that it was just time for me to leave room for new bassists to contribute."

As the amateur bassist participation expanded beginning in the late 1970s, so did the coaching repertoire, going far beyond the well-known works by Beethoven and Schubert. Now, a bassist's assignments would include mixed wind, string, and piano ensembles of all sorts of combinations: trios by Macchia, Schulhoff, Stern, and Wuorinen; quintets by Milhaud, Nielsen, Onslow, Prohaska, Prokofiev, and Strauss; a sextet by Reznicek; septets by Berwald and Hummel; octets by Badings, Ferguson, Françaix, Hindemith, and Wellesz; nonets by David, Farrenc, Feld, Martinů, Piston, Spohr, and Stanford; and even a dectet by Britten or Reizenstein.

week's composer. Additional visiting composers were included as well. Between 1998 and 2001 alone, the CMC faculty presented twenty-two works by American composers, including Kathryn Alexander, Arnold Black, Chen Yi, John Harbison, Stephen Jaffe, Steven Stucky, and Evan Ziporyn.

The Composers' Forum, Enhanced

In addition to hiring a new music director, the conference had to face the issue of Frank Wigglesworth's 1995 resignation from the board. Wigglesworth had essentially run the Composers' Forum during his board years. The conference continued to host composers-in-residence, but now the Composers' Forum needed someone like Wigglesworth, or Luening before him, to guide the program from year to year.

Guibbory, seeking to stabilize the management and enhance the impact of the Composers' Forum, recruited composer Martin Bresnick as a potential leader for the Composers' Forum. Bresnick was composer-in-residence during Week 1 in 1997, and he returned for all three weeks in 1998. At the time, Bresnick was on the faculty of the Yale School of Music, and early in 1998 he received the first Charles Ives Living award from the American Academy of Arts and Letters. During Bresnick's three-week residency in 1998, Guibbory began rethinking the Composers' Forum.

One of the most significant changes was the creation of a "senior composer-in-residence" staff position, so that the Composers' Forum would be directed by a composer hired on a renewable (initially, three-year) schedule (like the music director or other staff positions), thus providing continuity. The senior composer-in-residence would be responsible for direction of the Composers' Forum and would attend the

conference during those weeks. Composers would continue to be in residence each week, writing a new work for participants and coaching them on it, with a view toward performance by the participants. At least one of their works would be included on a faculty concert during their residency.

Bresnick recommended that the conference should find a way to host "composition fellows"—graduate school-level, "emerging" composers, typically early in their careers but already showing significant promise—in each Composers' Forum week as well. The composition fellows would also bring a work for participants to be coached on, and they

In 1998, the conference began including in the Composers' Forum what were later called "composition fellows"—young, emerging composers. Here, from left, Ian Honeyman, Senior Composer-in-Residence Martin Bresnick, and composer Chen Yi attend a rehearsal of a new work by Honeyman.

Photo by Claire Stefani

CMC Composers-in-Residence, 1998–2019

Composers are listed in order of week of attendance. From 2002 on, except in years when a guest or visiting senior composer-in-residence is listed, Donald Crockett held that position.

1998: Kathryn Alexander, Martin Bresnick, Chen Yi, Evan Ziporyn

1999: Chen Yi, Donald Crockett, James Mobberley, Salvatore Macchia

2000: Zhou Long, Chen Yi, Michael McFerron, Allen Shawn, Steven Stucky, Salvatore Macchia (visiting composer)

2001: Chen Yi (senior composer), John Steinmetz, Gregory Mertl, Stephen Jaffe

2002: Donald Crockett (senior composer), Victoria Bond, Tamar Diesendruck, John Steinmetz, Keith Fitch, Peter Scott Lewis

2003: David Schiff, William McGlaughlin, Reza Vali, Libby Larsen

2004: John Steinmetz, Gabriela Lena Frank, Stephen Hartke, Jennifer Higdon

2005: Roberto Sierra, Daniel Godfrey, Steven Mackey

2006: Keith Fitch, Paul Moravec, Stephen Hartke, John Steinmetz, Gabriela Lena Frank

2007: Derek Bermel, Gabriela Lena Frank, Robert Dick

2008: John Steinmetz, Jeffrey Mumford, Dan Welcher, Evan Chambers

2009: Lisa Bielawa, Daniel Godfrey, John Fitz Rogers

2010: Pierre Jalbert, Paul Moravec, Gabriela Lena Frank

2011: Kenneth Frazelle, Harold Meltzer, Susan Botti

2012: Daniel Godfrey (visiting senior composer), Andrew Norman, John McDonald, Keeril Makan

2013: Caroline Mallonée, Jeffrey Mumford, John Fitz Rogers

2014: Ted Hearne, Sean Shepherd, Laura Schwendinger

2015: Kurt Rohde, Hannah Lash, Dan Visconti

2016: Jesse Jones, Sean Friar, Amy Williams

2017: Marc Mellits, Susan Botti, Harold Meltzer

2018: Lei Liang, Pierre Jalbert, Paul Moravec

2019: Allen Shawn, Scott Wheeler, Judith Shatin, Pierre Jalbert (guest senior composer)

would be mentored by the composers-in-residence. In effect, this innovation, which was tried out in 1998 with Ian Honeyman and Yoko Nakatani attending as "apprentice" composers, would more than double the number of composers in residence each of the three weeks.

The Composers' Forum included "composition fellows" for the first time in 2001, with Marc Faris, Hannah Lash (who was to return as a composer-in-residence fourteen years later), and William Lackey. In 2003, Senior Composer-in-Residence Donald Crockett further refined the composition fellows' role, explaining to the board the advantages of recruiting fellows who were also capable instrumentalists. Emphasizing that the fellows' "primary function is to interact," Crockett explained that "it's a bonus" when the composition "fellow also plays and joins the participant community."

Bresnick, however, did not stay on as senior composer-in-residence, but instead was succeeded by Chen Yi in 1999. Despite having lived through China's Cultural Revolution, a time of official hostility to traditional music studies, Chen went on to be the first Chinese woman to receive a master of arts degree in music composition from the Central Conservatory of Music in Beijing. After immigrating to the United States in 1986, she studied with two composers previously associated with the CMC: Chou Wen-chung and Mario Davidovsky, both at Columbia University.[101] She was teaching at the University of Missouri-Kansas City when she first joined the conference. In 2000 and 2001, she shared the senior composer-in-residence responsibilities with her husband, Zhou Long, who would receive a Pulitzer Prize in 2011. She was the second recipient, after Bresnick, of the Charles Ives Living award, in 2001.

In 2002, Donald Crockett, who had been a composer on the faculty of the University of Southern California Thornton School of Music since 1981, and a CMC composer-in-residence in 1999, returned as senior composer-in-residence, attending for all four weeks. In an email, Crockett recalled his first summer at the conference in 1999:

In 2009, Donald Crockett, in his eighth year as senior composer-in-residence, during a coaching session. (Pictured in background: Albert Wray.)

Photo by Claire Stefani

> I met [Music Director] Shem [Guibbory], worked closely with Joel Berman and Jack Glick who were performing . . . [Crockett's violin and viola duo] "to be sung on the water," and hung out upstairs in Noyes [college house] sharing some libations with Zhou Long in the heat after a long day of coaching and teaching. Zhou Long and Chen Yi were also composing music—each in a corner of their dorm in Bingham—which was quite fun to observe. Shem realized that, to get a Senior Composer in Residence willing to do three weeks at the festival, he had to provide composing time in the schedule.

By 2003, the Composers' Forum was organized in much the form in which we know it today. Managed by Donald Crockett as the senior composer-in-residence, the forum takes place during Weeks 2, 3, and 4, and typically provides for one composer-in-residence and one composition fellow for each week, resulting in the composition of six new works that are coached as part of the regular coaching schedule and scheduled for performance by participant ensembles. Crockett explains whom he invites to the CMC as a resident composer:

> What I am looking for, in addition to "fabulous composer": a composer with a fairly significant chamber music output and activity in the field, perhaps even a composer/performer such as Susan Botti, Gabriela Frank and Hannah Lash. Someone committed to the idea of coaching young composers and adult amateur musicians in brand new pieces, and to sharing their unique artistry with the CMC population.

Recording Virgil Thomson

In 2000, the conference faculty included brass players—Nathan Durham, trombone, and James Stubbs, trumpet—instruments not often scheduled during the previous twenty-five years. They made possible the faculty concert programming of a chamber music rarity by Virgil Thomson—the *Sonata da Chiesa* (1926), a quintet for the odd combination of viola, E-flat clarinet, D trumpet, horn, and trombone. Thomson had been a friend of the conference's founder, Alan Carter, and was the first senior composer-in-residence in 1971. This programming choice was then rolled into the CMC faculty recording of chamber music by Virgil Thomson, released in 2002 on Composer Recordings, Inc. (CRI). The recording was the idea of Charles Fussell of the Virgil Thomson Foundation, which then funded the recording.

In addition to the *Sonata da Chiesa*, the CD included both of Thomson's string quartets; *The Feast of Love*, for baritone and piano; and the *Stabat Mater* for soprano and string quartet. Although it lacked participant involvement (which Guibbory had proposed for a 1996 CMC recording that was never made), it was an opportunity to showcase the conference's faculty on what Guibbory called "some of the best chamber works Thomson composed."

The Intensive "Week 0"

At the board's February 2001 meeting, Guibbory proposed a new initiative responding to the desire of some participants for a program that would provide a deeper and more thorough coaching experience.

The basic coaching schedule, which had been in place for roughly twenty-five years, had a morning session (two hours) and an afternoon session (one and one-half hours). One piece was coached in the morning, another in the afternoon. After the first three days, Monday through Wednesday, work would begin on two new assignments, again, one in the morning and one in the afternoon for the next three days, Thursday through Saturday. This format generally worked well, but some works could only be given cursory study due to length or complexity; hence, the proposed new schedule. This intensive week format was not intended to be limited to more advanced participants, but to allow participants to choose to dive more deeply into a smaller number of works.

With the basic coaching schedule format, participants could (and did) request to work on a piece for a second or even a third summer. Alternatively, a large work could be scheduled across six days, instead of the usual three, as was done in 1992 when then-Music Director Jack Glick led participants through Schoenberg's *Kammersymphonie*, opus 9, a highly complex work for fifteen "solo instruments." But some participants wanted something even more in-depth, and the new "intensive" week was the result.

Limitations on the availability of Bennington College's campus in 2001 for four full, consecutive weeks provided the impetus for testing an alternative site. The first intensive week was scheduled not at Bennington College, but instead at Colgate University, a private, liberal arts university founded in 1819 in Hamilton, New York, roughly 140 miles directly west of Bennington. Like Bennington, Colgate is situated in a rural area, and it was a highly attractive host site featuring vintage nineteenth-century buildings, a campus that was tidier and better groomed than Bennington's, and a very accommodating concert space, Colgate Memorial Chapel, built in 1917.

The conference's interest in Colgate University dated back to 1991. That June, the board convened there, having spent the night on campus, touring the campus and playing music. On the downside, Colgate's campus was viewed as more "spread out" and had more "elevations—hills and stairs—for the older participants," but on the positive side, it had "better dorms and housing for families," and an "adequate" number of rooms. Music Director Glick noted the "nice grounds and the chapel as a performance space." Although the conference decided to stay at Bennington, Colgate was already a possible alternative. The conference returned to Colgate again in 1999, operating a weekend workshop that included coachings, readings, and informal faculty and participant performances. When there was a need for another site in 2001, Colgate was the natural choice.

And it would be needed again two decades later, when the conference relocated from its long-term site, Bennington College, following the 2019 session. This experimentation with sites other than Bennington was the result of the work of the board's site committee, led for many years of seemingly endless research by participant pianist and board member Rebecca Lee.

The new intensive week at Colgate was scheduled for the week *before* the start of the conference's usual Week 1 at Bennington. The college was available to host these first three weeks as usual; the scheduling conflict was with the conference's "strings only" Week 4, so it was abandoned. To distinguish the first, newly designed, week at Colgate from the former Week 1 (which remained on the schedule at Bennington), the new week was dubbed "Week 0." The three succeeding weeks back at Bennington kept their numbers, so that participants could still sign up for their same Week 1, 2, or 3.

That first Week 0 had only three, instead of the usual four, coaching assignments. Two of the works were scheduled for double the usual coaching time: an afternoon coaching for one and one-half hours extended through the entire week, for a total of six coaching sessions; another work had both morning and evening coaching sessions scheduled over three days. The third work was scheduled for only three coaching sessions, although it, like the two other assignments, had time slots for additional rehearsals. The schedule was indeed intense, leaving almost no time for free-time playing. Subsequently, the first week schedule evolved to be less strenuous; today there are the same total coaching hours as in the other weeks.

Composer and double bassist Salvatore Macchia in Colgate's Memorial Chapel during a rehearsal of his Continuita for Five Instruments *for its first performance in 2001. Faculty clarinetist Marianne Gythfeldt is in the foreground.*

Photo by Claire Stefani

The expanded coaching schedule made it possible to dig deeper into unusual works such as Benjamin Britten's *Sinfonietta*, for ten instruments, coached by double bassist Salvatore Macchia, or Stravinsky's *L'Histoire du Soldat*, coached by percussionist James Preiss. Seminars on "How to Rehearse," including a Sunday night introductory session on that topic, intended to support the participant rehearsals without the coach, were led by faculty bassoonist and Composer-in-Residence John Steinmetz.

The first intensive week also kept up the CMC's commitment to living composers, as Steinmetz's *War Scrap* (2000) and the first performance of Macchia's *Continuita for Five Instruments*, with the composer performing, were both included on the one faculty concert of the week.

This commitment to programming living composers, during Week 0 as well as Weeks 1–3 back at Bennington, resulted in the CMC's receipt of two Awards for Adventurous Programming from Chamber Music America and ASCAP for "innovative approaches to presenting contemporary music for small ensembles" for 2001 and 2002.

Although the week at Colgate University was a success, the burden of staffing and managing two program iterations was significant. After setting up and running the conference for a week at the new location, the staff then had to move their operations back to Bennington as soon as the Colgate week finished. The Week 0 format, however, was well received and would continue as an integral part of the conference.

Despite this major administrative inconvenience, the following year (2002) the conference undertook another "new site" Week 0 experiment, this time at Vassar College, in Poughkeepsie, New York, as a result of neither Bennington College nor Colgate University being available as sites for that week. The Week 0 schedule, now slightly modified, was repeated. The conference returned Week 0 to Vassar for another year in 2003. The program was a success, and in particular, Vassar's outreach to the local community brought in far more local concertgoers than had ever been seen at Bennington's Greenwall Auditorium. But beginning with the 2004 session, Bennington College was again available for all four weeks of the conference, so Week 0 was hosted back at Bennington where it was followed directly by Weeks 1–3.

The "Week 0" nomenclature, an oddity resulting from the conference's fear of disrupting participants' expectation about the familiar, and one that must have puzzled most outsiders, remained in place for thirteen years, long after that week was joined with the other three back at Bennington. Finally, in 2017, the conference, with no fanfare, simply re-numbered its weeks to 1 through 4. Although for a time there seemed to be a feeling that clarification was necessary—as in, "I'm attending Week 1 (formerly Week 0)"—the conference community seems to have accepted the change.

The Jacob Glick Memorial Endowment Fund

At the board meeting when Glick resigned as music director in 1994, Laufman requested that the board "create something to commemorate Jack's contribution." But as the minutes of that meeting note, the "motion was made and seconded without specifying what the commemoration would be." Five years later, after Glick's death, the board found an appropriate commemoration: the Jacob Glick Memorial Endowment Fund.

The Glick Fund was established as an endowment for three purposes: providing scholarships for participants, supporting participation by composers at the conference, and commissioning chamber music works for performance at the conference.

The fund was intended "to perpetuate the memory of the conference's former music director and long-term coach, advocate of amateur chamber music playing and study, and champion of the performance and appreciation of contemporary music." As a sign of the conference community's high regard for the former music director, the fund's $100,000 initial fundraising goal was met in less than two years, through the leadership of participant pianist and violist Kay Cynamon.

The Jacob Glick Memorial Endowment Fund Commissions

Once the Glick Fund goal was met, the fund was put to work supporting a series of chamber music commissions, which began in 2002. (In fact, the fund has been used almost exclusively for new music commissions since its creation—other donations established a separate financial aid fund specifically to support scholarships.) The focus of the Glick Fund was to commission previous composers-in-residence who were thus already known to the CMC community. These new works received their first performances by the faculty—typically on one faculty concert, then repeated again in a later week's concert, giving rise to the CMC's unusual neologism, "second premiere performance"—but they were also included in participant coaching sessions. In general, the commissions deferred to the composers' choice of instrumentation, within the bounds of ensembles typically coached at the conference.

The first of the Glick Fund commissions was awarded to CMC Senior Composer-in-Residence Donald Crockett for his piano quartet, *The Ceiling of Heaven* (2004), a co-commission with the Los Angeles County Museum of Art and Xtet, a Los Angeles-based new music ensemble. Subsequently, Crockett's quartet was the title work for the conference's 2005 recording project.

The second Glick Fund commission was awarded to Gabriela Lena Frank in 2005. Frank had been a composer-in-residence for the first time in 2004; she was to return as composer-in-residence in 2006, 2007 (for the first performances of her commission), and 2010. The commission resulted in her quintet for piano and strings, *Tres Homenajes: Compadrazgo* (2007). The first performances included the composer at the piano.

The next Glick Fund commission went to Paul Moravec (composer-in-residence in 2006, 2010, and 2018) for his 2010 Wind Quintet. In 2013, John Fitz Rogers (composer-in-residence in 2009) received the fourth Glick Fund commission for a string quartet, *Book of Concord*. The most recent Glick Fund commission went to Pierre Jalbert for his *Wind Dances* (2018) for wind quintet and piano. He had been composer-in-residence in 2010 and returned as composer-in-residence for the first performances of *Wind Dances* in 2018.

The Mallory Commission

In addition to the ongoing Glick Fund commissions, the CMC undertook a special, one-time commission in honor of Frank Mallory, a highly accomplished amateur clarinetist who first attended the conference in 1986, and who served on the board of directors for many years during which he served on the executive committee and chaired the nominating committee. The latter committee's work in tracking board member terms and vacancies, years of service, geographic location, and instruments played, and in recruiting and recommending new board members from the community, was foundational in developing a high-functioning, democratically governed organization. And,

Frank Mallory, pictured here in 1995, was a participant clarinetist, board member, and founder and leader of the Casual Sax Sextet. Upon leaving the board, he was honored for his service to the conference with a commission from composer Daniel Godfrey in 2009.

Photo by Claire Stefani

as previously noted, Mallory was the leader and arranger for the celebrated CMC party ensemble, the Casual Sax Sextet.

As the board explored the idea of honoring Mallory with a new composition, the commission was planned to reflect his personal musical interests. In August 2007, Dianne Mahany reported to the board of directors that "Frank has expressed a preference for a clarinet quartet" (clarinet, violin, viola, and cello) or a "quintet with piano." The commission was awarded to Daniel Godfrey, who had been composer-in-residence in 2005. Mallory liked his compositions. The resulting quintet, *Dances in Checkered Shade*, for clarinet, string trio, and piano, received its first performances in Weeks 0 and 2 in 2009, when Godfrey returned as composer-in-residence. It was funded both by individual donations in honor of Mallory and by the Glick Fund.

The Conference at Sixty

In 2004, to commemorate the CMC's sixtieth-year anniversary, the conference produced a compact disc recording on Albany Records of CMC faculty performing works by composers closely associated with the conference. The title work, Donald Crockett's *The Ceiling of Heaven*, had been the first Glick Fund commission, and was inspired by a Kenneth Rexroth poem that contains the lines:

> . . . *The hawks scream*
> *Playing together on the ceiling*
> *Of heaven. The long hours go by.*

The recording also included Crockett's Horn Quintet "La Barca" (1999) in its first recording. Allen Shawn, a composer long associated with the conference, was represented by his movement for string quartet, *Sleepless Night* (1996), and his Wind Quintet no. 2, a work that had been commissioned by CMC participants.

Nicholas Cords, one of the three CMC faculty violists on *The Ceiling of Heaven*, shared these comments with the CMC board: "Besides being a valuable project for the conference, and the composers, recording is always a valuable learning tool for musicians. I think just about everybody involved in the process went the extra mile. I think it's something we can all feel pretty proud about."

As the conference turned sixty, it could now look back at what it had accomplished since its half-century mark. The preceding decade had indeed been exceptionally productive. The conference continued, summer after summer, to maintain a stable attendance, attracting new amateur musicians as well as nurturing a loyal population of returning players. A highly reliable funding base was established.

At the same time, its "experiments" proved, after some fine-tuning, to be highly successful. The conference successfully managed the innovation—in answer to participant needs—of designing and testing an "intensive" coaching schedule for one of its weeks. That intensive week had now become a permanent feature of the conference.

The conference also defined a newly prominent yet integral role for composers in a redesigned Composers' Forum, now under the leadership of a senior composer-in-residence. The Composers' Forum now offered a new "composition fellow" role especially for young, early-career composers. The conference's commitment to new music was demonstrated by its many commissions. All those changes, too, became permanent features of the conference.

Composer Allen Shawn and cellist Maxine Neuman, North Bennington friends long associated with the conference, shown here in 2015.

Photo by Noa Shawn, courtesy of Allen Shawn

The release of two compact discs, showcasing the conference's commitment to contemporary American music, documented—as if anyone who had attended the conference could have doubted it—the high artistic standards of the conference's faculty.

Bennington Chamber Music Conference
Chamber Music Conference and Composers' Forum of the East
73 Summers of Music – July/August 2018
Tobias Werner, Music Director   Donald Crockett, Senior Composer-in-Residence

Afternoon Musicale
Carriage Barn   Bennington College
Bennington, Vermont

Wednesday, August 1, 2018 at 4:00 p.m.

String Trio in D major, Op. 9, No. 2   Ludwig van Beethoven

   3.   Menuetto: Allegro

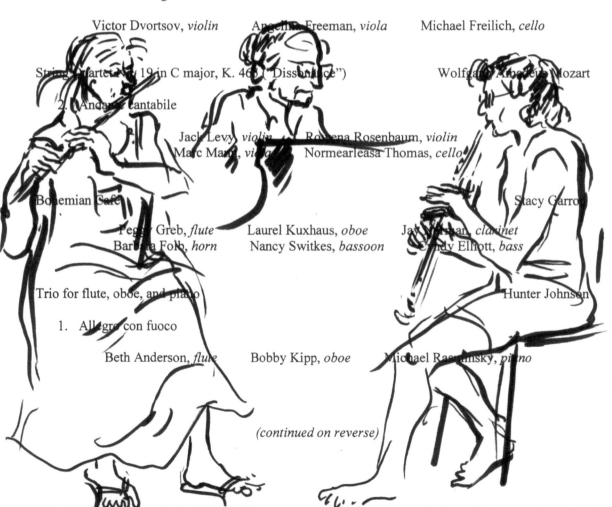

      Victor Dvortsov, *violin*   Angelina Freeman, *viola*   Michael Freilich, *cello*

String Quartet No. 19 in C major, K. 465 ("Dissonance")   Wolfgang Amadeus Mozart

   2.   Andante cantabile

      Jack Levy, *violin*   Rowena Rosenbaum, *violin*
      Marc Mann, *viola*   Normearleasa Thomas, *cello*

Bohemian Café   Stacy Garrop

      Peggy Greb, *flute*   Laurel Kuxhaus, *oboe*   Jay Nathan, *clarinet*
      Barbara Folb, *horn*   Nancy Switkes, *bassoon*   Sandy Elliott, *bass*

Trio for flute, oboe, and piano   Hunter Johnson

   1.   Allegro con fuoco

      Beth Anderson, *flute*   Bobby Kipp, *oboe*   Michael Rassimsky, *piano*

(continued on reverse)

X. Toward Seventy-Five

*The Bennington Chamber Music Conference
enables committed chamber musicians to learn
and grow, and supports new chamber music
composition and performance. We offer an
intensive summer program that includes coaching
sessions, seminars, formal and informal playing
opportunities, commissions, composer residencies,
and performances by our distinguished faculty.*

—Mission statement, adopted by the board of directors,
October 24, 2015

A S THE CONFERENCE was about to enter its sixth decade, it had achieved a new level of stability and maturity as a high-functioning nonprofit organization. From then on, the conference was essentially the organization that exists today.

Within the space of a few years, the CMC board would develop and adopt a strategic plan, which set not just the operational direction for the conference for the future, but finally explicitly articulated the conference's mission and identity. The conference would redesign its administrative staff roles and then address the controversial issue of faculty retention. The board would elect a new chair, a new music director would

*A program for a participant musicale in 2018, decorated with
sketches of one of the performing groups by Miriam Katin, a
graphic artist and wife of clarinet participant Geoff Katin.*

Courtesy of Miriam Katin

come from outside the CMC, and a new executive director would take over the administrative responsibilities. The strategic planning process would be re-initiated. These were certainly eventful years, yet the conference managed these changes smoothly.

At the same time, the conference continued to nurture what really mattered: a culture of musical learning and growth, integrating both new music—newly created as well as newly discovered—and works from the canon of chamber music masterpieces. What made all this possible was the increasing professionalization of the organization's staff. Although the CMC still relied heavily on volunteers for some crucial functions, volunteer and staff functions were better delineated, much as Max Lehman had hoped for forty years earlier. In short, the CMC had gained adaptability and organizational resilience.

Several factors supported this resilience. Staff members served for long periods, providing continuity—though they were able to shift roles, or leave and return, to prevent burnout. The administrative staff also often drew on years of experience as conference participants. Staff and board members brought relevant "day job" skills as educators and businesspeople to their work with the conference. No one person was responsible, or could have been responsible, for what the conference had achieved; their efforts were effective, but only because of the efforts of many others. It was as though the model of chamber music itself had been adapted to organizational functioning.

Going back several decades, the conference staff had been developing year-to-year continuity, drawing almost exclusively on musicians who had already been at the conference as participants. Beth Anderson, for example, first attended as a participant flutist in 1981. By 1983, then-Administrative Director Marilyn Bell pressed her into service—as the "party organizer," an indispensable volunteer function. By 1985, she took over as administrative director, a role she shared with participant pianist Dorothy Kalson. Kalson played in the Huntington Trio, which performed for many years on Long Island and in New York City, along with violinist Jo Margaret Farris and cellist Stephen Reid. Farris was for many years a violinist and violist at the CMC and served as a co-administrative director from 1988 to 1990.

Administrative staff were not only recruited from among participants; they generally continued as participants, getting coached and engaging in free-time playing, albeit on a reduced schedule. From 1985 through 2007, administrative leadership was provided by combinations of Beth Anderson, Dorothy Kalson, Jo Margaret Farris, and (filling gaps in staffing while also serving as board chair) Stephen Reid. Maintaining continuity in staffing throughout this period, Anderson was an administrative director for twenty out of twenty-three years.

In 2005, participant violist and manager of the winter reunion, Louise Lerner, having retired from her full-time employment as an attorney, took over as the conference's on-site office manager, responsible for day-to-day functioning of the conference office and coordinating housing for participants on campus.

The board of directors itself had long terms of service from its volunteer members, yet another factor supporting the stability of the organization. Frank Mallory, as chair of the nominating committee, reported regularly on this attribute of the board. In 2006, for example, the average board term of service was over eight years; the longest serving board member (and, at the time, chair of the board) was Stephen Reid, at twenty-seven years.

Cora Gordon, violinist, and Cathy Hall, violist, in 2017. For years, they have led the conference's auditor program, which benefits the dozens who attend the conference but do not sign up for coaching.

Photos by Claire Stefani

Louise Lerner, pictured here in 2010, has coordinated the conference's winter reunion for many years as well as managing the functioning of the conference office.

Photo by Claire Stefani

Phillip Bush Music Directorship

In 2006, Shem Guibbory left the music director position after nine seasons, while continuing as a faculty violinist. Beyond the conference, he continued to pursue his longstanding interest in interdisciplinary art forms.

The board of directors initiated a national search for a new music director, and, for the first time in CMC history, hired an outsider: the pianist Phillip Bush. Bush shared many of Guibbory's interests, such as performing music by living composers; since the 1980s, he too had played off and on with Steve Reich as well as with Philip Glass. His chamber music and solo activities included, as Bush described it, "a lot of newer music and involvement with various composers" in New York City, "but often elsewhere, festivals and the like." His Carnegie Hall debut, for which he received laudatory reviews, took place on short notice, when he replaced an indisposed Peter Serkin as soloist with the London Sinfonietta in concerti by Igor Stravinsky and Alexander Goehr.

In many ways, Bush took over a program that was fully formed and thoroughly vetted through the years. Without urgent concerns about successful day-to-day functioning or year-to-year survival, the conference could look to "quality of life" improvements. Artistic continuity was also provided by Crockett's tenure as senior composer-in-residence; he had already held that position for five seasons and would continue beyond Bush's time as music director. Bush continued the conference's commitment to programming living composers and lesser-known works. During his last season as music director, Bush added a Wednesday faculty concert in the second week to allow for the programming of Schoenberg's *Pierrot Lunaire*.

Phillip Bush during a coaching session in 2014. Bush, the first outsider hired as music director of the conference, served as music director for the 2007 to 2016 sessions, and then continued as a faculty pianist.

Photo by Claire Stefani

224

In early 2008, Bush recommended that the conference design and print full concert programs for the series of faculty concerts, in place of the modest one-page individual program handouts that had been used since the conference's founding. That summer the new *Artist-Faculty Concert Series* booklets, designed by participant violinist Niki Matsoukas and featuring photographs by viola participant Claire Stefani, ran to almost thirty pages and included performer and resident composer biographies, notes from those composers on their works, and revenue-generating advertisements from local businesses as well from others, such as instrument makers, of special interest to the conference community.

The new concert programs were intended to promote the series beyond the conference itself, much as titling the series the "Chamber Music Festival of the East" had been intended to put the series on the New England map for music-loving tourists almost ten years earlier. The local *Bennington Banner* picked up on this theme with an article that summer about the conference, which began, "It's one of Bennington's best kept secrets—and it has been, for more than 60 years."[102]

The booklet format provided an opportunity for Phillip Bush, as music director, to introduce the concert series ("to assemble this six-concert series from our roster of over 50 performing artists is an embarrassment of riches") and for Stephen Reid, as chair of the board of directors, to say something about the conference itself ("perhaps [we have] been too discreet about publicizing our organization and its concerts"). The conference also used the program as an opportunity to acknowledge its donors. In subsequent years, a message from the executive director completed the communications from conference to community.

Beginning in 1992, violist participant Claire Stefani (shown here in the Carriage Barn in 2001) began photographing conference activities. She has continued to do so as the conference's official photographer, providing many of the images used in this history.

Courtesy of Claire Stefani

The *Artist-Faculty Concert Series* booklet, which has been produced every year since 2008, quickly became a fitting memento for the entire four-week conference. A collection of obituary notices for the past year was subsequently added as a regular feature, along with listings for the conference's public lectures and seminars. Thoughtfully engaging program notes were added by participant violinist Larry Kohorn and later also by participant violinist Robert Matsuda.

Early in Bush's tenure as music director, he identified to the board one of the areas that "has gnawed at him," and that reflected his commitment to the conference concert experience. He explained at a 2008 board meeting that "in addition to the fact that Greenwall [Auditorium] acoustics and heat and humidity are bad . . . the chairs are squeaky, and this has started to have a serious impact on the listening experience." He went on to note that "even the stage chairs make noise." Board Chair Stephen Reid offered to look into this problem, and soon 100 new, quieter, and far more comfortable chairs for the audience appeared in Greenwall for the concerts, were stored during the year, and brought out for CMC use the following summer. (The Greenwall chairs are just one example of equipment and amenities—including fans, Manhasset music stands, floor lamps, and chairs for coaching rooms—that the conference routinely purchased because Bennington College's supply was inadequate.) Going further on the topic of extraneous noise during concerts, faculty representative Maxine Neuman provided a seemingly sinister report that her husband, the conference's recording engineer Reinhard Humburg, had "got[ten] rid of crickets (mowing lawns around the building)." The crickets, however, persisted as an enduring stage presence, and the occasional Bennington Battle Day fireworks—and wild mountain thunderstorms—have proved to be a background to faculty concerts well beyond the conference's control.

Defining the Conference's Mission and Future

At the same time in 2007 that the conference was bringing on a new music director, the board was wrapping up a strategic planning process that had started two years earlier. The board had engaged a nonprofit consulting firm, undertaken a variety of participant and faculty surveys, including interviews with non-returning participants, and sought input from five board working groups on governance and administration, faculty, finance, marketing, and facilities. The board met at a weekend strategic planning retreat, which generated a twenty-two-page report, complete with photos of the "individual visions" of the CMC's future, created by board members from arts and crafts materials—thus: "Frank explained that he created a purple sculpture and then figured out what it meant, noting that purple is a color that reminds him of music."

The strategic planning effort ultimately resulted in a remarkably succinct and coherent report—only five pages—which was presented to the board at their meeting during the 2007 session. The planning committee reported that at the conclusion of the planning retreat, the board had lacked consensus on three fundamental issues: how musically inclusive the conference should be, whether education is central to its mission, and what the role of new music is at the conference. The report recommended resolutions for these issues.

As it turned out, the second and third issues were the more easily answered.

On the issue of whether the conference's focus should be educational—learning through coached sessions as opposed to simply "playing for fun"—the answer was that the conference did emphasize education. Far more participants were attending and paying for coached sessions than there were auditors, and participant and faculty surveys put "quality of coaching" as a "foremost priority." So the CMC chamber music program was not, to paraphrase Otto Luening from twenty-five years earlier, mere "fun and games."

On the question of new music, in a remarkable echo of the board's consideration of keeping or dropping the Composers' Forum more than twenty-five years earlier, the survey results indicated that "commitment to new music was not ranked as particularly important," and "many inputs to the planning process did not mention the Composers' Forum." On the other hand, the Composers' Forum was "a vital part of what we do" for some stakeholders, while "no inputs voiced any objection or negativity regarding the Composers' Forum." The conference's role as a commissioning organization was noted as "among our most lasting positive impacts on the art of chamber music." And, perhaps surprisingly, the Composers' Forum was seen as "potentially self-funding or revenue positive." The Composers' Forum had passed its second test and remained a component of the conference.

Finally, the issue of "musical inclusiveness" was essentially a question about whether the conference should be only for "advanced" amateurs. The conference community was clearly divided on this question, although the majority was in favor of inclusivity, perhaps remembering the time when they themselves were something less than "advanced." The proposed answer was that the "learning and growth that the conference provides is more fundamental to our mission than the level of participants." Conceding that "the level of ability in our participant population is certainly an important attraction to some," the report asserted that "exclusivity need and should not be considered core to our mission and values."

As the minutes state, "after a lively discussion"—which the minutes understandably make no attempt to summarize—"the Board agreed that the issue of 'advanced' playing ability should not be part of the conference mission statement, but that 'learning' and 'new music' should be." As board chair, Stephen Reid then asked "for volunteers to wordsmith our mission statement." He later reported that his invitation had not been taken up, and the mission statement would be another eight years in the making, with final adoption in 2015, as quoted as the epigraph for this chapter.

If there were any doubts about the board's approach in defining the conference's mission and values, the board was later vindicated, to judge from the results of participant surveys as part of further strategic planning activity in 2015. This activity, which also included analysis of organizational strengths, weaknesses, and opportunities, led to the development and adoption of a set of core values and strategic priorities, in 2018.

On the question of "learning," an overwhelming majority of survey respondents "felt that most faculty members are effective coaches," and the high number of responses to this question suggested that quality coaching was an important criterion for participants, with a large segment reporting that coaches were very important or the most important factor for attending.

On the controversial question of the conference as serving only "advanced" players, a significant portion of respondents "cited the high quality of participants' playing as the most important reason for attending the conference," but almost as many "cited players' friendliness, enthusiasm, and personal compatibility as more important than skill." And almost as many respondents "felt that weaker players should be given the chance to play with stronger ones." The notion of inclusivity, and that the conference is not just for "advanced" players, seemed to have taken hold. Despite this, the survey also disclosed that many respondents "perceived an informal hierarchy of players." Similarly, a significant group of respondents reported that the conference has a "snobby," "cliquish," or "exclusive" reputation—although a smaller group of respondents noted that this reputation was undeserved—and many reported that they felt that the formerly cliquish atmosphere has improved.

Regarding the Composers' Forum, the 2015 survey found that the "prevailing sentiment overall seems to be that new music is an important part of the conference . . . and that working with composers is worthwhile for those who do so." A small number of respondents, who said new music was "not my thing," nevertheless conceded that they enjoyed exposure to it. The view that the Composers' Forum could be dropped from the conference was held by only a very small minority of the respondents.

The board's focus on these organization identity issues was soon reflected in conference publications. The conference brochure, which in one format or another had been distributed each year to promote the upcoming session, abandoned any reference to the conference being for "advanced chamber music players" or "experienced" amateurs; instead, the brochure stated that "our common denominator is a passion for chamber music." Newcomers were advised that if they wanted to "enjoy the Conference experience fully," they should be "able to play [their] instrument(s) skillfully, have good sight-reading ability and have some chamber music experience."

Within two years of the board's mission-focused discussions, Music Director Bush addressed another aspect of the conference, the longstanding Wednesday and Saturday participant concerts. He renamed them "Afternoon Musicales," returning to a term that had been used earlier in the conference's history. As Bush commented, this change was "really part of larger goals having to do with the culture of the conference, lessening the 'competitive' nature (or perception of same) of playing on the 'Recitals.'" In a one-page memo, which has been a standard enclosure in participant materials every summer since then, Bush explained that

> these Musicales are not meant to display perfection, nor are they in any way 'Honors Recitals,' reserved only for the most experienced and advanced players. On the contrary, these are open to any group who would like to play, and they are just for our community…not advertised to the general public, and a few clams or even a 'reboot' in the middle is absolutely no big deal in this context. It's just us, after all!

Bush's memo also explains that when a coached group comes to decide whether to ask to perform in a musicale, requesting to perform "is completely optional, and our long-standing CMC policy has been that ALL members of a group must unanimously agree." And to leave no doubt about this orthodoxy, Bush went on to stress that "no participant should ever feel pressured to play in front of others when they would rather not, for any reason at all."

Throughout this period, the board was conscious of its role in representing the participant community in organizational governance. Mahany's "lunch with the board" had been introduced many years earlier, but most participants—unless they were already on the board—did not know who the current board members were. In 2006, Secretary Karen Greif suggested—crediting participant violinist Stephen Lustig with originating the idea—that board members be identified on their nametags so that participants would know who, among their colleagues, could be addressed with praise or blame or asked questions about the conference's governance. The board took the suggestion under consideration—certainly a concern would have been that this would look like some form of elitist labeling. The next year, the issue came up again, with board member Ruth Alperson now asking "that we identify Board members with dots on their nametags." Result: "A sense of the Board was taken." The "Board member dot" policy was introduced in Week 3 that summer and has been a regular feature of the conference since then.

Staff Leadership Transitions

When Beth Anderson stepped down as administrative director after the summer of 2007, the conference found a replacement in Jack Chan, a professional bassoonist from Brooklyn who had first attended the conference as a participant in 2002. He completed his first summer as administrative director with several successful efforts. He helped the conference refine its administrative structure and improved conference communications through the increased use of email and the relatively new conference website, which had been launched only about four years earlier. The board looked forward to working with him in future years.

But Chan, and the board, may have underestimated the demands of running the conference. Facing the stressful prospect of a second year managing the conference, and with attractive professional playing opportunities beckoning, Chan resigned, leaving it to Stephen Reid—once again—to step in, now with the title "executive director."

At its meeting during the conference that year, minutes reflect the board's befuddlement when it came to the chief administrative employee—not only not knowing who, but also not even knowing what or how many: "Our immediate need is for an Administrative Director, or two Administrative Directors, or an Executive Director plus an Administrative Director."

The problem turned out to be surprisingly easy to solve, as the board identified Marilyn Bell as the leading candidate. In 2010, she was hired as executive director. To say she was qualified for the position seems an understatement. She had been a participant at the conference almost every summer for thirty-five years. She had served on the board of directors and worked as a paid staff member on two previous occasions. During an interview as part of the hiring process, she was asked what her biggest professional challenge had been, and how she handled it. She did not hesitate in replying: "On September 11, 2001, I was the principal of a public elementary school on the Upper West Side, and while the smoke poured out of Lower Manhattan, we made sure every child was safely evacuated."

Bell would serve as executive director for the next nine years, leading an administrative staff during the conference itself that typically included five other people. This was in keeping with the 2007 strategic planning goal of "ensuring effective, efficient and customer-focused administration," which shifted the conference from dependence on volunteers to more paid staff positions for key functions. Not all crucial functions were taken over by paid staff, however; the board treasurer, Dianne Mahany, for example, began in 2010 as a volunteer responsible for managing the CMC finances. Mahany established a paid accountancy relationship with John Howell, a participant violinist, who as a professional accountant still shares bookkeeping responsibilities and provides general accounting support to the conference. Bell resigned after the 2018 session, although she, like so many other former staff members, continued as a participant.

In the fall of 2018, the conference appointed Susie Ikeda as executive director to take over beginning with the 2019 session. Ikeda had been a violinist participant at the conference for over twenty years and previously served two terms on the board of directors. She had served in varying administrative staff roles since 2012, including working with the scheduling team, and had been attending all four weeks of the conference since 2015. Like her predecessor, Ikeda is committed to public education. During the off-season, she is a highly successful math and physics teacher at Boston International High School, where her students are non-English-speaking immigrants. Before her career as an educator, Ikeda held a progression of leadership positions, primarily in the field of information technology.

Susie Ikeda in 2012, the year she took on various staff roles. In 2018 she was appointed executive director.

Photo by Claire Stefani

The Amateur as Composer

Just as Moses Kligsberg attended the conference for twenty-some years beginning in the 1950s, working away at his day job while also writing music on his own time, with the conference as his primary, if not only, outlet for readings and performances, other non-professional composers have flourished at the conference. After the Composers' Forum was reorganized in the 1990s and then under Crockett's leadership as senior composer-in-residence, the avocational or amateur composers again began to find their place at the conference.

Among these composers was Zeke Hecker, who first came to the conference as a last-minute substitute participant oboist in the 1980s. A self-taught composer—or, as he prefers to say, "untaught"—he threw himself into writing music with little formal instruction, although he admits to "a few weeks of counterpoint." He now has a catalog of more than 120 works, which displays his special interest in art songs and musical theater.

In 2014, Hecker started attending as an oboe participant—along with his wife, Linda, on violin and viola—and his music has found a place at the conference as well. His Sextet for Piano and Wind Quintet (2012) has been included frequently in Sunday night Round Robin sessions, and, in 2019, it was scheduled as a coached work. A few years before that, Hecker's Woodwind Quintet (2009) was coached, with him in the group, resulting in an afternoon musicale performance. When faculty flutist Sue Ann Kahn, during a coaching session on Madeleine Dring's Trio for Flute, Oboe, and Piano that included Hecker, lamented the lack of works for that instrumental combination, he wrote one, and dedicated it to Kahn.

Among the most active and accomplished participant composers at the conference is Jonathan Newmark. He first attended the conference in 1981 as a violist and pianist, but his interest in composing went back many years earlier. The conference, with its composers-in-residence, and later, composition fellows, did not seem to have a place for a participant, "amateur composer" at the time.

In 1998, Newmark offered his newly composed string trio to the conference for coaching, and it was assigned with Martin Bresnick as the coach. But in 1999, Newmark explained that he "arrived at Bennington with a brand-new piece" as a "composer student," a role that was not yet well-defined. Newmark's breakthrough came in the form of a commission from two participants who knew of his willingness to compose for amateurs: oboist Jan Jakob Mooij and bassoonist Hans Cats. They requested the commissioned trio for oboe, bassoon, and piano, as a pre-formed group, which was coached by Kermit Moore, a respected composer in his own right. The trio was premiered at a participant concert, which Newmark describes as "a very emotional experience for me; for the first time I was presenting my own stuff in front of people who had known me for decades."

Composer-in-Residence Lisa Bielawa was a significant influence in suggesting in 2009 that Newmark attend graduate school in composition. After he retired as a colonel in the U.S. Army Medical Corps in 2013—a neurologist by training, he was a leading military authority on medical response to chemical warfare and terrorism—he took Bielawa's advice and pursued his master of music degree from the College-Conservatory of Music, University of Cincinnati, which he received in 2015.

Rosemary Waltzer (horn and later violin) was another participant who brought her compositions to the conference. In 2000, she worked with Senior Composer-in-Residence Chen Yi, who Waltzer recalls "was amazing" as a mentor. The most thrilling moment came when Chen Yi, introducing Waltzer as "the composer, Rosemary," left Waltzer glancing about for someone else named Rosemary who was a composer, until she realized she had taken on a new identity at the conference. Several summers later, Waltzer returned with a new song cycle, scored for soprano, clarinet, and horn. Valerie Matthews, a participant cellist and soprano, agreed to take on the soprano part for the work to be scheduled for coaching, and Dianne Mahany on clarinet joined Waltzer on horn. Daniel Godfrey, the composer-in-residence, coached the group. The trio went on to perform four songs from the cycle at the participant concert that week.

The Amateur as Commissioner of New Music

Norman Reiss, an amateur double bassist and for many years a CMC board member, reported at a board meeting in 1971 that he had commissioned a work by Joseph Ott "for [my] family to play last year." He added that he planned on doing this every year by himself, not through the conference. Ott had been a composer at the conference in 1967, and then again in 1969 and 1970, and is now remembered chiefly as a pioneering composer of electronic works.[103] Given that other participants have requested commissions directly from composers, as Reiss proposed to do, our knowledge of these commissions is almost certainly incomplete.

There are some notable commissions by participants that we do know about. Ardith Bondi, an avid participant flutist with an interest in new music, first attended in 1980, then returned for additional years, including 1988 when she joined her brother, Eugene Bondi, a professional cellist on the staff. Although she held a doctorate in pharmacology from Columbia University, and later was at New York University engaged in research on neuromuscular electrophysiology, Bondi was certainly an accomplished musician: Allan Kozinn referred to her in the *New York Times* as an "excellent flutist" for her playing in an Aaron Jay Kernis premiere with her brother at Merkin Concert Hall in New York City.

During her first year at the conference, Bondi commissioned Lionel Nowak's *Four Green Mountain Sketches* for flute and cello. For the CMC sixtieth anniversary in 2005, Music Director Shem Guibbory programmed this work as the first piece on the first concert of the session, with Sue Ann Kahn, flute, and Kermit Moore, cello. With that, this participant commission seems to have entered the permanent repertoire at the conference. It was programmed again in 2016, again with Sue Ann Kahn, and with Maxine Neuman, cello.

A participant wind quintet, "The Usual Suspects"—in score order: Roger Brooks, Karen Greif, Frank Mallory, James Dunne, and Abby Wells—is an example of the abiding friendships formed and fostered at the conference. This quintet, complete with customized Usual Suspects T-shirts designed by Dunne, played together every summer in a pre-formed coaching session—one of the great advantages of having a scheduling system that allows pre-formed ensembles—for 18 years,* until Frank Mallory's final illness prevented him from attending in 2014.

One summer the Usual Suspects quintet was working on Allen Shawn's Woodwind Quintet (no. 1) in a session coached by faculty oboist Pat Stenberg. Shawn, who was on the Bennington College faculty and living in North Bennington, was able to sit in on one of their coaching sessions. The quintet decided to ask Shawn if he would be interested in writing a quintet for them, and as Karen Greif put it, "Allen agreed, and no doubt dropped his usual fee quite a lot so we could make it happen."

The summer after he completed that commission, Wind Quintet no. 2 (2001), Shawn worked with the quintet during free-time playing. The first performance of the work was at Bryn Mawr College in May 2002 as part of a chamber music series that Mallory and Greif (both were on the faculty at Bryn

---

* As James Dunne pointed out in an email to the author, "To be clear, that was one different work per year, not the same work for 18 years."

Mawr; he in chemistry, she in biology) helped to establish on campus. CMC faculty bassoonist Lauren Goldstein Stubbs came for a weekend at Frank and Sally Mallory's Bryn Mawr home to help prepare the work for its premiere. Sadly, at the time of the commission, Pat Stenberg had been diagnosed with cancer, and she died two months before the first performance. At the quintet's request, Shawn dedicated it to her memory. The conference faculty recorded this quintet for its *Ceiling of Heaven* CD recording in 2005.

Another participant commission went to Andrew Norman for his wind quintet *Tongue and Groove*. Norman first attended the conference as a composition fellow in 2002, bringing with him a work for flute and string trio, *Light Screens*, now in the Schott Music catalog as one of Norman's first published works. Participant flutist Trish Maxson recalls getting a phone call from Administrative Director Beth Anderson, asking if she was willing to be coached on a work for flute and string trio. "Of course I said yes—what flute player wouldn't—and so met Andrew for the first time." Maxson and her usual second week wind quintet "liked him and his music so much we asked to commission a quintet and bring him back." As hornist Emily Fine explained, "we had essentially 'adopted' him during his first summer, introducing him to all sorts of quintet literature and encouraging him in that direction!" Norman returned the next year, and the quintet (Maxson and Fine plus Scott Brodie, oboe; William Holl, clarinet; and David Halpert, bassoon) premiered *Tongue and Groove*. In 2012, Norman returned to the CMC yet again, now as a composer-in-residence.

A more recent participant commission went to John Steinmetz, a CMC faculty bassoonist and composer. Steinmetz attended the first Week 0 at Colgate University in 2001, and

The Participant Chamber Orchestra

During the first three decades of the conference, amateurs and professional staff regularly joined together for readings and performances of traditional chamber orchestra literature. During the early years, when many resident composers were writing works scored for orchestra, there seems to have been no question about the relevance of an orchestra at a chamber music conference. But over the years, interest in the chamber orchestra waned, despite efforts to keep the orchestra sessions. Finally, it was up to Music Director Phillip Bush in 2007 to endorse the "continued absence of orchestra."

The story of the chamber orchestra reflects the changing interest among amateurs, away from orchestral playing and toward exclusively playing chamber music. The orchestra sessions meant taking time out from chamber music free-time playing. Finding a conductor willing to work with amateurs in a reading orchestra, and keeping amateur players interested—string players in particular—was an ongoing challenge.

But in 1975, for example, the orchestra was featured in the conference brochure as a regular item on the schedule ("11:30–12:30 Full Orchestra reading"), described as "daily reading sessions of symphonic works under the direction of the Director, Alan Carter."

After 1975, identifying a successful conductor—one adequately tolerant of amateur skill levels—seems to have been difficult. Maxwell Lehman's 1977 proposed reorganization plan makes this point—perhaps in reference to the imperious Myron Levite, who expressed, perhaps too freely, his frustration with the amateurs: "The conductor must realize that he is working with educated, intelligent adults who love music, even though they may not have the technique to carry out their musical desires to the fullest extent." The reorganization plan goes on to explain that a performance opportunity might enhance the orchestra experience, proposing a short concert of works "within the orchestra's reach" for each Friday night. These orchestra sessions would continue in various forms for almost thirty years.

As the conference reorganized in the late 1970s, the versatile musician Norman Pickering took over conducting duties from Levite, but after Pickering resigned in 1981, the orchestra's direction was again unclear. By 1984, a "new modus operandi" was proposed for the orchestra: assigning parts to specific participants and meeting three times a week.

Conducting duties soon fell to faculty cellist Kermit Moore, who first came to the conference in 1988. He had a distinguished career, not just as a cellist and composer, but as a professional conductor, having studied with Koussevitzky. He was a frequent guest conductor for the Brooklyn Philharmonic and the Symphony of the New World, among others.

Moore included faculty members in the CMC chamber orchestra—one way to improve the orchestra and attract amateur players as well—and actively recruited participant

Kermit Moore conducting the participant orchestra in the Carriage Barn in an undated photo.

Photo by Claire Stefani

string players. He made excursions into the New York Public Library for the Performing Arts at Lincoln Center to retrieve unusual orchestral works (board minutes note a particularly successful Cherubini session, presumably the rarely played Symphony in D Major) to bring to the conference. These efforts seem to have revived interest in the orchestra.

But by 1994, interest in the chamber orchestra again waned, and orchestra sessions were trimmed back to two per week; it was necessary to "appoint" lead players. Nevertheless, in 1995, the orchestra had a "mixed reception, although it was a fairly good year in terms of participation." As early as 1996, music director Shem Guibbory was reporting complaints from string players that "having an orchestra is inappropriate for a chamber music conference." By 1997, the orchestra was pared back to one meeting per week, despite what was reported to be an excellent session with Moore conducting the Elgar *Introduction and Allegro*, opus 47, featuring guest faculty Charlotta and Paul Ross (cello and violin, respectively) in the solo string quartet.

Faculty oboist and Carl Nielsen devotee Pat Stenberg also led many orchestra sessions, including a reading session of Nielsen's rarely performed *Aladdin Suite*. In another popular repeated session, she conducted the two Brahms orchestral Serenades, opus 11 and 16, on Friday evenings. The Serenades were especially liked by wind players, who often rotated playing responsibilities for each movement,

while the absence of violins in the opus 16 Serenade reduced the need for string player recruitment. The regular Friday night Brahms sessions, however, came to an end in 1999, as a result of Stenberg's final illness.

Although Moore continued to lead the orchestra sessions, board minutes note "mixed results" through 2002, and by 2005 no one seemed to care when Music Director Guibbory announced that the time had come to drop the orchestra. Indeed, in his report to the board the next year, Guibbory commented that *not* having an orchestra appeared to be successful. But, he added, a "spontaneous" reading of Robert Schumann's *Konzertstück in F Major* for four horns and orchestra, opus 86, had been a "resounding success." The next year, however, the conference's new music director, Phillip Bush, concurred in the decision not to continue the orchestra as a scheduled conference activity. A long tradition had come to an end. Larger ensemble works—the *Brandenburg* concerti, for example—continue to be played at the conference as more spontaneous, and often late-night, free-time sessions.

then returned for several years. In 2009, Renée Redman, horn, Stephen Kamin, piano, and Jeannine Burky (later Webber), clarinet, were coached by Music Director Phillip Bush on George Rochberg's Trio for B-flat clarinet, F horn, and piano. (Rochberg had been a composer at the conference in 1952; his unusually scored Trio was written not long after, although he revised it in 1980, but making few changes.) According to Webber, the participant trio "really enjoyed the combination of instruments, and were disappointed to learn that there were almost no other available pieces for this combination." Webber and Redman knew Steinmetz from his coaching and playing at the conference, and he was an ideal composer for an amateur ensemble. He had a special affinity for the CMC amateur scene, as he explained in *Chamber Music* magazine in 2005, in an article prominently featuring the CMC:

> We think that the late Beethoven and Mozart quartets survived because professional groups kept performing them, but that's only the tip of the iceberg. The bulk of preservation work of keeping that music alive in our ears and in our hearts was done by people who weren't getting paid to play it.[104]

As Webber explained, "I decided to reach out to John to see if he'd be willing to write a piece for clarinet, horn, and piano. I was thrilled when he accepted the commission." The resulting work, *A Little Traveling Music*, was completed in 2010, and the same three conference participants, after some preparation with Kermit Moore, whom they already knew as a CMC faculty cellist, premiered the piece in New York City early the next year.

Board Leadership in Transition

In a significant change in board leadership, and in conference leadership more generally, Stephen Reid announced that upon the expiration of his term in 2015 he would retire—after twenty-three years—as chair of the board of directors. He had taken over the job when the conference was not sure what to call it. He stayed on as a board member, providing important continuity and remaining accessible to the board, with intimate knowledge of the workings of the conference. Two years later, in 2017, he announced that he would retire from the board itself in 2019. His service to the organization spanned forty-two years, exceeding even the terms of Luening and Nowak. For two generations of participants, Reid led the conference, in a wide range of roles and functions—even stepping in as the organization's executive director—in effect as the CMC's chief executive officer, always quietly and without bravado. At his last board meeting, in October 2019, he was elected director emeritus in recognition of his extraordinary service.

Following Reid's announcement, the board's nominating committee immediately commenced its search for a new board chair, and put out a call to current or former participants or other conference community members for applications, noting the "position is held on an unpaid/volunteer basis."

The nominating committee quickly identified a candidate, and the board unanimously confirmed the nomination of Mike Kong. The succession was well-planned: Kong returned to the board as "chair-elect" in November 2014, one year before his term was to start, thus enabling him to shadow Reid for that year, and then assume his role "familiar with current issues and with the chair's duties."

A pianist, violinist, and violist, Kong had first attended the conference in 1983, and was experienced with a variety of conference activities and operations. Early on, he worked with Eve Cohen on the scheduling team, and, a little later, he created and managed the conference's first website. He first joined the board of directors in 1993 and served until 2008, chairing, at different times, both the site committee and the strategic planning committee, and serving on the board search committee that recommended Phillip Bush as music director. In his career in software engineering management, Kong developed leadership, communication, and interpersonal skills—all of which a non-profit organization such as the CMC looks for in a board chair.

Tobias Werner Music Directorship

After Mike Kong became chair-elect of the board, the conference needed to find a replacement for Phillip Bush, who had submitted his resignation, effective after the 2015 season. Like Shem Guibbory before him, Bush served for nine seasons as music director. He resigned from the conference so that he could devote more time to his duties as associate professor of piano and chamber music at the University of South Carolina, a post he had held since 2012, but continued on the conference's faculty. As posted to the conference email list by then-chair Stephen Reid on behalf of the board, news of Bush's resignation included the acknowledgment that:

> The Conference is a special place and environment, and Phillip has maintained and enhanced that specialness with his administration of our musical activities, bringing in excellent new faculty to join our wonderful veterans, programming exciting concerts,

and extending CMC's reputation in the world of
chamber music generally.

Once again, the board took up a national search for a key
staff member. A search committee, balanced by participant
representatives who attended each of the conference's four
weeks, and including pianists and string and wind players,
was co-chaired by Frank Daykin, faculty pianist and lecturer,
and Trish Maxson.

Soon, a new post to the conference email list announced the
appointment of Tobias "Tobi" Werner as music director, upon
a unanimous board vote. During the 2015 session, Werner
was a guest faculty member during Week 2 and the start of
Week 3, to observe conference activities and meet conferees,

*Tobias Werner became the
conference's music director
beginning with the 2016 season.*

Photo by Claire Stefani

thus assuring a "seamless transfer of our artistic leadership in time for the 2016 season."

Werner had a distinguished career as cello soloist and chamber musician. He studied at the Musikhochschule Freiburg in his native Germany, then later at Boston University. Residing in the Washington, DC, area, he had taught at Georgetown University and, reflecting his commitment to new music, he was a member of the Verge Ensemble, a DC-based new music ensemble. Werner was also the artistic director of the Pressenda Chamber Players, the ensemble in residence at the Washington Conservatory of Music, and the cellist in residence and co-artistic director at Garth Newel Music Center from 1999 until 2012.

In his first season as music director, Werner retained the new Week 2 Wednesday faculty concert that had been added by his predecessor Phillip Bush the year before, and he also added a Wednesday concert in Week 1. The conference's public faculty series now included eight concerts.

The "Core Faculty" Concept

In 2016, the board determined to address the "faculty tenure" issue, which had been discussed for two decades but not satisfactorily resolved. The tenure issue had been central to the "ideological differences" underlying Jack Glick's resignation in 1994, and Phillip Bush had exhorted the board to address the issue at the final board meeting he attended in 2015. The professional musicians on the CMC faculty—accomplished performers who are also outstanding coaches of amateur musicians—are in many ways the conference's most valuable asset. The conference needed a policy that would ensure faculty security but give sufficient hiring flexibility to the music director.

On the one hand, participants valued the regular return of faculty, year after year, often for the long term. For many participants, one of the joys of returning to the conference for successive years was seeing and working with the same faculty again. Faculty members, too, appreciated this aspect of the conference, since they could plan their future summer schedules knowing that the conference was committed to having them back. Plus, they valued their involvement—perhaps becoming personally attached to their summer experience the same way participants did—and looked forward to returning.

On the other hand, this desire for faculty stability and continuity could be seen as conflicting directly with the genuine—perhaps even pressing—need for new faculty to be engaged, to experience what the CMC offered, and then, if all went well, to return in the future. Having new musicians join the faculty is one way that the conference has renewed itself and maintained its vitality.

Since the 1980s, there had been a poorly documented faculty "tenure policy" whereby, if a faculty member were invited back for a third year in a row, he or she would attain "tenure" and have the "right of first refusal" for a slot going forward. Under this policy, with automatic grant of tenure based on consecutive years of service, the percentage of slots held by tenured faculty tended to increase, leaving the music director with little flexibility in hiring and few opportunities to invite new faculty. To preserve flexibility, the music director had to avoid inviting non-tenured faculty members for too many consecutive years; when faculty members were not invited back, they sometimes resented these decisions and perceived them as arbitrary.

A committee of three board members, two faculty members, and Music Director Tobias Werner set out to craft guidelines that would better serve all constituents at the conference. The term "core status" replaced "tenure," to avoid the confusion with academic tenure that had occurred in the past. Core status carried the same assurances as defined in the old tenure policy. However, core status was achieved not automatically upon a series of consecutive invitations, but after three distinct steps: decision by the music director and the board to create a new core slot for a given instrument; determination that a faculty member on that instrument is eligible for core status, based on recent years of service; and evaluation of the candidate by the music director, based on faculty and participant input. The core faculty guidelines also defined procedures for evaluating

Dianne Mahany performs with the Casual Sax Sextet in 1995. To her right is David Halpert, a clarinet and bassoon participant, who initiated the 2013 Halpert fundraising challenge, and to his right is Martin Frank, who attended for many years as a clarinet participant.

Photo by Claire Stefani

a faculty member—when the music director considers either granting or removing core status—that previously had been unspecified. The creation of a core slot as an explicit step, rather than an implicit effect of an automatic tenure grant, allowed the conference to manage the balance between continuity and change on the faculty. The committee's approach, informed by many years of institutional experience, embraced the values of stability and continuity while providing opportunities for new faculty; its proposal for core faculty guidelines was adopted at the October 2017 board meeting.

As board member Dianne Mahany, who had been involved in those decades-long discussions, described it, there was "nothing bureaucratic about this, it was done with love."

The Music of Friends—and Families

One of the historical features of chamber music has been the involvement of members of the same family, often hearkening back to a culture of music making in the home that has been passed down from generation to generation. One might think in this context of Franz Schubert, learning the quartet literature when playing with his father and two brothers, and later, writing his first quartets for these same players. No history of the conference would be complete without noting how this chamber music tradition extends to the present day, and the way that the conference becomes a significant part of the lives of these families.

According to Marc Wager, participant hornist and a pediatrician, when he and his wife, Terry, "joined the Conference back in 1982, there were few children who attended the Conference." The next year, they brought their son Adam with them—"and he has not missed a single summer since." The number of parents bringing their children soon began to grow, and it was apparent that the Bennington campus and environs was an ideal setting for kids, with its open space, informal dining facility, and dorms—back when the dorms were unlocked, and the kids could come and go as they pleased—and with the Bennington Early Childhood Center summer camp and Lake Paran—what Wager refers to as "lots of Vermont outdoorsy and Bennington artsy activities." As the crowd of youngsters grew, Wager explained, "some kids got in trouble, and in order to enforce the policy that kids need supervision, I was invited on the board." He was to become an informal liaison with families with children, as well as an advocate for the conference being more child-friendly in its approach. By 1991, board minutes reflect that Judy Lacker, Terry Wager, and Peggy Dumouchel were working on an "improved/enhanced children's program." As the site committee looked at other possible locations for the conference, compatibility with the needs of families was assessed during site visits.

Photo by Claire Stefani

As the population of children increased, and they grew older, "kids' concerts," instituted by faculty cellist Maxine Neuman in the early 1990s for the last two weeks of the conference, became a regular part of the conference experience. Neuman—she was "Auntie Maxine" to violinist Imani Congdon, daughter of faculty violist Lisa Whitfield—would herd the kids together, make customized arrangements of appropriate skill-level music that accommodated the instruments the children could play, and lead rehearsals and coachings throughout the week. Taking place after the Saturday afternoon participant concert, the kids' concert would draw enthusiastic, standing-room-only audiences.

Among the celebrated ensembles was the "Total Twenty-One Trio" (Elisabeth Cohen, violin; Joanna Schor, cello; and Julia Neuman, piano). Billed as "A Trio for this Century and the Next," the Trio's name was purportedly the sum of the player's ages, although Maxine Neuman has recently conceded that twenty-one "was actually incorrect: Julia was only six, while Elisabeth and Joanna were seven. But we thought Total Twenty-One sounded cool, and she would have been seven in November." The Trio made its debut in 1991. Neuman's son Mark Humburg, now a professional cellist, made his CMC debut as a pianist in the Total Nine Duo, along with cellist Emma Cohen. Many of the kids who played at these concerts went on to have lasting involvement in chamber music, and some returned as adult-level participants.

Pairs of siblings have often attended the conference together, hinting again at the family origins of chamber music making. Notable are the sisters, Avra and Niki Matsoukas, both violinists, and who, although they are not twins, have a sufficiently strong resemblance to each other that Avra has frequently

Poster for the Total Twenty-One Trio (Elisabeth Cohen, violin; Joanna Schor, cello; and Julia Neuman, piano) from 1991 for its debut performance at a kids' concert.

Courtesy of Maxine Neuman

Conference faculty member Maxine Neuman coaches the Total Twenty-One Trio.

Photo by Sylvia Lipnick

received the praise intended by other participants for her sister's playing in afternoon musicales. After years of enduring this mistaken identity, she explains that "I don't even bother to correct people anymore, I'm happy to get the compliment." Other siblings include Ardith Bondi, flutist, and her faculty cellist brother, Eugene; violist Maurice Kouguell and his brother, faculty cellist Alexander; bassoonist Hans Cats and his sister, flutist Henneke; the brothers Robert Osborn, violist, and Howard, violinist and violist; flutist Peggy Holleran Greb and her brother, pianist Steve Holleran; and violinist, violist, and pianist Mike Kong and his sister, pianist Diana Hagerott.

The number of parents and their children in attendance is so large that any attempted catalog is necessarily incomplete. One example is the father and son violinists and physicians, F. William Sunderman and F. William Sunderman Jr., who were in attendance in 1957 and other years as well. Faculty members Lauren (bassoon) and James (trumpet) Stubbs brought their children to the conference for many years. Their son Matt recalls the Bennington campus as "remarkably beautiful . . . [t]he mountains, forests, streams, wildlife, etc. together created an exciting and magical atmosphere." He played in many kids' concerts—his last and most remarkable performance was the Stravinsky Piano Concerto, with his teacher and conference faculty pianist David Oei accompanying him on the piano— and then first attended as a participant at age fifteen in 2010. Looking back, Matt Stubbs cites the conference as "the inspiration for my growth as a musician and importantly, ground zero for my love of chamber music." Faculty double bassist Lewis Paer recalls how his younger son Jeff "took some of his first steps down the path from Commons to the volleyball net." Both his two sons "benefited immeasurably from playing piano (both), trumpet (Jeff), and bass (Nate) during Maxine Neuman's most wonderful family concerts for the kids."

The Cohen family—parents Eve and Don, daughters Elisabeth and Emma—was also a familiar presence at the conference for more than forty years. On their home turf in Cheviot Hills, Los Angeles, the Cohens hosted legendary chamber music play-ins every spring—eighty musicians filling their home for an afternoon and evening of playing—including a backyard Gilbert and Sullivan operetta performance. These events, which continue to this day, are often organized according to some musical theme, such as a specific composer, as Eve Cohen explained: "we thought Hindemith—instead of Brahms or Beethoven—would drive them away, but when we scheduled him as a composer a few years back, even more came."[105] They brought that same chamber music marathon-party enthusiasm

Eve Cohen

Photo by Marilyn Bell

Violist Eve Cohen finished her last summer at the conference in 2012. Although seriously ill at the time, she managed to handle the scheduling of coaching sessions, and she played in almost all the sessions of the conference's four weeks—all, as Stephen Reid put it, "at her accustomed level of excellence." Knowing that her time was short, she took care to pass her scheduling acumen on to a new team so that operations could continue without interruption. She died roughly a month later.

Eve's daughters, Elisabeth and Emma, organized a memorial to take place on November 24, 2012. Musicians and friends gathered for chamber music parties in numerous locations, including Bennington, District of Columbia, Los Angeles, New York, Boston, and Philadelphia, to play music and honor Eve's memory. The "official memorial quartet" for the occasion—Eve's favorite—was the Brahms Quartet in A Minor, opus 51, no. 2—the same quartet that the Silvermine Quartet had played at its final conference concert in 1999.

Eve Cohen, whose work on scheduling transformed the conference, was a highly accomplished violist. The pianist in this 1992 photograph is then-Administrative Director Dorothy Kalson.

Photo by Claire Stefani

to the conference, and both Elisabeth and Emma, after growing up at the conference, later returned as participants.

A Culture of Giving

The conference's history offers many examples of generous giving of time, intellect, and financial support by participants and faculty members who are passionate about the conference's mission. The Jacob Glick Memorial Endowment Fund is by no means the only instance of such community generosity.

The support of individual donors has been, from the early years, a necessary feature of the conference's success. Although the conference has always charged a fee to participants, and, at least theoretically, these fees can be adjusted to support the conference's projected expenses, overall expenses always exceed what can reasonably be covered by participant fees. These fees must be kept in a range that participants can afford and that is in line with what is charged by similar chamber music programs. Expenses that lend themselves particularly to donor support include participant financial aid—a fund seeded by a donation from Carl Tretter in 2001—and support for the Composers' Forum, including commissions for new works such as those supported by the Glick Fund. Donors may also choose to target their gifts for several other specific funds or for the conference's general operating fund.

Documents from the early Bennington years reference efforts made at the time to raise funds from donors. A Carriage Barn "Special Sponsors Concert" program in 1957, for example, lists ten sponsors, including "Mrs. David Karrick," a frequent cello participant; the composer and North Bennington resident Elsa Golbin; and Carl Stern, principal cellist of the New York Philharmonic, who had been a CMC faculty cellist for two previous summers, 1955 and 1956.

Among the earliest, focused, community-wide fundraising campaigns was one undertaken for the conference's 50th anniversary, led by participants Ann Franke and Stephen Fillo. For that campaign, board member Franke developed a T-shirt bearing Music Director Jack Glick's portrait and motto, "Music is too important to be left entirely to professionals." The 50th anniversary campaign proved to be highly successful, reaching its goal of $50,000 on schedule.

The next campaign, only about three years later, was for the Glick Memorial Endowment Fund. This effort, led by participant pianist and violist Kay Cynamon, also reached its $100,000 goal.

Carl Tretter, an amateur violinist from the Washington, DC, area with a successful career in commercial real estate, who started attending the conference in 1997, made a generous gift to the conference in 2001 to generate income for a scholarship for a needy participant each year. This was the beginning of the Financial Aid Fund. Tretter and others have made additional gifts to the fund over the years, thus ensuring that the CMC is accessible to all musicians without regard to financial need. Gifts made in memory of Mort Raff, a violinist who was deeply committed to welcoming newcomers to the conference, and who left his valuable violin to the conference, are added to the Financial Aid Fund.

Conference participants Fan Tao and Tara Kazak provide full financial aid to one participant each year in Eve Cohen's

Violinist Mort Raff, pictured here in 1994, was a conference participant with a great passion for giving newcomers opportunities to join in free-time playing. The namesake Mort Raffle, a weekly contest that encourages inclusion of newcomers in playing opportunities, carries on Raff's commitment to making the conference a welcoming place.

Photo by Claire Stefani

memory. Every year several other donors earmark their gifts for financial aid.

When Pat Stenberg, oboe coach, conductor of the conference participant orchestra (which included her highly popular Friday evening readings of the two Brahms Serenades for orchestra), and assistant music director, died in 2002, an endowment fund was launched to support an oboe faculty chair position for the third week, her usual week of attendance. To this day, gifts in Stenberg's memory are added to this fund, which is now part of the Named Chair Fund. When faculty pianist Marya Sielska, who was at the conference from 1969 to 1998, died, she left a substantial legacy to the conference, and the board voted to use it to endow a piano faculty chair position for one week each summer. Additional gifts made in her memory support this endowment, which is also now part of the Named Chair Fund.

Among the most generous post-mortem gifts in conference history was that of Robert Maguire, retired chair of the Department of Slavic Languages at Columbia University, who gave cash, musical instruments, and royalties from his translations of Russian and Polish fiction. An avid violist, he first attended the conference in 1975, served on the board of directors from 1978 to 1985, and returned almost every year until 2005, the year of his death. Because of his generosity in making this very substantial bequest—today the Maguire Risk Reserve Fund, ensuring a financial "rainy day" backup in case of unpredicted difficulty—the conference established the Robert Maguire Legacy Society in his memory. Individuals who name the conference in their wills or make other legacy arrangements are members of this society.

Jerry and Barbara Hulka—horn and violin, respectively— first came to the conference in 2005. Both worked in academic medicine at the University of North Carolina. They endowed a fund in their names that currently supports lectures and special events in the second week of the conference.

In 2013, Stephen Reid, board chair, wrote to the conference community, via its email list, about "a wonderful fund-raising opportunity." David Halpert, a clarinet and bassoon participant, offered to match donations, up to $50,000, including a two-to-one match for any new or increased donations over the donor's past-year donation history. One purpose of the Halpert Initiative, as Reid called it, was "to encourage a culture of giving to the Conference." Reid noted that all board members had already pledged to support it. Apparently that "culture of giving" did not need very much encouragement, as a little more than two months later, in early January 2014, Reid was posting on the email list again, sharing a "big collective 'thank you'" because "the Conference has already received many gifts that qualified for matching under this initiative, and as a result the full amount of David's gift to CMC ($50,000) has already been achieved ... more than 7 months ahead of the anticipated end date for this campaign!"

In addition to the gifts from the estate of Robert Maguire, the conference has also benefited from gifts of instruments and accessories from other participants. A particularly generous gift of instruments was received in 2013 from Robert Levine—two violins and a viola, with bows and cases. Levine, a prominent pediatric cardiologist in the New York City area, attended the conference on and off for many years. Stephen Reid recalls playing in the "lunch time concert series centered around string quartet performances" that Levine ran at his New Jersey hospital center. When Levine retired from playing, he donated his instruments to the conference. Participants Mort Raff and Albert

Wray also left their instruments to the conference. These gifts have been offered for sale to conferees, as wished by the donors. In early 2014, Stephen Reid was able to report to the conference community that "quite a number of instruments and bows and cases were sold to Conference members—a great response to the thought that these items could remain with Conferees and thus continue the connection to their former owners."

Many participants at retirement, or their heirs after their death, have donated their music libraries to the conference, as was the case when Frank Mallory's extensive library of clarinet-inclusive parts and scores, along with his own inimitable arrangements of diverse works for saxophones and other ensembles, was donated by his widow, Sally Mallory, in 2018. Norman Pickering's extensive collection was also donated to the conference, as were Pat Stenberg's library and Albert Wray's collections, which Wray had opened to the conference before it organized its own library. Drawing on the conference's library for parts for free-time reading sessions, participants are likely to experience a rush of nostalgia upon opening the music and finding the former owner's name—a musical friend or acquaintance no longer at the conference.

Jennings
Music
Building

XI. Postlude

All things shall perish from under the sky.
Music alone shall live,
Music alone shall live,
Music alone shall live—never to die.

—"Himmel und Erde," traditional folk song
sung as a round at conference welcome meetings

I N EARLY 2019, Mike Kong, chair of the conference
board of directors, received an email from the conference services coordinator at Bennington College
requesting an in-person meeting. Kong immediately knew something was wrong—this was certainly "an
odd and unprecedented request," in Kong's experience in
negotiating renewals of the conference's rental agreement
with the college.

In a phone call the next day, Kong learned that starting in
2020, the Bennington campus would no longer be available
to the conference. As Bennington College later announced
publicly, it had agreed to make its entire campus available to
Middlebury College for the operation of several of Middlebury's
summer language programs. After a total of sixty-seven years
at Bennington, including a highly successful run since 1975, the
conference would have to find a new home.

Participant free-play sessions in the Jennings music
building at Bennington College often continued
well into the evening, as seen here in 2008.

Photo by Claire Stefani

A week later, Kong shared this information with the conference community via the conference email list, and while noting that the 2019 conference at Bennington would go ahead as planned, he further explained that a committee of the board was hard at work identifying a new site.

Although moving to a new site was an eventuality that the conference board had long considered and planned for, as much as such a situation could be planned for—recall that as long ago as 1991 the board visited Colgate University, and the conference had held successful alternative weeks at both Colgate and Vassar University in 2001 and 2002, respectively—such a change was fraught with significance, both logistically and, for many conferees, emotionally.

By mid-July, during the conference's final Week 1 at Bennington College, Kong announced on behalf of the board that the site committee, after considering 350 candidate sites and making visits to fourteen, had unanimously recommended Colgate University as the conference's new location following the 2019 session.

An Endless Summer

Two generations of musicians have attended the conference during its time at Bennington College, and more than fifteen years have passed since any have attended the conference anywhere else. The conference has become so strongly associated with the location that it is often referred to simply as "Bennington," as in "are you going to Bennington this summer?" The conference even wrapped the location name into its brand; in 2013, it started using "Bennington Chamber Music Conference" as its name—then dropped "Bennington" in 2019 in anticipation of relocating.

Over the decades, the conference, held on the same campus and only in July and August, has given returning conferees the experience of a timeless, seemingly unchanging season of summer. Memories of Bennington are likely to be not just of making music and new friends, but of the place itself, and its place in nature.

Multiple walks daily from the college houses or dining hall to the Jennings music building, and back again, took participants past the campus pond, perhaps with mist hanging over it in the cool of the morning, a great blue heron carefully stalking among the cattails. Or returning from Jennings after the last reading session of the night, the stroll along the gravel path was accompanied by the clunking and roaring, snoring and peeping, clicking and chirping sounds of green frogs, chorus frogs, wood frogs, bullfrogs—all manner of pond-resident Bennington amphibians.

The Jennings music building surely has a special place in the memory of every past conferee. From year to year, the trumpet vine seemed to extend its reach even further, as though it would soon enter the third-floor windows, returning the entire granite structure back to nature. Summer rainstorms racing up the valley could be counted on to erupt violently—as if on schedule in the middle of an afternoon coaching session—and then end just as suddenly.

Jennings was perhaps most dramatic at night. With open windows brightly lit, it was like a giant music box gone berserk, emitting multiple simultaneous streams of music. Passing by, one might hear a Brahms piano quartet dominating the Charles Ivesian mix, which would then phase into a Dohnányi sextet, which in turn would be supplanted by a Mozart wind serenade.

Just down the hill, the Carriage Barn—old-timers might recall that it was once the Paul Robeson House, but later came to be called the Deane Carriage Barn—cast a special spell. Faculty clarinetist Allen Blustine remembers the Carriage Barn as having "the best acoustics of any place I've played." When composer and violinist Alison Nowak (later a conference faculty member) played the tape of her 1970 Bennington College senior year concert for Charles Wuorinen at Columbia University, Wuorinen listened and then recalled, "That sounds like the Carriage Barn—with its fine acoustics."

Glancing skyward on the walk to a faculty concert in Greenwall Auditorium, participants could marvel at the cerulean sky, the moon rising over the mountains to the east, and, perhaps during the conference's last week, just a tinge of color in the trees to remind one that fall comes early in Vermont. Later at night, urban-dwelling participants in particular, accustomed to their light-polluted environments, were astonished at the well-defined Milky Way and constellations. Those hoping for a glimpse of the annual Perseid meteor shower were more often disappointed than not. It is no wonder that amateur astronomers frequently set up their telescopes on the Commons lawn, with conferees lined up to take turns viewing the rings around Saturn or craters on the moon.

If the conference seemed like an endless summer at Bennington, that was of course an illusion. Change—indeed, the finality of change—has always been part of the conference experience. As every musical performance comes to an end, what remains is silence and a memory. At the conference, just as newcomers are welcomed, friends who no longer return are missed, and remembered in necrologies in the conference concert program. Beloved faculty oboist Pat Stenberg, whose death in 2002 was a very painful change for many conferees, referenced the persistence of memory in, of all things, a limerick she titled "Melancholia":

> *The Bennington campus is dark;*
> *Cold silence . . . places to park.*
> *Dear friends have gone home,*
> *Where they think of this poem,*
> *And the lingering call of the lark.*

On every musician's path is the point where the music making ends. Marty Lipnick, who first attended in 1964, decided to retire from playing at a certain age, after logging roughly half a century at the conference. The oboe, Lipnick said—he remained his own toughest, outspoken critic—was "not fun . . . for me or anyone who might be listening to me!" After seventy years of violin playing, muscle pain forced former Administrative Director Judith Ensign to retire from playing in 2015. She found a new avocation in writing, including the essay quoted as the epigraph to the first chapter of this book. Ensign's essay has this conclusion: "Memories are all that are left to me now. . . . My music room holds only echoes of the past. Its silence is a sound I will have to get used to."

But as Music Director Tobias Werner said, out of concern that a sense of sadness and loss might weaken commitment to the conference, "nostalgia can be a dangerous thing." Indeed, recollections of the past must lead to imaginings of the future. Ultimately, remembering the conference's long stay at Bennington College also leads to recalling that the place, while a signature aspect, was always subsidiary to the music making itself.

The Last Notes

Like a jilted lover who begins to catalog newly apparent deficiencies in the former beloved, the conference community quickly found ways to begin to distance itself from its long-term site and look to the future. In the last summer at Bennington College in 2019, the long-awaited reopening of the renovated Commons dining hall, for example, proved to be an abject acoustic failure, where it was impossible to converse without shouting. Greenwall Auditorium seemed to go out of its way to confirm its reputation as an inappropriate venue for faculty concerts—as a sweatbox with abysmal acoustics. "We won't miss this!" became a commonly spoken phrase in the summer of 2019. And of course the college's stultifying coaching and sleeping spaces provided a fine reason for participants to celebrate the prospect of Colgate's air-conditioned venues.

During that last summer at Bennington, the Saturday night parties were an occasion for participants to treat the topic of relocation with humor and satire. Participant pianist Richard Friedberg, in mock-serious monologue, disclosed that the actual reason for the decision to move to Colgate University was Bennington College's failure to honor the conference's request for a long-sought-after addition to dorm bathroom amenities: toothpaste. Participant flutist Peggy Greb shared with partygoers some of the questions that had come up at the "lunch with the board" session earlier in the week. Participants, it appeared, wanted assurances that Colgate would be up to Bennington's standards when it came to features like dorm room doors that close themselves with a loud slam in the middle of the night, leaving the room occupant locked outside without a key.

Even Joel Berman's lecture on Beethoven's opus 135 string quartet was adapted to address the relocation, with the title "Farewell to Bennington—Muss es sein?" Berman described the work thus, giving new relevance to this great masterpiece:

> The [viola] and [cello] ask the grim question "Muss es sein?" from the depths of their instruments. Response is worried as the upper three voices dither in canonic disarray. Tension grows and responses become shrill, then terrified. Fear subsides and players are drained, 'til in joyful surprise the Allegro ... brings us the true answer.

On the afternoon of August 10, 2019, the final Participant Musicale in the Carriage Barn concluded with a performance of the Composers' Forum participant work with cellist Anne Taylor playing alone the last note. Not long after, the final kids' concert ended with a rendition, by the entire contingent, of Rodgers and Hammerstein's "So Long, Farewell," with successive groups of kids exiting the stage, one by one, waving goodbye. That evening, Heinrich Isaac's "Innsbruck, ich muss dich lassen" (Innsbruck, I must leave you) was included in the madrigal singing outside Greenwall Auditorium before the faculty's last concert.

Resonant with Potentiality

If there is a lesson in the conference's history, perhaps it is that change is ceaseless, and while conferees might on occasion savor the sadness that accompanies change, they are just as likely to look forward with positive anticipation to what is next. After all, this is what the experience of musicians is all about.

Chamber music players, although they enjoy returning to long-familiar favorites, are also on the lookout for the next thing—a previously unfamiliar work that is not much more than a minor addition to the literature; a fun one-time read; or that yet unknown masterpiece. As Otto Luening put it in 1977, "every piece may not be a hit," but hoping to find those that are motivates many participants to engage with experiments in new music. The Composers' Forum, as it was redesigned about two decades ago into the form in which we know it today, provides opportunities for precisely that. Today's Composers' Forum brings together the two sides of the conference that had for so many years been divided—the composer and the amateur player sides.

Making music—whether new or old—is an act of bringing something to life, creating it anew each time. New music at the conference is an explicit invitation to engage in an experiment, but even the most familiar music offers an opportunity for discovery. In keeping with this commitment to what is new, while referencing the past, the conference will greet its seventy-fifth year with four new chamber music commissions from Donald Crockett, Hannah Lash, Elizabeth Ogonek, and Kurt Rohde.

There is little question that the conference itself is, as Lionel Nowak put it in 1978, "alive and well"—with stable, ongoing management, representing the interests of participants and faculty and engaging with the future through a thoughtful planning process; a reliable funding base and sustainable financial plan; involvement of a large number of volunteers in a wide range of functions that add value to the organization; and a program, developed over many decades, that meets the deep need that participants have for personal musical enrichment and learning. But most important, the conference is supported by a vibrant community of musicians, as evidenced by a very high rate of participant longevity and by faculty who similarly return year after year.

Are there broader cultural or demographic trends on the horizon that might affect the conference's future? In the culturally diverse environment of the early twenty-first century, some say that classical music inherently perpetuates a racist, class-based, and gender-biased culture, worthy of abandonment. Could it be that classical music is already well on the way of being discarded as an irrelevant historical artifact? Worrying rumors about the demise of classical music are certainly persistent (as Charles Rosen reportedly put it, "The death of classical music is perhaps the oldest tradition of classical music"), but they remain rumors only. Indeed, the perception that the conference has an increasingly older population has been a source of concern within the conference—for decades. The disappearance of music instruction in so many public schools is a cause of despair among many musicians who were first introduced to music making as schoolchildren, although there is no discernible impact on the number of musicians coming to the conference. At the same time, a music critic in an arts and culture magazine circulated nationally can refer in 2014 to this as the "golden age of the string quartet."[106] And it is likely that most, if not all, conference participants will know exactly what he meant in saying that.

For a delineating perspective on how things have changed, the conference was well into its first decade before the widespread availability of chamber music recordings on long-playing vinyl records. Similarly, when the conference started, chamber music parts and scores were available only from specialized music retailers or chamber music collections in public or academic libraries. And the available editions of works were limited. The Peters Edition, with its iconic and immediately recognizable cover design, dominated the field and defined for many musicians the chamber music canon.

All that has changed—and in ways that the first generation of conference participants could not have imagined. Remember that set of string quartets by F. X. Richter, referenced in the introductory chapter to this book, that Dittersdorf delighted in playing at his chamber music party in 1757? The parts to those quartets, in the original edition, are now available for free online, as is a professional quartet recording.

Now, in the digital age, music streaming services make multiple professional recordings, including archival recordings, of many works (including the most obscure) readily available for listening and study. Since 2006, IMSLP (International Music Score Library Project/Petrucci Music Library)—founded by an amateur musician—has revolutionized open access to public domain scores and parts. At the same time, traditional publishing houses have replaced older editions (indeed, those Peters Editions are among them) of standard works with new, urtext editions, giving players the option of playing the music as notated and intended by the composer. Playing directly from these or other digital parts is the inevitable next step. Nothing more needs to be said about how the present seems resonant with potentiality for the conference as an organization with a mission of "learning and growth" for amateur musicians.

If there is something timeless about this history, with its references to the distant musical past and the anticipation of music in the future, that timelessness resides in the memories of everyone who has been touched and moved by the music,

by their own music making, and by the fellowship of the conference—the shared common language of chamber music.

Acknowledgments

The publication of *The Music of Friends* is just one of the ways in which the Chamber Music Conference is celebrating its 75th anniversary. The board of directors began planning for these activities five years in advance, in 2015. By early 2016, the board's 75th anniversary committee, co-chaired by Barbara "Bobby" Kipp and Claire Stefani, was reporting to the board not just on a written history of the conference, but also on several other ambitious, coordinated projects. Among these was the review and organization of archival photographs and recordings as part of a potential online history archive, an oral history project (also available online), the commissioning and performance of new works during the 2020 session, and an anniversary-focused fundraising campaign.

By the fall of 2016, the anniversary committee had refined its proposed anniversary plan to include "a number of activities and initiatives to commemorate and celebrate this important milestone." The goals were preserving and honoring the past, gathering in celebration of the present, inspiring and implementing a vision for future success, and raising funds to ensure the conference's future. The committee's strategy of chronicling the conference's history and "telling the story" was intended to enhance the conference's learning from its past to aid future planning, to be a means of recruiting new participants, faculty, and composers, and to expand the conference's donor base. And by early 2017, through a request-for-proposal process, I was chosen to research and write the organizational history.

The writing of this history was overseen by an editorial board of volunteer conference participants. Serving in various ways and at different times as a content focus group, a collective fact-checker, a book design and production directorate, a knowledge and resource bank on all manner of historical detail—and, perhaps most important, as a cheering section—the members of the editorial board continuously oversaw the book's writing.

Each member of the committee deserves to be individually thanked. Early on, Richard Beales provided a healthy dose of skepticism about the entire undertaking, persuasively advised on many matters of style, helped identify a book designer and printer, and later oversaw crucial aspects of the final production. Zeke Hecker made many practical suggestions about how to approach the writing and exercised a keen editorial eye. I quickly learned I could count on his warm encouragement, no matter what, and, as a relative newcomer to the conference, he offered a uniquely important non-insider's view. Dianne Mahany, a long-time participant and conference board member, not only provided her own valuable viewpoint on the organizational changes that took place over more than forty years, but also brought her nuanced sense of editorial propriety to the manuscript review. Dan Rodgers shared his helpful experience as a published author, and when my focus on historical matters was not quite what the editorial board had envisioned, he gave the needed redirection with extraordinary courtesy. He also helped reorganize several chapters, making the book a far more coherent narrative than it would be otherwise. Hugh Rosenbaum, another long-term conferee, provided feedback that kept the story relevant to the conference and theme-focused, instead of following the irresistible but far-reaching story lines that present themselves to a curious author.

Two members of the editorial board deserve special acknowledgment and thanks. First, Bobby Kipp—project manager extraordinaire—took on the leadership of the editorial board, guiding every step of the writing and editing, as well as the production schedule, while also keeping up with reading and commenting on drafts and revisions, and contributing her own "conference by the numbers" sidebar to the book. She did all that with a boundless enthusiasm for the project and a seemingly endless supply of positive energy and patience. It is no exaggeration to say that without her, this book would not have been completed on time, if at all. Next, after the board had reviewed and commented on the draft manuscript, Theresa Schlafly, who had already been closely involved in selecting a designer and printer, took on the enormous task of final editing and proofreading, as well as compiling the indices of musical works and names. Her attention to detail and careful, thoughtful editing improved the manuscript immeasurably. She also assembled the final text for the designer, including placing numerous sidebars and integrating the more than seventy captioned photos, and coordinated the final review of the designer's page proofs.

In sum, the members of the editorial board were indispensable to the process of bringing this book into existence. They were always a pleasure to work with, and I cannot thank them enough. But if my description of this process suggests that this book was "written by a committee," I want to emphasize that both as a group and as individual readers, the editorial board always respected my own judgments as a researcher and author about how the conference's story should be told.

Several members of the conference community who have important perspectives on this history were involved as well. Marilyn Bell, as a former staff member and long-time conferee, served as an unofficial member of the editorial board, and generously read drafts as they went through several stages of writing and revision. In interviews, she called on her own recollections going back to 1975 and provided many valuable corrections and additions to the manuscript with encouragement in equal measure. The almost-final draft benefited immensely from thoughtful and detailed comments from conference Executive Director Susie Ikeda and from Mike Kong, chair of the conference's board of directors. Marilyn, Susie, and Mike provided their long-term insiders' perspective on the conference's workings and ensured factual accuracy on many, many important historical points, as well as offering useful comments on style and expression. We all owe them our deepest gratitude.

Laura Lis Scott of Book Love Space was responsible for the design of this book, a painstaking process to which she brought a high level of professional expertise combined with personal enthusiasm.

Special thanks go to Judith Ensign, not only for taking the time to meet me for a lengthy interview in North Bennington during the conference in 2018, but also for her generosity in sharing her unpublished essay, "Echoes of a Violin," which is quoted in the first and final chapters.

I thank Stephen Poppel for his thoughtful advice, for sharing a variety of informative documents from his early years at the conference, and for assisting with the retrieval of scores and other documents relating to composer Moses Kligsberg.

Quite a few conference outsiders deserve thanks. Dona Brown, professor of history at the University of Vermont, generously shared information on source materials for her insightful article "Vermont as a Way of Life," which covers Alan Carter's early years in Vermont and his founding of the Vermont Symphony Orchestra. Early in the writing, Michael Harrington drew on his many years of experience as a professional journalist and editor to provide valuable advice and editorial insights on the first several chapters. Thomas Schuttenhelm shared his perspective as a music historian and composer, providing encouraging feedback on those early chapters as well. Tyler Resch, currently librarian at the Bennington Museum (and formerly the editor of the Bennington Banner and one-time director of publications at Bennington College—surely a more knowledgeable source for local history does not exist) commented on historical sources, reviewed excerpts, and shared his own recollections about people at the conference.

One great personal disappointment for me was that, due to his final illness in 2019, I was not able to interview a central figure in the conference's history—the composer Mario Davidovsky. Martin Brody and Anne Shreffler, however, interviewed Davidovsky in 2015, and that interview focused on his involvement in the conference both before and after the 1974 organizational split at Johnson State College. I thank them for sharing their interview with me and for granting permission to quote from it.

Before his death in 2019, the composer Chou Wen-chung, with the help of his assistant, Belinda Quan, very generously provided materials, including correspondence, music parts and scores, and recordings, from composer Moses Kligsberg. Chou also provided photographs from his personal collection, which are gratefully acknowledged.

Research for this history benefited significantly from a number of institutional resources, and I have nothing but appreciation for the generosity of the staff who have assisted me in a wide variety of ways—facilitating my visits, answering my many questions, and providing copies of photographs and documents:

Ray Banas, Department Head, Music Department, and Leanne Fallon, Chamber Music Librarian, Parkway Central Library, Free Library of Philadelphia

Gunnar Berg, Archivist, and Vital Zajka, Information Manager, YIVO Archive, Institute for Jewish Research

Raymond Brior, Technical Services Librarian, and Lauren Philie, Director of Development and Alumni Relations, Northern Vermont University–Johnson

Prudence Doherty, Public Services Librarian, Special Collections and University Archives, Howe Memorial Library, University of Vermont

Karson Kiesinger, Reference and Adult Services Librarian, Bennington Free Library

Eleanor Long, Orchestra Manager, Vermont Symphony Orchestra

Laura Payne, Public Service Coordinator, Crossett Library, and Susan Reiss, Jennings Music Librarian, Bennington College

Bernard Schwartz, Director, Unterberg Poetry Center, 92nd Street Y

Mikaela Taylor, Postgraduate Fellow, and Joseph Watson, Preservation Manager, Special Collections and Archives, Middlebury College

Special thanks are due to the Special Collections and University Archives of the University of Vermont for providing access to their collection, *Alan Carter and the Vermont State Orchestra Papers*, and for allowing me to quote from Carter's unpublished autobiographical writings. Thanks are due as well to Middlebury College's Special Collections and Archives for the copies of images from the College's 1946 and 1947 conference bulletins and for copies of the images originally published in 1955 in *Vermont Life* magazine. Thanks, too, to the Archives of the YIVO Institute for Jewish Research for providing a photograph of composer Moses Kligsberg.

Throughout its history, the conference was documented by its own highly skilled photographers—including the celebrated Clemens Kalischer—and these images alone tell much about the conference. John F. Smith Jr. took what are among the earliest surviving photos from the conference, published originally in *Vermont Life* magazine in 1955. I thank his daughter Sandra Roberge and her siblings, Karen Smith and Matthew Smith, for graciously giving us permission to reprint those photographs.

The outstanding contributions of the two most recent conference photographers deserve acknowledgment. Alice Berman provided access to her extensive collection of photographic materials, covering 1976 to 1993, and assisted with the identification of the subjects in those revelatory images. From 1992 on, Claire Stefani photographed the conference, resulting in a huge collection of film and digital images, which she cataloged and made available for this history. With such a rich archive of images, the effort involved in organizing, sorting, and selecting images for publication was an enormous one—with often the most difficult decision being what *not* to include. Claire and Bobby Kipp joined me in spending many, many hours in that effort.

So many people helped in so many other ways. They provided interviews, answered follow-up questions, volunteered advice on important topics, suggested leads for information and sources, shared personal photos, press clippings, and concert programs, and, in one case during an archival research trip, even housed me in their home. Many of them are quoted directly while many others provided useful background information and confirmed information I had obtained elsewhere. I am grateful to them all: Norman Abrams, Beth Anderson, Dane Anderson, Robert Baksa, Edwin Barker, Eric Bartlett, Larry Bell, Marilyn Bell, Melvin Berger, Joel and Alice Berman, Allen Blustine, Ardith Bondi, Neil Boyer, Roger Brooks, Phillip Bush, Kathy Canning, Zita Carno, Gerald Carp, Eric Chasalow, Chou Wen-chung, Don Cohen, Elisabeth Cohen, Emma Cohen, Jeffrey Cornelius, Donald Crockett, Frank Daykin, Jane Deckoff, James Dunne, Emily Fine, Ann Franke, Gina Genova, Cora Gordon, Peggy Greb, John Greenwood, Karen Greif, Shem Guibbory, Zeke Hecker,

Jennifer Higdon, Reinhard Humburg, Susie Ikeda, Melvin Kaplan, David Karrick, Keith Kendig, Janel Kim, Bobby Kipp, Ralph Kirmser, Larry Kohorn, Mike Kong, Alexander Kouguell, Hannah Lash, Cheryl Lawson, Jacqueline Leclair, Louise Lerner, Marty and Sylvia Lipnick, Susan Lurie, Stephen Lustig, Dianne Mahany, Stephen Manes, Pat Manley, Trish Maxson, Victoria Miller, Maxine Neuman, Jonathan Newmark, Alison Nowak, Robert Nowak, Tina Pelikan, Lewis Paer, Katie Morton Peña, Stephen Poppel, James Primosch, Belinda Quan, Daniel Raff, Linda Reichert, Stephen Reid, Susan Reiss, Sandra Roberge, Hugh and Rowena Rosenbaum, Charlotta Ross, Howard Rovics, Frederic Rzewski, Theresa Schlafly, Anita Schmukler, Vivien Schweitzer, Robert Sharon, Allen Shawn, Martha Somach, Claire Stefani, Suzanne Stevens, Lauren Goldstein Stubbs, Matt Stubbs, Fan Tao, Judy Tobey, Emily Toll, Joshua Tonkel, Raymond Tonkel, Rosemary Waltzer, Abby Wells, Tobias Werner, Robert Wigness, Julie and Brian Wolfe, Maurice Wright, Anne Zindars, and Helene Zindarsian.

I have saved for last my most important acknowledgment of heartfelt thanks to my wife, Jeannine, who has been unstinting in her enthusiasm and support for this project—and whose patience with me during the long-term distraction of this project knows no bounds. Our shared love of music brought us together, and, as it happened—yet another episode in the music of friends—that coming together took place at the conference, too.

Notes on Sources

The conference celebrated its fiftieth anniversary with its first published history, *Fifty Vermont Summers of Chamber Music*. Written by Francis Church and Harold Laufman, that historical account—although not without its flaws—was an invaluable starting point for my own research, particularly with the addition of annotations and comments from Dianne Mahany or collected by her from others.

In September 2007, board member Kay Cynamon undertook an organizational archiving project. Unknown at the time to anyone on the board or staff, including Cynamon herself, her activities would prove to be crucial for my research. Reporting to the board in August 2008, she noted how she "retrieved materials from CMC storage room in Jennings and also from Joe Schor's basement," a reference to the North Bennington home of the conference's long-term violin faculty member and several-times music director. A call was put out to all conferees to donate materials relating to the conference to the archive. "All retrieved materials are currently stored in Steve Reid's attic," she explained. Eventually, through her efforts, scanned documents and electronic files were uploaded to an online repository, thus making it possible for me to access these materials remotely.

The conference's attendance directories—we have them for all but six years in the conference's history—provide a reasonably reliable account of who was in attendance, although a full listing indicating each person's role (staff, composer, or amateur player?) did not begin until 1960. Although we do not have directories from the Middlebury College years (1946–1950), or for the first year at Bennington College (1951), much can be pieced together from Middlebury's annual conference bulletins and brochures. Published accounts, including those by writers such as Alfred Frankenstein and Theodore Strongin, also provide many details about the conference's early years. Concert programs for the early years are another source of information about who was in attendance. By about 1960, we have board minutes for almost every board and executive committee meeting, and although these documents, varying as they do in formality, level of detail, and inclusion of background context, sometimes present their own very special puzzles, they give an inside look at how the conference was run.

The comprehensive listing of composers and faculty members included in the appendices was based primarily on annual conference directories. Conference directories, however, do not exist or were unavailable for six of the seventy-five years. Promotional brochures and flyers issued prior to that year's conference, faculty concert programs, internal conference documents, and news media accounts were relied on to fill any apparent gaps. But those materials, too, are not entirely complete in the conference's archives for all years. While extensive efforts have gone into making these lists as accurate as possible, errors and omissions are certainly possible, and we regret them.

Although I have cited many published sources in the endnotes, the editorial board and I agreed it would be wise to dispense with citations to materials not accessible to the general reader—for example, conference board minutes or similar internal organizational documents—in order not to overburden the reader. Readers should be able to infer easily from references in the text when the narrative draws from these materials. Images without source identification were drawn from the conference's own archives.

In researching and writing *The Music of Friends*, I have relied on some outstanding recent publications, among them Edward Klorman's *Mozart's Music of Friends* and Marie Sumner Lott's *The Social Worlds of Nineteenth-Century Music*. For those interested in a deeper read about amateurs in the history of music, I recommend them both as excellent sources on chamber music in the context of social settings that involved a significant amateur population. Although the focus is by no means exclusively on amateur music making, every serious student of chamber music should be familiar with John H. Baron's *Intimate Music: A History of the Idea of*

Chamber Music (his first chapter alone, "The Idea of Chamber Music," is a highly engaging discussion of the concept itself). And not just for string players is Christina Bashford's essay, "The String Quartet and Society," in *The Cambridge Companion to the String Quartet*—one of the first attempts to take a serious look at the social context for chamber music. Similarly, Leon Botstein's chapter on Beethoven's "patrons and publics," in *The Beethoven Quartet Companion*, provides fascinating details about amateur musicians in that context.

Author's Note

My work on this history was informed by my own experience as a conference participant. I first attended in 1992 as a double bassist whose previous experience was largely limited to orchestral playing.

As the saying goes, I was hooked, and have returned every summer since.

The conference supported my eager exploration of the major thoroughfares and the far more numerous byways in the chamber music literature that includes the bass. Illustrative of the heady experiences that seemed to come my way every summer, in 1993 I asked to be coached on Charles Wuorinen's *Turetzky Pieces*, a trio for clarinet, flute, and double bass. The coach was Bertram Turetzky himself, the bassist that Wuorinen had written for, and one who was for me, ever since my high school days, legendary. And if that were not remarkable enough in itself, Turetzky turned out to be an extraordinarily supportive and generous mentor. Another faculty bassist and composer, Salvatore Macchia, not only was a wonderful mentor to me, but became a dear family friend. He was to write *Kvell*, a birthday trio for the birth of my son Dylan, which I first performed at the conference in 2001. Salvatore went on to write other pieces for me—a quartet for my daughter Elena's birth, and, later, a duo piece as a wedding present for my clarinetist wife Jeannine and me. Indeed, the conference has literally been for me, as for so many others, the music of friends.

This history project was an opportunity for me to turn from a career in public interest law, public health advocacy, and nonprofit fundraising, and to return to music history—a field of study I had abandoned long ago, having dropped out of the graduate program in musicology at New York University to pursue a law degree. I must confess, it has been an enormous pleasure to leave the law behind, and to trade writing and updating legal treatises for researching and writing about the evolution of a nonprofit organization in the

In this photo from 1992, my first year at the conference, participant violinist Arthur Newmark, a friend of mine from Philadelphia, and I are consulting our dance cards, no doubt to schedule a free-time reading session.

Photo by Claire Stefani

context of contemporary musical culture. This project has also been an opportunity to work with many of my long-time friends, to renew old friendships that had languished, and, at the same time, to make new friends and acquaintances, both at the conference and in the world beyond it. I will always be grateful for having been given this opportunity.

Like most if not all conferees, I knew next to nothing about the conference's history when I first arrived as a participant—and the conference was already forty-seven years old at that point. I served on the board of directors for about thirteen years beginning in 1996, so that provided me somewhat of an insider's view, at least for those few years. But as I began to research the earlier years that I knew nothing about, I realized that the conference's early history is a keyhole view of the post-war new music scene, a scene that extends to the present. This project did indeed involve the discovery of a place that was unknown to me, yet—perhaps like stepping through a mirror—no matter how unknown or different it is, you already know it. The conference's story really is like that. If you think of the first year, it is a mix of musicians, amateur and professional, with composers—and, in 2020 and beyond, no matter how much it has changed (and there have been profound changes over the years), it is still that mix of musicians, amateur and professional, with composers. And it remains the music of friends.

Conference Faculty 1946–2019

Years indicate the first year of attendance. This listing includes all professional musicians identified as conference "staff" or "faculty" including guest and visiting faculty members.

Violin

Allen, Doris (1964)
Allen, Sanford (1987)
Anderson, Rebecca (2018)
Beal, Gerald (1972)
Berman, Joel (1967)
Berofsky, Aaron (2007)
Black, Arnold (1982)
Briesmeister, Ernestine (1963)
Brooker, Anita (1980)
Bruce, Diane (1990)
Buswell, James (2016)
Chung, Sonya (2017)
Cohen, Diana (2009)
Cohen, Isidore (1992)
Coonce, Phillip (1989)
deBlasiis, Virginia (1946)
Diaz, Gabriela (2012)
Dimmick, Charles (2013)
Eisenberg, Marcella (1994)
Eissenberg, Judith (2005)
Fortes, Alex (2019)
Fransen, Delbert (1968)
Freyhan, Michael (1970)
Fryer, Anne H. (1964)
Fuks, Mauricio (1981)
Fukuhara, Mayuki (1990)
Galluzzo, Amy (2015)
Genova, Joana A. (2007)
Gibson, Jerre (1965)
Goldstein, Nathan (1954)
Graf, Vera (1963)
Graybeal, Melissa (1989)
Guibbory, Shem (1982)
Gussow, Olga (1985)
Hamilton, Laura (2004)
Hegyi, Julius (1965)
Ideler, Edwin (1946)
Ingraham, Jeanne (1983)

Jenner, Joanna (1982)
Jolles, Renée (1994)
Judd, Kathy (2016)
Kadlubkiewicz, Veronika (2001)
Kalisch, Joan (1967)
Kantorowicz, Lilo (1985)
Kobayashi, Kenji (1966)
Kornacker, Thomas (1988)
Lenski, Kathleen (1999)
Lester, Joel (1992)
Levite, Myron (1977)
Lewis, Megumi Stohs (2013)
Lieberman, Carol (1980)
Lim, Sunghae Anna (2008)
MacLean, Janet (1966)
Macomber, Curtis (1992)
Marder, Samuel (1973)
Mark, Bob (1973)
Marx, Karen (2000)
Monosoff, Sonya (1984)
Namkung, Yuri (2018)
Nemkov, Solomon (1953)
Nowak, Alison (1969)
Nowinski, William (1961)
Oakland, Ronald (1975)
Ohmes, Alan (1960)
Otani, Muneko (2016)
Pepper, Joseph (1964)
Picard-Dunietz, Shelly (1992)
Pitchon, Joel (2007)
Pollikoff, Max (1953)
Rogers, Alvin (1970)
Rosenberg, Sylvia (1998)
Rosenblith, Eric (1981)
Rosenthal, Linda (1999)
Ross, Paul (1970)
Sato, Eriko (1995)
Sawyer, Priscilla (1952)

Schiller, Alan (1964)
Schleuning, Maria (2012)
Schor, Joseph (1959)
Schultz, Andrea (1999)
Schwartz, Cornelia (2010)
Schweigart, Stephanie (2005)
Shapiro, Rachel Kitagawa (2018)
Sherba, Charles (1996)
Smiley, Alice (1984)
Spencer, Peggy James (1982)
Steen, Marjorie Hill (1970)
Stern, James (2017)

Svilokos, Andrew (1961)
Tong, Kristopher (2017)
Tower, Marjorie (1954)
Trépanier, Annie (2009)
Waterbury, Susan (2007)
Wetherbee, Charles (2015)
Wiersma, Calvin (2007)
Wilk, Maurice (1948)
Wolfe, Paul C. (1956)
Wong, Deborah (1994)
Yanagita, Masako (1984)
Yannatos, James (1985)

Viola

Adams, Sarah (2000)
Albers, Rebecca (2010)
Azikiwe, Amadi (2011)
Becker, Eugene (1997)
Benjamin, Robert (1970)
Berger, Melvin (1957)
Caldwell, Brenton (2009)
Carbone, Ronald (1995)
Cline, Jennifer (2000)
Coletta, Harold (1995)
Consiglio, Catherine (2002)
Cords, Nicholas (2000)
Elsevier, Désirée (2004)
Fader, Laurence (1964)
Farina, Danielle (2000)
Fay, Paula (1978)
Flagg, Russell D. (1953)
Fujiwara, Korine (2015)
Glick, Jacob (1964)
Gottesman, Joseph (1996)
Grossman, George (1953)
Gustavsson, Marka (2008)
Hansen, Jennie (1989)
Holtz, Deborah (1982)
Horner, Jerry (1973)
Huebner, Christof (1996)
Insell-Staack, Judith (1999)
James, Mary Elliott (1972)
Kaplan, Ynez Lynch (1960)
Koppell, Olivia (1998)
Kozupsky, Willa (1988)
LaMariana, Angelo (1953)
Larson, Steve (2009)
Levine, Caroline (1995)

Loft, Abraham (1952)
Luce, Gregory (2018)
Neu, Ah Ling (1996)
Page, Raymond (1978)
Pelikan, Tina (1988)
Perich, Guillermo (1983)
Pickering, Norman (1979)
Reinhold, Sheila (1999)
Ritscher, Karen (1996)
Rosenblum, Myron (1982)
Royer, Ellen S. (1977)
Rudiakov, Ariel (1994)
Sabinsky, Raymond (1952)
Sachs, Leonard (1977)
Salas, Veronica (1994)
Smith, Derek (2016)
St. Amour, Susan (1988)
Stalberg, Kenneth (1980)
Ting, Liuh-Wen (1996)
Trampler, Walter (1956)
Uscher, Nancy (1987)
Vincent, Kate (2004)
Votapek, Kathryn (2010)
Wheeler, Lawrence B. (1976)
Whitfield, Lisa (2001)

Cello

Anderson, Dane (1970)
Anderson, Donald (1963)
Arron, Edward (1999)
Avins, Styra (1999)
Baun, Nancy (2002)
Bondi, Eugene (1988)
Bryant, Claire (2011)
Chapman, Susannah (2000)
Contino, Adriana (1985)
Esch, Joan Brockway (1963)
Eskin, Jules (1957)
Farnsworth, Dan (1949)
Finckel, Christopher (1965)
Finckel, George (1946)
Finckel, Michael (1969)
Gardner, Robert (1964)
Grinhauz, Leo (1998)
Herren, Matthew (2008)
Horvath, Janet (2008)
Jackson, William (1961)
Jacobsen, Eric (2008)
Kouguell, Alexander (1958)
Krosnick, Joel (1962)
Laufman, Laurien (1982)

Lee, Andrea (2012)
Lipscomb, Ronald (1966)
Moore, Kermit (1989)
Morganstern, Daniel (1965)
Neuman, Maxine (1983)
Ou, Carol (2016)
Oxman, Ralph (1975)
Parke, Nathaniel (1992)
Rath, Lutz (1986)
Rosenfeld, Peter (1965)
Ross, Charlotta Klein (1972)
Scripp, Ashima (2010)
Sebastian, Michael (1980)
Seidenberg, Peter (1999)
Seligman, Susan (1985)
Shuman, Mark (2002)
Stehn, Leonard (1965)
Steinbock, Evalyn (1961)
Sturm, Harry (1977)
Tekula, Joseph (1960)
Tilley, Bettina Roulier (1952)
Wells, David (1995)
Werner, Tobias (2015)
Wilson, James (2009)

Double Bass

Andre, George (1975)
Batchelder, Jane T. (1952)
Berlind, Gary (1961)
Brehm, Alvin (1960)
Doty, Karl (2017)
Gladstone, Robert (1951)
Jacobsen, Alexander (2018)
Kruvand, Gail (1990)
Levine, Jeffrey (1971)
Macchia, Salvatore (1991)
Manzo, Anthony (2017)

Mathews, John (1989)
O'Brien, Orin (1956)
Paer, Lewis (1980)
Petty, Warren (1968)
Powell Eig, Jessica (2018)
Reichler, Ronald (1970)
Shapinsky, Murray (1954)
Turetzky, Bertram (1972)
Walter, David (1964)
Wilson, Barbara (1969)

Flute

Asin, Nadine (2001)
Blaisdell, Frances (1953)
Cohen, Joseph (1952)
Fedele, David (2008)

Fukushima, Mary (2008)
Giese, Richard (1951)
Gilbert, David (1969)
Höskuldsson, Stefán (2004)

Jones, Harold (1992)
Kahn, Sue Ann (1979)
Kershaw, Jean (1960)
Kraber, Karl (1965)
Laughlin, Marilyn (1961)
Lesser, Erin (2010)
Malosh, Tim (1973)
Miller, Sandra (1976)
Mueller, Zizi (2001)
Nelson, Conor (2012)

Nugent, Bärli (1996)
Palma, Susan (1986)
Schaefer, Lois (1957)
Sollberger, Harvey (1963)
Sollberger, Sophie (1964)
Solum, John (1968)
Spencer, Patricia (1975)
Vinci, Jan (1998)
Wykes, Robert (1954)
Zuber, Patricia (2004)

Oboe

Bloom, Robert (1946)
Breczinski, Stuart (2014)
Cohen, Fred (2005)
Cole, Roger (1977)
Dallessio, Richard (2001)
Díaz, Pedro (2002)
Fay, Thomas (1976)
Gatwood, Elden (1975)
Greene, Brian (2000)
Ingliss, Robert (2003)
Kaplan, Melvin (1958)
Kozenko, Lisa (2005)

Lai, Winnie (2008)
Leclair, Jacqueline (2002)
Lehrfeld, Robert (1952)
Marx, Josef (1964)
Pearson, Peggy (2004)
Schuman, Henry (1970)
Schuster, Earl (1957)
Stearns, Anna Petersen (2012)
Stenberg, Patricia (1979)
Sullivan, Matt (2008)
Wilson, Keve (2010)

Clarinet

Ambrosini, Armand (2001)
Blackwell, Virgil (1987)
Blustine, Allan (1965)
Dumouchel, Michael (1975)
Eig, Jeremy (2018)
Faria, Richard (2014)
Fingland, Benjamin (2017)
Flax, Laura (1987)
Guy, Larry (2000)
Gythfeldt, Marianne (2001)
Hartman, Steven (1999)
Heffner, Diane (2001)
Hill, Thomas (2001)

Kay, Alan (1999)
Kirkbride, Jerry (1987)
Lowenstern, Michael (2004)
Martula, Susan (2007)
Palmer, Todd (2017)
Russo, Charles (1959)
Shapiro, Wallace (1951)
Sherry, Morrie (1998)
Smith, Jerry Neil (1992)
Sternberg, Jo-Ann (1997)
Stoops, Meighan (2010)
Vinnitsky, Pavel (2012)
Waldman, Stanley (1964)

Horn

Anderer, Joseph (1979)
Anderer, Virginia Benz (1999)
Benjamin, Barry (2001)

Boden, John (2016)
Byrd-Marrow, David (2016)
Cowan, Daniel (1963)

Donaruma, Frank (1966)
Ellsworth, Ann (2016)
Froelich, Ralph (1959)
Grabois, Dan (2005)
Happe, Richard (1964)
Kramer-Johansen, Karl (2015)
Martin, Jean (1997)
Martin, Michael (1997)

Myers, Philip (1978)
Richman, Albert (1951)
Richmond, Albert (1967)
Rife, Jean (2002)
Snyder, Christine (1975)
Vegter, Alana (2013)
Wakefield, David (1998)
Wions, Dan (2018)

Bassoon

Benjamin, Alice (1990)
Bial, Bert (1954)
Cantor, Lester (1959)
Carroll, David H. (1975)
Dickie, James (1953)
Finn, Michael (1992)
Garfield, Bernard (1951)
Goeres, Nancy (1977)
Kolkay, Peter (2009)
Kushner, Sylvia (1953)
Lawson, Richard (1957)

Lyman, Jeffrey (2009)
Pachman, Maurice (1961)
Rosenberg, Sidney (1989)
Shubin, Matthew (1994)
Steinmetz, John (2001)
Stubbs, Lauren Goldstein (1982)
Taylor, Jane (1979)
Walt, Stephen (1996)
Whipple, James (1976)
Zirkuli, Bernadette (1976)

Piano

Adler, Cynthia (1975)
Andersen, Stell (1951)
Asuncion, Victor Santiago (2016)
Bannister, Tanya (2019)
Berger, Jean (1949)
Bjerken, Xak (2011)
Bogin, Abba (1986)
Bush, Phillip (2007)
Carno, Zita (1967)
Daykin, Frank (2001)
Frugoni, Orazio (1947)
Gainsford, Read (2016)
Goldsworthy, James (1992)
Golka, Adam (2018)
Gordon, Judith (2007)
Grant, Cameron (1999)
Haines, Edmund (1948)
Huebner, Eric (2013)
Kahn, Denise (2010)
Klibonoff, Jon (2008)
Kompass, Lynn (2011)
Laimon, Sara (2018)
Lee, Genevieve Feiwen (2017)

Manes, Stephen (1978)
Marantz, Frederick (1967)
McMillen, Blair (2014)
Miller, Robert (1964)
Muzijevic, Pedja (2009)
Nitsch, Paul (2017)
Nordli, Douglas (1960)
Nowak, Lionel (1951)
Oei, David (1997)
Pessl, Yella (1953)
Ritt, Morey (1990)
Rodríguez, Carlos César (2016)
Rubinsky, Sonia (2001)
Shawn, Allen (1987)
Sielska, Marya (1973)
Spivak, Raul (1946)
Spottiswoode, Daphne (1976)
Tahmizian, Emma (2000)
Wong, Debby (2013)
Wright, Elizabeth (1990)

Accordion

Banic-Curcic, Dragica (2006)

Voice

Bettina, Judith (2015)
Bryden, Jane (1985)
Eyton-Jones, Susanna (2002)
Ferrante, Maria (1999)
Lavanne, Antonia (1963)
Lynch, Ynez (1962)

Harp

Chang, Jocelyn M. (1972)

Saxophone

Regni, Albert (1998)

Trumpet

Anderson, Ronald (1964)
Benedetti, Donald (1962)
Lisenbee, Thomas (1967)
Nagel, Robert, Jr. (1952)

Trombone

Braverman, Fred (1963)
Durham, Nathan (2000)
Fromme, Arnold (1963)
Pearlstein, Abraham (1972)

Percussion

Beiro, Joseph (1977)
Carno, Zita (1972)
Centanni, Barry (2006)
Cook, Richard (1968)
desRoches, Raymond (1964)
Means, Jeffrey (2010)

Improvisation

Nachmanovitch, Stephen (2002)

Markussen, Arne (1961)
Meyer, Carol (2001)
Nickel, Matilda (1957)
Rogers, Earl (1953)
Sollek-Avella, Kirsten (2001)
Turash, Stephanie (1951)

Jolles, Susan (1986)

Shainman, Irwin (1953)
Stubbs, James (2000)
Tanenbaum, Elias (1953)

Philips, Elliot (1951)
Shanman, Jay (1967)
Swallow, John (1953)
Wigness, Robert (1973)

Pearson, Phyllis (1973)
Preiss, James (2000)
Smith, Warren (1965)
Zindars, Earl (1963)

Conference Composers 1946–2019

The year for each composer is the first year of attendance.

Addiss, Stephen (1959)
Adolphe, Bruce (1996)
Aitken, Hugh (1957)
Albright, William (1965)
Alexander, Kathryn (1998)
Ames, Richard (1968)
Ames, William (1953)
Anderson, Beth (1992)
Andrews, Michael (1971)
Arel, Bülent (1959)
Armer, Elinor (1987)
Auznieks, Krists (2015)
Babin, Stanley (1964)
Baker, Larry (1972)
Baksa, Robert (1975)
Baley, Virko (1972)
Ballou, Esther Williamson (1949)
Barbera, Aceste J. M. (1949)
Barnes, Joseph (1967)
Barnes, Larry (1970)
Beale, David (1972)
Bean, Calvert (1954)
Beasley, Rule (1962)
Beck, Frederick W. (1951)
Beckstrom, Xenia (2013)
Beecher, Lembit (2008)
Bell, Larry (1972)
Benavides, Nick (2013)
Benjamin, Thomas (1987)
Benoliel, Bernard (1969)
Berger, Arthur (1966)
Berger, Jean (1949)
Bermel, Derek (2007)
Bertchume, Gary (1971)
Betjeman, Paul (1973)
Bialosky, Marshall H. (1951)
Bielawa, Lisa (2009)
Biscardi, Chester (1973)
Blank, Allan (1962)
Blauvelt, Ralph J. (1970)
Blewett, Quentin, Jr. (1955)
Bloom, Robert (1951)
Blumenfeld, Harold (1970)

Boagni, Edward V. (1961)
Boehnlein, Frank (1970)
Bolaños, Gabriel (2015)
Bond, Victoria (2002)
Boswell, William, Jr. (1970)
Botti, Susan (2011)
Bouchard, Linda (1982)
Brant, Henry (1956)
Bresnick, Martin (1994)
Brezina, William (1972)
Broer, Fred (1970)
Brooks, Richard (1973)
Brouwer, Margaret (1996)
Brown, Elizabeth (1992)
Brown, James E. (1966)
Bruckner, Howard (1959)
Buechner, Margaret (1954)
Bunger, Richard (1967)
Burnham, Cardon V. (1954)
Burrows, David L. (1955)
Calabro, Louis (1953)
Callaway, Ann (1971)
Camacho, Hermes (2008)
Castaldo, Joseph (1953)
Chadabe, Joel (1986)
Chambers, Evan (2008)
Chambers, Stephen (1964)
Chan, Alan (2006)
Chapman, Frederick Harold (1946)
Chen Yi (1998)
Chen, Ying-Lung (2000)
Childs, Barney (1963)
Chinn, Genevieve (1956)
Cho, Sabang (2000)
Chou Wen-chung (1953)
Christoff, Gerald (1967)
Clay, Carlton (1992)
Clayton, Harold (1957)
Cohen, Marcia (1969)
Coker, Wilson W. (1957)
Consoli, Marc-Antonio (1969)
Contreras, Juan Pablo (2017)
Cooper, John (1964)

Corman, Brenda (1962)
Cory, Eleanor (1972)
Cox, Thomas (1971)
Crane, Thomas (1971)
Crego, Clifton (1972)
Crockett, Donald (1999)
Curtis-Smith, Curtis O.B. (1973)
D'Angelo, Nicholas (1973)
Dahl, Ingolf (1948)
Dalgleish, James (1951)
Dashow, James (1968)
Davidovsky, Mario (1969)
Davidson, Tina (1981)
Davis, David (1963)
Day, Fred (1955)
deJong, Conrad (1965)
Del Monico, Alfred (1969)
Denhard, David (1986)
Derr, Ellwood S. (1953)
Diamond, Arline (1963)
DiBerardino, Nick (2016)
Dick, Robert (2007)
Dickman, Stephen (1967)
Diesendruck, Tamar (2002)
Dodge, Charles (1963)
Donovan, Richard F. (1946)
Dority, Bryan (1951)
Dortort, Marcel (1965)
Dougherty, Tommy (2018)
Downey, John (1984)
Duncan, John (1956)
Dure, Robert (1965)
Eaton, John (1974)
Efrein, Laurie (1965)
Eller, Daniel (1960)
Endrich, Thomas J. (1970)
Erb, Donald (1959)
Esmail, Reena (2011)
Fairlie-Kennedy, Margaret C. (1957)
Faris, Marc (2001)
Farmer, Peter (1971)
Feldman, Morton (1965)
Fetner, George (2016)
Fewell, C. Marvin (1953)
Fields, Robert (1968)
Finckel, Michael (1978)
Fine, Vivian (1976)
Firszt, Joseph (1965)
Fisher, Kenneth (1959)
Fishman, C. Marian (1967)

Fitch, Keith (2002)
Fitz Rogers, John (2009)
Fodi, John (1973)
Franceschini, Romulus (1965)
Franco, Clare (1969)
Frank, Gabriela Lena (2004)
Frazelle, Kenneth (2011)
Friar, Sean (2016)
Furrer-Münch, Franz (1969)
Gaber, Harley (1968)
Gamer, Carlton (1953)
Gardner, Mildred (1947)
Gates, Steve (2004)
George, Willard (1950)
Gervais, Aaron (2009)
Ghent, Emmanuel (1962)
Gibson, Sarah (2012)
Girdon, Peggy (1954)
Godfrey, Daniel (2005)
Goeb, Roger (1950)
Golbin, Elsa (1951)
Goldstein, Malcolm (1959)
Golub, Peter (1979)
González, Luis A. (1972)
Goode, Daniel (1973)
Gorbos, Stephen (2005)
Gunderson, Helen (1953)
Gyring, Elizabeth (1951)
Haimo, Ethan (1971)
Haines, Edmund (1948)
Hannay, Roger (1963)
Harbison, John (1964)
Harris, Daniel (1967)
Hart, Jane S. (1961)
Hartke, Stephen (2004)
Hartman, Peter (1960)
Hartway, James (1986)
Hausrath, Lucas (2011)
Hayden, Joel (1947)
Hearne, Ted (2014)
Hedwall, Paul (1969)
Heiss, John (1978)
Helm, Everett (1948)
Henderson, Lorraine (1946)
Henkin, Robert I. (1961)
Higdon, Jennifer (2004)
Hill, Phillip (1959)
Hoffman, Allen R. (1966)
Hollister, David (1960)
Holmes, Jeffrey (2002)

Honeyman, Ian (1998)
Hsu, Chiayu (2008)
Hudson, Joseph (1971)
Israel, Brian (1968)
Itoh, Takuma (2010)
Jaffe, David (1980)
Jaffe, Stephen (2001)
Jalbert, Pierre (2010)
Jankowski, Loretta (1987)
Johnson, David (1956)
Johnson, Hank (1968)
Johnson, Marvin (1966)
Johnson, Thomas (1965)
Johnston, David (1955)
Johnston, Donald (1991)
Jones, Jesse (2016)
Jordan, Roland (1971)
Kang, Jonghee (2016)
Karlins, M. William (1959)
Kates, Morris (1995)
Kaufmann, Henry (1947)
Kennedy, John R. (1951)
Kern, Marcia (1999)
Kestenbaum, Myra (1994)
Kirby, Suzanne (1954)
Kirchoff, Leanna (2006)
Kish, Anne (1959)
Kligsberg, Moses (1953)
Koblitz, David (1972)
Kochins, Thomas (1963)
Koopmans, Tjalling C. (1953)
Koplow, Philip J. (1971)
Korte, Karl (1958)
Kosteck, Gregory (1971)
Kotcheff, Thomas (2015)
Kraft, Leo (1991)
Kramer, Jonathan D. (1970)
Krause, Benjamin (2018)
Laba, Kevin (2012)
Lackey, William (2001)
Laderman, Ezra (1952)
Laird, Helen L. (1949)
Lakner, Yehoshua (1952)
Lam Bun-Ching (1995)
Lang, Thomas (2014)
Larsen, Libby (2003)
Lash, Hannah (2001)
Laske, Otto E. (1969)
Lauer, Elizabeth (1952)
Laufer, Edward (1968)

Lawergren, Bo (1968)
Layman, Pamela (1973)
Lee, Eugene (1971)
Lee, Jookang (1999)
Lehrman, Leonard J. (1970)
Leich, Roland (1976)
Lenel, Ludwig (1947)
Levine, Caroline (1995)
Levine, Elliot (1952)
Levine, Jeffrey (1983)
Levitan, Daniel (1984)
Levitch, Leon (1956)
Levy, Marvin David (1955)
Levy, Paul A. (1969)
Lewis, Peter (1965)
Lewis, Peter Scott (2002)
Liang, Lei (2018)
Lille, Barry (1968)
Lissauer, Fredric (1968)
Littledale, Harold (1951)
Lockwood, Normand (1948)
Loiacono, Loren (2011)
Lowry, Philip W. (1966)
Lubin, Ernest (1950)
Luening, Otto (1946)
Lukewitz, Joseph (1957)
Lusterman, Don-David (1961)
Lutyens, Sally (1968)
Macchia, Salvatore (1999)
Macero, Attilio "Teo" (1955)
MacInnis, Donald (1957)
Mackey, Steven (2005)
Macklay, Sky (2013)
Makan, Keeril (2012)
Mallonée, Caroline (2013)
Mamlok, Ursula (1958)
Manno, Robert (1973)
Mar-Haim, Joseph (1967)
Mårtensson, Bo (2004)
Martin, Judith (1973)
Maslanka, David (1990)
Mathis, James (1970)
Mauzey, Peter (1953)
Mayer, William R. (1951)
McCulloh, Byron (1955)
McDonald, John (2012)
McDowell, John Herbert (1958)
McFerron, Michael (1999)
McGilvra, Douglas (1967)
McGlaughlin, William (2003)

McKinney, Mathilde (1946)
McLean, Barton (1985)
McLennan, John (1951)
McMahan, Herbert C. (1951)
McNulty, Robert (1962)
Mellits, Marc (2017)
Meltzer, Harold (2011)
Merten, Eric (2009)
Mertl, Gregory (2001)
Meyers, William (1977)
Meynaud, Michel (1970)
Miller, Alexander (2009)
Miller, Cynthia (1969)
Miller, Michael (1969)
Miller, Robert (1960)
Mobberley, James (1999)
Moevs, Robert (1992)
Moore, Carman (1967)
Moravec, Paul (1994)
Morrill, Dexter G. (1962)
Morris, Franklin (1968)
Morrow, Charles (1967)
Moryl, Richard (1967)
Mukai, Kohei (2000)
Mumford, Jeffrey (2008)
Murray, Bain (1960)
Nagel, Robert, Jr. (1949)
Nakatani, Yoko (1998)
Nelson, Jordan (2010)
Nelson, Kalvert (1972)
Newmark, Jonathan (1999)
Norman, Andrew (2002)
Nowak, Alison (1973)
Nowak, Lionel (1951)
Nowak, Robert (1976)
O'Brien, Hod (1963)
Olan, David (1973)
Orenstein, Joyce (1970)
Orloff, Natalie (1969)
Osborne, Tom (2003)
Ott, Joseph (1967)
Overton, Hall (1967)
Paccione, Paul (1973)
Payne, William (1967)
Peck, Russell (1967)
Pepe, Carmine (1967)
Perera, Ronald C. (1970)
Perry-Parrish, Josh (2007)
Perskin, Amelia (1953)
Peters, Richard (1956)

Phillips, Burrill (1954)
Pitton, Robert (1954)
Pleskow, Raoul (1964)
Polin, Claire (1964)
Pollock, Robert (1971)
Poor, Harris (1958)
Post, Jennifer (1972)
Powell, Mel (1966)
Powell, Morgan (1971)
Praetorius, Emily (2017)
Price, John E. (1967)
Ptaszyńska, Marta (1973)
Quintanar, Héctor (1973)
Raksin, David (1972)
Raid, Kaljo (1954)
Randall, James (1965)
Rausch, Carlos (1971)
Redding, James (1959)
Reitell, Elizabeth (1952)
Retzel, Frank (1984)
Rhie, Kay (2004)
Richter, Marga (1960)
Rochberg, George (1952)
Rodriguez, Robert Xavier (1982)
Rogers, Patsy (1979)
Rohde, Kurt (2015)
Rollin, Robert Leon (1969)
Roosevelt, J. Willard (1952)
Rosenberg, Philip (1973)
Rosenzweig, Morris (1982)
Roussakis, Nicolas (1959)
Rovics, Howard (1961)
Rutledge, Logan (2017)
Rzewski, Frederic (1954)
Saperstein, David (1967)
Sarvello, Frank (1964)
Saul, Walter B. (1971)
Schiff, David (2003)
Schimmel, Carl (2006)
Schramm, Harold (1964)
Schwartz, Elliott (1961)
Schwendinger, Laura (2014)
Scott, Eric J.Y. (1961)
Sear, Walter (1957)
Shapey, Ralph (1962)
Shapiro, Don (1954)
Shapiro, Nancy (1999)
Shatin, Judith (1997)
Shawn, Allen (1983)
Shepherd, Sean (2014)

Sierra, Roberto (2005)
Silver, George (1956)
Sims, Ezra (1959)
Singleton, Alvin (1968)
Sirulnikoff, Jack (1960)
Slates, Philip M. (1956)
Smith, Russell (1955)
Snider, Sarah (2005)
Snyder, Theodore (1954)
Sollberger, Harvey (1961)
Somer, Avo (1965)
Son, Yung Wha (1996)
Southard, Keane (2019)
Steinke, Greg (1972)
Steinmetz, John (2001)
Stephens, John E. (1957)
Stern, Arthur (1963)
Stevens, Halsey (1946)
Stewart, Robert (1960)
Stires, Ernest, Jr. (1967)
Stock, David (1966)
Stölzel, Ingrid (2004)
Stonaker, Ben (2014)
Strandberg, Newton (1968)
Strilko, Anthony (1954)
Stroh, Virginia (1959)
Strongin, Theodore M. (1947)
Stucky, Steven (2000)
Susser, Peter (1989)
Suter, Anthony (2007)
Sydeman, William Jay (1955)
Tan, Su Lian (1991)
Tanenbaum, Elias (1953)
Tanrikulu, Orhan (1968)
Taylor, Clifford (1958)
Tenney, James (1956)
Thomas, Alan (1955)
Thomas, David Evan (2018)
Thome, Diane (1988)
Thomson, Virgil (1971)
Thórarinsson, Leifur (1964)
Todd, George B. (1966)
Tonkel, Stanley (1951)
Tosar Errecart, Héctor Alberto (1946)
Tower, Joan (1961)
Townsend, Douglas T. (1949)
Toyama, Michiko (1957)
Trimble, Lester (1955)
Trombly, Preston A. (1971)
Ultan, Lloyd (1961)

Usmanbaş, İlhan (1952)
Ussachevsky, Vladimir (1951)
Vali, Reza (2003)
Vandervalk, Bruce (1970)
Varèse, Edgard (1964)
Vazquez, Álida (1970)
Vazzana, Anthony E. (1957)
Visconti, Dan (2015)
Walker, George (1967)
Wallner, Mimi (1949)
Waltzer, Rosemary (2000)
Warren, Kristina (2019)
Washburn, Robert (1961)
Waxman, Donald (1976)
Weidenaar, Reynold (1972)
Weigl, Vally (1951)
Weille, F. Blair (1956)
Welcher, Dan (2008)
Wendelburg, Norma (1951)
Weyandt, Michael (2003)
Wheeler, Scott (2019)
White, LJ (2014)
Whittenberg, Charles (1961)
Wiener, Ivan (1961)
Wigglesworth, Frank (1951)
Wilcox, A. Gordon (1965)
Williams, Amy (2016)
Williams, Edgar (1969)
Williams, Glenn (1963)
Williams, Howard (1966)
Wilson, Donald M. (1967)
Wilson, Dorothy (1951)
Wilson, Richard (1967)
Wilson, Thomas (1973)
Winsor, Philip G. (1969)
Wolfe, Julia (1990)
Wolpe, Stefan (1965)
Wright, Maurice (1970)
Wright-Fitzgerald, Jesse (2007)
Wuorinen, Charles (1956)
Wykes, Robert (1954)
Xi Wang (2005)
Yannatos, James (1962)
Young, Nina (2012)
Yount, Max H. (1966)
Yttrehus, Rolv (1971)
Zhou Long (1999)
Zhou, Zheng Selvester (2018)
Zindars, Earl (1963)
Ziporyn, Evan (1998)

Conference Chronology 1946–2019[*]

1946 Founding and first year, August 17-31. *Middlebury College Composers' Conference and Chamber Music Center*. Alan Carter, professor of music at Middlebury, is founder and director. Conference operates as a Middlebury College summer program. Halsey Stevens's Sonatina for Flute and Piano selected for publication by Broude Brothers under conference sponsorship. Richard Donovan and Otto Luening are staff composers.

1947 Halsey Stevens added as staff composer.

1948 Edmund Haines, Everett Helm, Normand Lockwood, and Otto Luening are staff composers. Composer and flutist Theodore Strongin first attends.

1949 Conference announces award of seven scholarships to composers and instrumentalists. Ingolf Dahl and Esther Williamson (later Ballou) added as staff composers. Robert Bloom placed in charge of woodwinds.

1950 Roger Goeb added as staff composer.

1951 Conference moves to Bennington College, August 12-25. *The Bennington Composers' Conference and Chamber Music Center, Inc.*, Alan Carter, director. The conference is incorporated as independent nonprofit for the "purpose of encouraging young and unknown composers of ability and furthering the knowledge of established composers by instruction, criticizing, and playing their untried works." Five public concerts added. Staff composers include Halsey Stevens, Richard Donovan, Otto Luening, Lionel Nowak, Esther Williamson Ballou, and Frank Wigglesworth. Composer Vladimir Ussachevsky attends.

1952 Conference expands inclusion of wind instruments, with faculty wind quintet in residence. Alan Carter, Otto Luening, and Robert Bloom are the conference executive committee. Luening and Vladimir Ussachevsky commence experiments in electronic music composition in the Carriage Barn. Conference initiates concert series at 92nd Street YM-YWHA, New York City, which continues through 1954. Max Pollikoff added as faculty violinist.

1953 Composer Chou Wen-chung attends; will return in 1954.

1955 Composer Charles Wuorinen attends; will return for eight years.

1956 Paul Wolfe added as faculty violinist and conductor. Amateur musician readings of new works by resident composers introduced.

1958 Alexander Kouguell added as faculty cellist. Melvin Kaplan added as faculty oboist.

1959 Henry Brant added as staff composer. Joseph Schor added as faculty violinist. Composer Donald Erb attends.

1962 Max Pollikoff appointed co-director of the conference.

---

[*] For clarity, references to the year of an event are to the summer session affected, not to the actual calendar date of the event. Thus, an action at a fall board meeting that affects the next summer's activities is referenced to the summer session year.

1963   Antonia Lavanne added as staff soprano and voice coach.

1964   Edgard Varèse, composer-in-residence. Jacob "Jack" Glick added as faculty violist.

1965   Stefan Wolpe added as staff composer.

1966   Conference executive committee votes to postpone conference for one year but is overruled by entire board of trustees. Efrain Guigui added as conductor.

1967   George Grossman designated head of the coaching staff. Joel Berman added as staff violinist.

1969   Mario Davidovsky and Donald Erb added as staff composers.

1970   Conference's twenty-fifth anniversary year. Twenty-five composers are in residence, plus four staff composers and twenty-seven faculty instrumentalists. Fifteen composers receive full tuition scholarships. Max Pollikoff appointed associate director. George Grossman appointed chief coach. Robert Moog is guest speaker.

1971   Virgil Thomson, senior composer-in-residence. George Grossman appointed associate director; Melvin Kaplan appointed chief woodwind coach. Michael Finckel added as faculty cellist.

1972   Conference moves to Johnson State College (Johnson, Vermont). Ernest Stires, executive director. Fifteen composer scholarships announced.

1974   Conference dissolves into two nonprofit organizations.

1975   Returning to Bennington College, conference is re-incorporated on July 15 as *The Chamber Music Conference and Composers' Forum of the East, Inc.* Alan Carter, president and director; George Grossman, vice president and associate director. After Carter's death in September, Grossman succeeds him as president and music director; Joel Berman, assistant music director. Michael Dumouchel added as faculty clarinetist.

1976   Bennington College opens its Visual and Performing Arts Center (VAPA), including Greenwall Auditorium. First documented participant musicales.

1977   Participant violist Eve Cohen assists George Grossman with participant scheduling, initiating what would become a software-supported advance scheduling process. Conference begins reorganization, shifting governance to amateur players, adopting plan by board member Maxwell Lehman.

1978   Paul Wolfe succeeds George Grossman (now president emeritus) as music director. Lionel Nowak, chairman of the board; Harold Laufman, president of the conference and vice chair of the board; Judith Ensign, administrative director. Stephen Manes added as faculty pianist.

1979   Stephen Reid joins board of directors. Patricia Stenberg added as faculty oboist. Sue Ann Kahn added as faculty flutist.

1980   Marilyn Bell succeeds Judith Ensign as administrative director. Gerald Carp appointed legal counsel.

1981   Harold Laufman is president and executive director.

1982   Jack Glick succeeds Paul Wolfe as music director. Conference expands from two weeks to three. Lauren Goldstein (later Stubbs) added as faculty bassoonist. First winter reunion, SUNY Purchase Guest House.

1983   Harold Laufman, executive director; Judith Ensign, deputy executive director; Joan Einhorn, assistant administrative director. "Buddy System" implemented to welcome new participants. Bylaws amended to include two faculty representatives on board of directors with full voting rights except for staff salary decisions. Maxine Neuman added as faculty cellist.

1984   Winter reunion moves to Wainwright House (Rye, New York). Composer Vivian Fine succeeds Otto Luening on board of directors.

1985   Beth Anderson succeeds Joan Einhorn as administrative director. Harold Laufman, chairman of the board and president; Judith Ensign, executive director; Erika Phillips, assistant executive director.

1986   Conference expands from three weeks to four. Pat Stenberg appointed assistant music director. Lionel Nowak coordinates the Composers' Forum.

1987   Marilyn Bell, executive director; Jo Margaret Farris and Dorothy Kalson, co-administrative directors.

1988   Frank Wigglesworth succeeds Lionel Nowak as coordinator of the Composers' Forum.

1990   Music Director Jack Glick on one-year sabbatical; Joseph Schor appointed acting music director.

1991   Beth Anderson and Dorothy Kalson, co-administrative directors.

1992   Stephen Reid succeeds Harold Laufman as chair of the board. First "Lunch with the Board." Haskell Edelstein succeeds Marilyn Bell as executive director.

1993   Louise Lerner assumes management of the winter reunion. Don Cohen introduces new printed dance card format.

1994   Jack Glick resigns as music director, citing ideological differences with board. Faculty tenure policy reformulated.

1995   Joseph Schor succeeds Jack Glick as acting music director. Music library initiated.

1996   Joseph Schor appointed music director. Bylaws amended. Fiftieth anniversary fund campaign exceeds goal of $50,000.

1997   Reinhard Humburg, recording engineer. Martin Bresnick added as composer-in-residence. Conference observes its fiftieth anniversary by issuing *Fifty Vermont Summers of Chamber Music*, authored by participant cellist Francis Church and Harold Laufman.

1998   Shem Guibbory succeeds Joseph Schor as music director.

1999   Chen Yi and Zhou Long appointed senior composers-in-residence through 2001.

2001   Intensive Week ("Week 0") is introduced at Colgate University, with remaining three weeks at Bennington College. Creation of the Jacob Glick Memorial Endowment Fund. Stephen Reid succeeds Dorothy Kalson as co-administrative director with Beth Anderson.

2002   Intensive Week held at Vassar College; remaining three weeks held at Bennington. Donald Crockett appointed senior composer-in-residence, continues in that position to the present. Brahms Requiem performed in memory of Pat Stenberg.

2003   Intensive Week repeats at Vassar College. Website launched.

2004   Intensive Week returns to Bennington as first week of four-week conference. Named chair fundraising launched as memorial to Pat Stenberg. Beth Anderson returns as administrative director. First Glick Fund commission awarded to Donald Crockett for *The Ceiling of Heaven*.

2005   Release of sixtieth anniversary faculty compact disc, *The Ceiling of Heaven*, presents works by Allen Shawn and Donald Crockett. Bequest from estate of participant Robert Maguire establishes Robert Maguire Legacy Society. Board commences strategic planning process. Second Glick Fund commission awarded to Gabriela Lena Frank for *Tres Homenajes: Compadrazgo*.

2007   Phillip Bush succeeds Shem Guibbory as music director. Daniel Godfrey is awarded commission in honor of Frank Mallory, resulting in *Dances in Checkered Shade*. Bennington College renovates Carriage Barn, adding air conditioning.

2008   Jack Chan succeeds Beth Anderson as administrative director. Bylaws amended.

2009   Stephen Reid appointed to position of executive director, succeeding Jack Chan. Lauren Stubbs appointed assistant music director. Music Director Phillip Bush re-envisions participant recitals as "Afternoon Musicales."

2010   Marilyn Bell succeeds Stephen Reid as executive director. Third Glick Fund commission awarded to Paul Moravec for his Wind Quintet.

2013   Fourth Glick Fund commission awarded to John Fitz Rogers for *Book of Concord*.

2014   Winter reunion relocates to Graymoor Spiritual Life Center (Garrison, New York).

2015   Mike Kong succeeds Stephen Reid as chair of the board. To facilitate transition to new music director, Maxine Neuman is appointed associate music director.

2016   Tobias Werner succeeds Phillip Bush as music director.

2017   Planning for seventy-fifth anniversary commences. Winter reunion relocates to Stony Point Center (Stony Point, New York). Maxine Neuman and Lauren Goldstein Stubbs continue as assistant music directors.

2018   Susie Ikeda succeeds Marilyn Bell as executive director. Fifth Glick Fund commission awarded to Pierre Jalbert for *Wind Dances*.

2019   Conference begins search for new site, as Bennington College announces 2020 summer program with Middlebury College, leaving no room for other summer programs on campus. Colgate University is selected as the conference's future site.

Notes

Chapter I

1. David Kemp, "A Summer Camp Where Musicians Work Hard at Playing," *New York Times*, May 24, 1981, Sec. 10, p. 5.
2. Barry Green, *The Inner Game of Music* (Doubleday & Co., 1986), p. 2.
3. *Joseph Haydn: Eighteenth-Century Gentleman and Genius* (University of Wisconsin Press, 1963), p. 13, translation by Vernon Gotwals of *Biographische Notizen über Joseph Haydn* (Breitkopf & Härtel, 1810) by Georg August Griesinger.
4. Goethe's correspondence with C.F. Zelter, Nov. 9, 1829, quoted in Edward Klorman, *Mozart's Music of Friends: Social Interplay in the Chamber Works* (Cambridge University Press, 2016), p. 20.
5. Karl Ditters von Dittersdorf, *The Autobiography of Karl von Dittersdorf, Dictated to his Son*, trans. A.D. Coleridge (Richard Bentley & Son, 1896), p. 90.
6. Edward Klorman, *Mozart's Music of Friends: Social Interplay in the Chamber Works* (Cambridge University Press, 2016), pp. 13–14.
7. Emily Anderson, ed. & trans., *The Letters of Mozart and His Family* (St. Martin's Press, 1966), pp. 885–87.
8. Klorman, p. 269.
9. Louis Spohr, *Louis Spohr's Autobiography, Translated from the German* (Da Capo, 1969), p. 150, quoted in Marie Sumner Lott, *The Social Worlds of Nineteenth-Century Chamber Music: Composers, Consumers, Communities* (University of Illinois Press, 2015), p. 81.
10. Lott, p. 194.
11. Lott, p. 194.

Chapter II

12. Theodore Strongin, "Composers at Bennington," *Vermont Life* (Summer 1955), p. 44.
13. Dona Brown, "Vermont as a Way of Life," *Vermont History Journal* (Vermont Historical Society, 2017) 85 (1), p. 57.
14. "History," *Vermont Symphony Orchestra*, vso.org/about-us/history.
15. "Concert and Opera Asides," *New York Times*, July 2, 1939, Sec. X, p. 5.
16. Alan Carter, "How It All Started," *UVM Special Collection, Carter/VSO Archive*, n.d., unpublished manuscript.
17. Brown, p. 57.
18. Otto Luening, *The Odyssey of an American Composer* (Charles Scribner's Sons, 1980), p. 476.
19. "Chamber Music Conference Gets Under Way Aug. 16," *Bennington Banner*, Aug. 14, 1976, p. 11.
20. "It Happens in the World of Music," *New York Times*, May 19, 1946, Sec. X, p. 5.
21. Theodore Strongin, "Working Together: Creators and Amateurs Meet in Bennington," *New York Times*, Aug. 26, 1956, Sec. X, p. 7.
22. Ernest Lubin, "Composers' Conference: Intensive Period of Study at Middlebury College," *New York Times*, Sept. 10, 1950, Arts & Leisure Sec., p. 103.
23. "Luening, Otto (Clarence)," *Baker's Biographical Dictionary of Musicians*, Nicolas Slonimsky, rev. (Schirmer Books, 8th ed. 1992), p. 1091.
24. "The Final Curtain: Ideler, Edwin," *The Billboard*, Aug. 29, 1953, p. 68.
25. The family name is spelled differently in various sources including the conference's documents. For consistency, the spelling used here is the correct spelling preferred by the family.

26. Rustin McIntosh, *Helen Rice: The Great Lady of Chamber Music* (Amateur Chamber Music Players, n.d.), p. 185.
27. "Raul Spivak, Pianist, Gives Program Here," *New York Times*, Nov. 24, 1945, Amusements Sec., p. 22.
28. "Marianne Finckel," *Bennington Banner* (obituary), Aug. 28, 2007.
29. Otto Luening, *The Odyssey of an American Composer* (Charles Scribner's Sons, 1980), p. 478.
30. Alfred Frankenstein, "A First Middlebury Conference," *Modern Music* (1946), pp. 300–02.
31. Frankenstein, pp. 300–02.
32. Ellen M. Baize, *The Life and Music of Frederick Harold Chapman 1909–1974* (thesis, 1989), p. 32.
33. "Helm, Everett (Burton)," *Grove Music Online*, doi.org/10.1093/gmo/9781561592630.article.12744.
34. "Edmund Haines, 59, Composer, Teacher," *New York Times*, July 7, 1974, p. 37.
35. James R. Heintze, *Esther Williamson Ballou: A Bio-Bibliography* (Greenwood Press, 1987), pp. 3–4.
36. "Seven Win Music Prizes," *New York Times*, Aug. 12, 1949, p. 12.
37. Allan Kozinn, "Carter Harman, 88, Composer, Music Critic and Record Producer, Dies," *New York Times*, Jan. 31, 2007, p. C15.
38. Eric Pace, "Richard Dana, Ex-Publisher and Rockefeller U. Executive," *New York Times*, Jan. 8, 1984, Sec. 1, p. 28.
39. Otto Luening, *The Odyssey of an American Composer* (Charles Scribner's Sons, 1980), p. 477.
40. Jean-Jacques Nattiez, ed., *The Boulez-Cage Correspondence*, trans. Robert Samuels (Cambridge University Press, 1993), pp. 60–75.

Chapter III

41. Ernest Lubin, "Composers' Conference: Intensive Period of Study at Middlebury College," *New York Times*, Sept. 10, 1950, Arts & Leisure Sec., p. 103.
42. Elizabeth McPherson ed., *The Bennington School of the Dance: A History in Writings and Interviews* (McFarland & Co., 2013), p. 13.
43. "Bennington: An Experiment in Progressive Education that Works," *Life*, Nov. 22, 1937, pp. 36–43.
44. Thomas P. Brockway, *Bennington College: In the Beginning* (Bennington College Press, 1981), p. 165.
45. *Virgil Thomson* (Alfred A. Knopf, 1966), p. 348.
46. Alan Arkin, *An Improvised Life* (Da Capo Press, 2011), pp. 32–33.
47. "Chamber Music Conference Gets Under Way Aug. 16," *Bennington Banner*, Aug. 14, 1976, p. 11.
48. Ross Parmenter, "The World of Music: Conference; Vermont Sessions for Composers and Chamber Ensemble Performers Shifted from Middlebury to Bennington," *New York Times*, Feb. 25, 1951, Sec. D, p. 95.
49. Allan Kozinn, "Frank Wigglesworth, 78, Writer and Performer of New Music," *New York Times*, Mar. 20, 1995, Sec. D, p. 24.
50. Allan Kozinn, "Roger Goeb, 82, Who Composed for Orchestra and Taught Music," *New York Times*, Jan. 12, 1997, Sec. 1, p. 31.
51. Ross Parmenter, "The World of Music: Conference; Vermont Sessions for Composers and Chamber Ensemble Performers Shifted from Middlebury to Bennington," *New York Times*, Feb. 25, 1951, Sec. D, p. 95.
52. Allan Kozinn, "Theodore Strongin, 79, a Critic; Championed Contemporary Music," *New York Times*, Dec. 3, 1998, Sec. B, p. 15.
53. Mario Davidovsky, Interview by Martin Brody and Anne Shreffler, Jan. 8, 2015.
54. C. Gerald Fraser, "Max Pollikoff, Violinist, Dies; Created 'Music of Our Time,'" *New York Times*, May 14, 1984, Sec. D, p. 18.
55. Theodore Strongin, "Working Together: Creators and Amateurs Meet in Bennington," *New York Times*, Aug. 26, 1956, Sec. X, p. 7.
56. "About Us," *Theodore Presser Company*, www.presser.com/about.
57. Neil W. Levin, *Ezra Laderman* (2015), www.milkenarchive.org/artists/view/ezra-laderman/.
58. Katherine Morrow Ford, *Quality Budget Houses; A Treasury of 100 Architect-Designed Houses from $5,000 to $20,000* (Reinhold Pub. Corp., 1954), pp. 124–25.

59.   Donna Gallers, *Guide to the Papers of Moses Kligsberg (1901–1975), 1937–1974*, YIVO Institute for Jewish Research, digifindingaids.cjh.org/?pID=109123.

60.   Lawrence Van Gelder, "Often Solo, Often Duo," *New York Times*, Feb. 20, 1983, Sec. II, p. 2.

61.   "Woodwinds, Too," *New York Times*, May 11, 1952, Sec. X, p. 7.

62.   Otto Luening Trust, *Otto Luening: Centennial* (2000).

63.   Otto Luening, *The Odyssey of an American Composer* (Charles Scribner's Sons, 1980), p. 516.

64.   Luening, p. 516.

65.   Luening, p. 523.

66.   "Dr. William Kolodney Dies at 76; Brought Arts to the 92d St. 'Y,'" *New York Times*, Jan. 19, 1976, p. 32.

67.   Harold C. Schonberg, "Composers Present New Chamber Music," *New York Times*, Dec. 1, 1952, p. 19.

68.   Harold C. Schonberg, "Bennington Concert Held at the Y.M.H.A.," *New York Times*, Mar. 2, 1953, p. 19.

69.   Harold C. Schonberg, "Trio by Calabro on Program Here," *New York Times*, Jan. 29, 1954, p. 15.

70.   "Aug. 14–28 Dates Scheduled for Composers' Conference," *Bennington Banner*, May 11, 1960, p. 8.

71.   Eric Salzman, "Performers Aid Creators on Mountain," *New York Times*, Aug. 27, 1961, Sec. X, p. 9.

72.   Eric Salzman, "Music: Rural Workshop," *New York Times*, Aug. 21, 1961, Sec. L, p. 18.

73.   Otto Luening, *The Odyssey of an American Composer* (Charles Scribner's Sons, 1980), p. 475.

74.   George Grossman, *I Don't Want You to Be a Bum! Some Incoherent Recollections of a Musician's Life* (Magna Graphics, 1983), pp. 36–39.

Chapter IV

75.   Keith Kendig, *Never a Dull Moment: Hassler Whitney, Mathematics Pioneer* (MAA Press, 2018).

76.   Susan Elizabeth Deaver, *The Group for Contemporary Music* (Manhattan School of Music DMA dissertation, 1993), p. 1, www.stokar.com/site/assets/files/1048/deaver.pdf.

77.   Allan Kozinn, "Henry Brant, Avant-Garde Composer, Dies at 94," *New York Times*, Apr. 30, 2008, p. B6.

78.   Eric Salzman, "Performers Aid Creators on Mountain," *New York Times*, Aug. 27, 1961, Sec. X, p. 9.

79.   Leslie M. Bigelow, "The Green Mountain Fiddlers – Early Years," 1974, University of Vermont Special Collections, Carter/VSO Archive (unpublished manuscript).

80.   Doris Severy, "Green Mountain Fiddlers," *Vermont Encyclopedia*, John J. Duffy et al. eds. (U. Vermont Press, 2003), p. 145.

81.   "Varèse, Edgard (Victor Achille Charles)," *Baker's Biographical Dictionary of Musicians*, Nicolas Slonimsky, rev. (Schirmer Books, 8th ed. 1992), p. 1942.

82.   John H. Baron, *Chamber Music: A Research and Information Guide* (Routledge, 2010), p. 714.

83.   Allen Hughes, "Surprise! It's Your Birthday!" *New York Times*, Aug. 9, 1970, p. D11.

Chapter V

84.   "Northern Vermont University," wikipedia.org/wiki/Northern_Vermont_University.

85.   Francis Church and Harold Laufman, *Fifty Vermont Summers of Chamber Music* (Chamber Music Conference and Composers' Forum of the East, 1997), p. 12.

86.   Aljean Harmetz, "David Raksin, the Composer of 'Laura,' Is Dead at 92," *New York Times*, Aug. 11, 2004, p. C13.

87.   "Imagine '96 – SCI Conference," Department of Music, University of Memphis, library.uta.edu/sci/sites/library.uta.edu.sci/files/nc_1996.pdf.

Chapter VI

88.   Robert Baksa, "Someone's Melody Is Another's Discord," *New York Times*, Oct. 27, 1996, Sec. 2, p. 14.

89.   Charles Wuorinen, *Simple Composition* (Longman, 1979), p. 3.

90. "Dr. Alan Carter, Founder of Symphony, Found Dead," *Burlington Free Press* (Burlington, VT), Sept. 23, 1975, p. 10.
91. Irwin Shainman, "Music," *Bennington Banner*, Aug. 4, 1973, p. 36.
92. Susan Chira, "Maxwell Lehman, 73, Helped to Draft New York Charter," *New York Times*, Sept. 14, 1982, p. A25.
93. Grossman, pp. 36–39.
94. Harold Laufman, "Profound Accidental Hypothermia," *Journal of the American Medical Association*, 147 (13), 1951, pp. 1201–1212 (doi.org/10.1001/jama.1951.03670300015004).

Chapter VII

95. Peter Babby et al., "Rufus Z. Smith In Fond Memory," *American Review of Canadian Studies* 21 (4), pp. 379–381 (1991) (doi.org/10.1080/02722019109481095).

Chapter VIII

96. David Kemp, "A Summer Camp Where Musicians Work Hard at Playing," *New York Times*, May 24, 1981, Sec. 10, p. 5.
97. Kemp, p. 5.
98. Mark Edmundson, "Bennington Means Business," *New York Times*, Oct. 23, 1994, Sec. 6 (Magazine), p. 40.
99. "Censure List," *American Association of University Professors*, www.aaup.org/our-programs/academic-freedom/censure-list.

Chapter IX

100. Albany Music Distribution #884 (2006).
101. "Chen Yi," *Theodore Presser Company*, www.presser.com/chen-yi.

Chapter X

102. Stephanie L. Ryan, "Chamber Music Conference is a Secret Worth Passing On," *Bennington Banner*, Aug. 7, 2008.
103. "Joseph Ott (1929–1990): A Brief Biography and Survey of His Career," *Claude Benny Press*, www.claudebennypress.com/html/biography.html.
104. Laura Schiller, "Professionals on the Amateur Scene," *Chamber Music*, March/April 2005, pp. 24–27.
105. Blair Tindall, "Ensembles for the Soul," *Los Angeles Times*, Mar. 25, 2007.

Chapter XI

106. Russell Platt, "Small is Beautiful," *New Yorker*, Oct. 24, 2008.

Index of Names

Index of Musical Works

CPSIA information can be obtained
at www.ICGtesting.com
Printed in the USA
BVHW090608260820
587142BV00004B/233